Praise for *The Prophetic Lens*

"Phil Allen Jr. is the ancient-present prophetic voice of our time. With surgical precision, Allen excavates the Black experience as it is historically ensconced in the narrative of America. He utilizes the camera as a historical living witness and considers its ethical implications in anti-Black injustice. Allen's prophetic voice and courageous hope deserve consideration in the halls of truth-telling ancestors. He is the one his ancestors prayed for. His is a courageous invitation into reimagination."

—Inés Velásquez-McBryde, co-lead pastor of
The Church We Hope For, preacher, reconciler, and speaker

"From a bridge in Selma to a backroad in Georgia to a street curb in Minneapolis, the camera has captured the truth of injustices against Black lives, from generation to generation. But perhaps until now, we've not dived deeply enough into the cultural, historical, and theological implications of the camera as an instrument of justice. In *The Prophetic Lens*, Phil Allen Jr. testifies to the power of the lens, through his own lens, as a Black man in America. Allen is an author and educator, but he's also a theologian and filmmaker. And it's in this creative collision and collaboration of varied vocations, alongside his own lived experiences, that Allen ushers forth a prophetic narrative that is timely, timeless, and true. Come to this work with ears to hear and eyes to see. In so doing, you will witness a truth teller in his element, guiding us to a justice that rolls like rivers and film reels, one movement at a time."

—Bobby Harrison, co-lead pastor of The Church We Hope For

"We all saw how an eyewitness's camera recording brought a modicum of justice to George Floyd's family. Phil Allen connects today's headlines to the ancient prophetic tradition in brilliant and evocative ways. He issues an inspiring call to take up a camera as a weapon against the principalities and powers that oppress our brothers and sisters. We will all begin to see far more clearly via his *Prophetic Lens*."

—Craig Detweiler, dean, Grand Canyon University's
College of Arts and Media

"This work is an excellent introduction to the life-giving force the camera has been and is in honoring the sacred journey of African Americans. This work extends the conversation that Frederick Douglass and Sojourner Truth started as they, like Phil Allen, see the camera lens as a witness to the dignity and sacredness of African American life. Powerful, inspiring, enlightening, and prophetic."

—Ralph Basui Watkins, The Peachtree Professor of Evangelism and Church Growth, Columbia Theological Seminary

"Phil Allen Jr. is the Howard Thurman of our time—a theologian, philosopher, educator, as well as an antiracism scholar. Allen brings a fresh and new perspective to the social justice movement. In this revelatory work, Allen animates the video camera as the protagonist in what he calls 'the prophetic movement for justice.' By breathing life into the video camera, he simultaneously breathes new life into those of us who've been shouting from the margins. This book is an essential companion as we continue our March to Zion."

—Rodney D. Smith, EdD, vice president for access and engagement, William Jewell College

"The Prophetic Lens reminds us that all truth requires a witness. When it comes to the reality of the Black experience in America, the camera lens has emerged as the urgent witness we have needed to tell our stories. Phil Allen Jr. is masterful with words. His writing in The Prophetic Lens is culturally relevant, historically accurate, and deeply theological. Anyone reading this will walk away in gratitude at the mastery of a camera's ability to capture injustice and equally troubled thinking of all those same injustices that have not been caught on camera."

—Khristi Lauren Adams, dean of spiritual life and equity, The Hill School, and author of Parable of the Brown Girl and Unbossed: How Black Girls Are Leading the Way

"The power of an image can influence a movement. For Phil Allen Jr., images from photography and film reveal incontrovertible stories about pain and creative hope, trauma, and resilience in the midst of Black bodies suffering under white supremacy. In The Prophetic Lens, Allen urges us to immerse in testimony of the camera as a prophetic witness to reveal and to challenge race-related violence against Black bodies, minds, and souls. He is clear: the time for the visual truth-telling movement is now."

—Lisa Withrow, leadership professor, independent scholar-author, founding coach and consultant at Clear Transition Strategies

The Prophetic Lens

The Prophetic Lens

*The Camera and Black Moral Agency
from MLK to Darnella Frazier*

Phil Allen Jr.

FORTRESS PRESS
MINNEAPOLIS

THE PROPHETIC LENS
The Camera and Black Moral Agency from MLK to Darnella Frazier

Cover image: Kristin Miller
Cover design: Top image: Black Lives Matter Mural, 9 June 2020, copyright Jason White from Charlotte, NC, United States. Bottom image: Civil Rights March on Washington, D.C., 28 August 1963, copyright Rowland Sherman, U.S. Information Agency. Press and Publications Service, NAID 542010.

Print ISBN: 978-1-5064-8419-8
eBook ISBN: 978-1-5064-8420-4

To all those braves ones who dare to expose racism in all forms and inspire a new generation toward a new normal, a new consciousness, and a new community.

Contents

Acknowledgments

Thank you to any and everyone who offered encouragement as I penned this project during a pandemic, with constant reminders and triggers of racial injustice, and while completing a doctoral degree. Shout-out to Will Bergkamp for believing in this project from the beginning and walking with me through its development.

Foreword

A few years ago, I wrote a letter to my children, partly to share with them a few aspects of my childhood that were different from theirs, but primarily to encourage them to take full advantage of the boundless possibilities that lay in store for them. The letter was in part a spiritual dowry of the values that were instilled in me by my parents and community when I was young but also a mini memoir of the life lessons I had learned as a result of my own experiences. I remembered sharing with them examples of how my parents often sternly instructed my brother and me to stay in close proximity to them when out in public spaces. I explicitly wanted them to know that my wife and I had intentionally done the opposite when they were young. I told them that we had made a conscious decision to allow them to roam free—at safe distances, of course—when we were out in public spaces like parks and shopping malls. We wanted them to feel and know that the world was theirs.

I mentioned that my parents had instructed my brother and me in an opposite way not because they were intentionally marginalizing us but because they wanted to protect us. They were protecting us from the irrational "White gaze" that would likely not have seen us as innocent children in the exploratory stages of life. I explained to them that I had grown up on the heels of an era where children of Color were often seen as public threats and not young explorers. I concluded the letter reassuring them that "the world is theirs, and they are free to make of it what they will."

The letter referenced above was written over five years ago. Since that time, I have trained my attention on our country with a heightened sense of vigilance. While there has been progress in recent years, and definitely since the years of my youth, there are obvious threats to our collective advancement. Unfortunately, one of those dangers, as recent events (i.e., the killings of George Floyd, Breonna Taylor, Ahmaud Arbery, etc.) have reminded us, is anti-Black violence. This violence in many ways stalks the Black community unrelentingly and can be found anywhere and everywhere—in schools, colleges and universities, and shopping malls and on random street corners. While this anti-Black violence and aggression has thrived for centuries in silence and under the cloak of darkness, it has in recent years begun to be exposed via the eyewitness of the video camera.

In the pages ahead, my dear friend and distant relative Phillip Allen Jr. not only brings to life the video camera as the "star" witness in our collective trial against anti-Black injustice; he equips the hands and hearts of the movement with a clairvoyant companion in the "cause for justice." While the video camera gives us an "indispensable" partner in our pursuit for justice and a battle buddy against the ubiquitous "White gaze," it, too, helps strengthen the gaze of Black America. This instrument that Phil calls "a prophetic tool for Black moral agency" will also cause African Americans to see ourselves with a bit more clarity. As I have often said, as an African American educator and social scientist, I am most interested in the gaze of Black America. Far too many of us have fallen prey to the four-hundred-year public relations campaign, as Tom Burrell calls it, that attempts to convince us that we are inferior beings and second-class citizens. I simply want Black people to see ourselves differently. Again, far too many of us believe, consciously and subconsciously, that we deserve second-class treatment. To be sure, Phil has written this book for the entire community; however, he has written this book especially for the African American community. This work has been created not to destroy any community but to energize and empower the "beloved" community. As you read through these pages, see yourself, see the good in all of humanity, but more importantly, see God.

Many of our South African brothers and sisters greet each other with the Zulu greeting *Sawubona*, which means "I see you." A deeper meaning of the greeting translates into "The God in me sees the God in you." For this reason, the greeting deeply resonates with me. I think it is a really powerful concept to "see others," to acknowledge their presence on earth, to recognize their humanity. It is even more powerful to see God in others. Enclosed in such a greeting is love. I believe, ultimately, that Phil has written this book in love. A love that acknowledges God in all of humanity.

I began this excerpt telling you about a letter that I wrote to my children some five or so years ago. You most likely discerned the unease that I feel regarding their future. Yes, I am a bit concerned for their future and for future generations that follow. You, too, perhaps share in this concern.

As we speak, our country is in the throes of an unforgettable stretch of unsettling years. We all have been forced to consider the deadly pathogens of a global pandemic, a contagion the likes of which hadn't been experienced for over one hundred years. We have also been dealing with similar human pathogens that many of us thought were long buried—the human pathogens of hatred, tribalism, and discontent. These bacteria had lain dormant just below the surface for decades, similar to the inactivity of a once-active volcano. What we have learned from both diseases is that we must always be aware of their ever-present threat; we must be prepared to protect ourselves from exposure, have knowledge of their propensity for longevity, and be attentive to their ability to mutate and hibernate until they are reawakened. It seems that the only potential antidote is, first, an awareness that these contagions are not easily destroyed—that they should never be underestimated or taken for granted and that they are, if nothing else, doggedly persistent. A thorough understanding of history would help with this awareness. We must train ourselves to learn from history instead of forbidding any mention of it. An embracing of history will no doubt help us navigate prior pitfalls, and it will in the end help us protect ourselves as well as subsequent generations from the dangers of the aforementioned pathogens. If we don't, my reassurance to my children that "the world is theirs, and they are free to make of it what they will" might very well be in vain.

Rodney D. Smith
Educator, Author, Public Servant,
Son, Brother, Husband, Father

Introduction

In the Black church, it is common to hear a preacher passionately share spiritual, theological, or practical insight during a sermon and then ask the congregation the question, "Can I get a witness?" He or she may substitute that question with phrases like "Help me somebody!" or "Somebody say *amen!*" As call-and-response is central to the Black church experience (and, one could argue, the Black experience outside of the church context as well), they are tapping into the collective expectation to allow for all and any in attendance to testify. When the Black preacher asks, "Can I get a witness?" she is asking if there is someone out there who agrees with her. "Is there someone who relates to what I'm preaching on this morning? Is there anyone who can testify that what I'm proclaiming is the truth?" When the preacher is done preaching, the same questions and comments could come from the worship leader, who artistically and seemingly effortlessly weaves those questions and statements in between song lyrics sung by either the worship leader, or the choir, or both.

This practice is not restricted to the church context. Marvin Gaye wrote a song called "Can I Get a Witness?" Although it was not written for church, which greatly influenced Gaye, he had the same intentions for his listeners as the pastor did for her congregants. Gaye sings these lyrics:

Listen everybody, especially you girls
Is it right to be left alone
While the one you love is never home?
I love too hard, my friends sometimes say
But I believe, I believe
That a woman should be loved that way
But it hurts me so inside
To see her treat me so unkind
Somebody, somewhere tell her it's unfair

Can I get a witness?
Can I get a witness?
Can I get a witness?
Somebody[1]

One could replace a few words, and it would sound like a sermon. Rather than the woman treating him so unkind and unfair, in a sermon, the preacher may speak about life (especially life without a relationship with Jesus) being unkind and unfair, leaving a person to feel lonely and unloved. Gaye echoes the sentiments regarding a woman who has broken his heart. He shares his feelings with great vulnerability, and like the Black preacher on a Sunday morning, he asks if there's anyone who agrees with him or thinks what he feels and is singing about is true. Is there another person who can relate to him and *testify* to the pain he feels, his plight, or him deserving better?

The congregation responds in agreement because their bodies have felt or sensed what the lyrics in the song testify to. They have heard painful words, seen suffering, felt in their bodies the hurt from loss or neglect, and even remembered the scents present during the traumatic events. They may not always know cognitively the experience the lyrics speak of, but their bodies often do.

A critical, though inanimate, and technological witness is the camera. It captures the Black experience with objective truth-telling and "testifies" to both the trauma and resiliency of African Americans living amid a violent reality. If I were to personify the video camera or the camera phone, it would be sitting in the figurative congregation of society responding with a resounding, "Yes!" The camera would testify boldly in the public and legal courts. The camera has much to say about the injustices and abuses in the underbelly of the United States that render African Americans vulnerable to continued trauma.[2] Its eye has seen the images. The camera is the witness that will attest to the pain and the plight of African Americans while making the case that we deserve better, we deserve justice, and we deserve our collective dignity to be recognized and honored. The camera's "testimony" is accurate and consistent each and every time it testifies. It can be misinterpreted, depending on who is doing the interpreting, but unedited, it will not give false information. Indeed, it cannot. It cannot be manipulated into giving contradictory testimony. Its content is reliable and compelling.

The Difference Footage Makes

What if there was no footage of George Floyd's murder? As I watched the trial of Derek Chauvin, the Minneapolis, Minnesota, police officer convicted of murdering Floyd on May 25, 2020, I realized how indispensable the footage on the camera phone recorded by Darnella Frazier had become. Had it not been for her courage to record this traumatic event, would Chauvin have been arrested, tried, and convicted of the crime and sentenced to twenty-two and a half years? The "star" witness of the trial, amid testimonies from all the witnesses, was the video footage. Eleven months earlier, this video circulating on social media, which captured the horrific event and (re)traumatized African Americans and other ethno-racial groups alike, became the single most important testimony that served to hold Chauvin accountable for his egregious actions. Footage that traumatized also became a symbol for justice and a multiethnic, multicultural social movement that touched countries across the globe and inspired a global movement under the banner of Black Lives Matter.

Prior to the release of the image of a White officer with his hands casually in his pockets while his knee is pressed into the neck of an African American man—George Floyd—while he cries out for his life, there was the video footage of the murder of Ahmaud Arbery. Arbery was jogging through a neighborhood before his run was interrupted by two White men—father and son—and another White man filming from a distance. He was shot on camera while attempting to defend himself. More than two months would pass before the video was released. Only then could the family, friends, community, and nation demand justice.

And what if there *was* video footage of Breonna Taylor's killing? Taylor, an ER technician, was asleep in her apartment when a barrage of bullets (thirty-two, to be exact) from the guns of law enforcement officers executing a no-knock warrant filled her apartment.[3] Six of those bullets pierced Taylor's body and took her life. The difference between Taylor's murder and those of Ahmaud Arbery and George Floyd was that there was no video footage. It was determined six months after her death by a grand jury that none of the officers were at fault for Taylor's death, with the exception of one officer who was charged with wanton endangerment for "firing shots that went into another home with people inside."[4] The neighbors whose lives appear to be more valued than Taylor's are White. Even they recognized the injustice that took place in charging an officer for bullets entering their home but not killing anyone, while bullets from those same guns killed Taylor—a Black woman.[5] We cannot be certain video footage would have changed the outcome, but we do know that anti-Black injustice thrives in the dark. What is not lost on many African Americans (and allies) is that the system found a way to place more value on White bodies than Black lives.

George Floyd's brother Philonise Floyd said in a television interview that people would approach him after he spoke or after a march and would say that the same thing that happened to his brother had happened to someone in their family. They would go on to say that people did not care about their family member like they care about his brother because they did not have a camera to capture the violence. In other words, the distinguishing factor in the response to the murders of or brutality faced by many unknown African Americans in contrast to the response to Floyd's murder is that there was a camera present to record the event and publish it on social media for the world to witness. While it would not have guaranteed justice, at least their family member would have been seen, remembered, and included in the national or global narrative of anti-Black violence.

The purpose of this book is to bring to light the imperative role that the camera has played in African Americans' quest to get justice for racially motivated tragedies, particularly those that happen at the hands of White people. This book aims to show that the video camera (and in some cases, still images) is not only a tool—an extension of Black moral agency for acquiring justice—but also a type of prophetic witness to inspire a countercommunity energized with subversive activism to dismantle the dominant White power structures.

The camera is indispensable to African Americans as a critical eyewitness in making our case for justice. What is most disheartening is the fact that it *has* to be. Historically, on one hand, when African Americans have insisted that they have been wronged or falsely accused in some way, particularly by White people, those cries for justice are far too often not believed. On the other hand, when a White person says an African American committed a crime or offense of some kind, they generally get the benefit of the doubt. The benefit of the doubt, in this sense, is dangerous to Black lives because it preserves racist practices and protects White offenders, while African Americans are disproportionately injured, falsely accused and imprisoned, or unjustly killed when the status quo of racist practices is not interrupted. Martin Luther King Jr. knew this. Darnella Frazier intuitively knew this. Christian Cooper—the African American birdwatcher in Central Park who filmed Amy Cooper while she falsely accused him of an assault—instinctively knew this.

The camera is not just technology that is indispensable for documentation; it is a prophetic tool for Black moral agency. It is a truth-telling instrument in the hands of those advocating for victims of violence, especially at the hands of self-assigned arbiters of oppressive authority and power. It introduces an alternative narrative that produces unwelcomed discourse for those in power, the "royal regime." The alternative narrative energizes those pushed to the margins and the bottoms of society and their allies to movements of resistance for the cause of justice.

Shooting a video has become as powerful a discipline as shooting a gun. While the gun can protect one from violence, it can also compound violence. The video camera can either deter violence or capture violence in action. As a prophetic tool for Black moral agency, its primary function is to reveal, to inherently criticize, and ultimately to energize a prophetic movement for justice. Walter Brueggemann outlines the "prophetic imagination" that will be used as a framework for this book to put language to and understand the implications of the camera as a social justice tool in the social media era (more on this in chapter 4).

Will Smith reminded the nation on *The Late Show with Stephen Colbert* that the anti-Black violence being witnessed in the last decade is nothing new; it's just being filmed for everyone to see.[6] The virality of the video of George Floyd's murder forced most people to see what African Americans have been testifying about for centuries. The video footage did not necessarily create a new narrative on anti-Black racial injustice, but it amplified what Michel Foucault describes as "subjugated knowledge,"[7] the narratives pushed to the margins of society. The footage itself was inherently a criticism of an anti-Black US society. But even further, it energized an unprecedented multiethnic and multicultural countermovement for justice and social reform in all spheres of society.

In this book, I aim to answer the "why" question behind the imperative of the camera for the African American community when they interact with law enforcement or other White citizens in spaces that lack accountability. History tells us why. When there has been injustice by Whites against

African Americans, White people still get the benefit of the doubt. The African American man, woman, or child must have done something to deserve what they received. Surely the White individual—terms synonymous with *patriot, upstanding,* and often *Christian*—had to have been provoked to defend themselves, if they did anything at all. The disproportionate amount of power that White people, under the spell of whiteness / white supremacy, collectively have over African Americans lends to the necessity of the camera. The presence of the camera has the potential to shift power dynamics.

This is in fact a book about power. When the camera is in the hands of the gatekeepers of White power structures, it is used for surveillance and the criminalization of African Americans. Because of the democratization of the camera—through the smartphone and social media—power is now decentralized. That power is further democratized by the production of documentaries and narrative films that dramatize anti-Black injustices and perpetuated social/racial inequities. This democratization of the camera decentralizes power and redistributes it to those on the margins. The video camera allows them to control their own narratives rather than be subjected to the narratives created by the gatekeepers of power structures. What was once a monologue controlled by a few now becomes dialogue.

This is a book about improvisation. The instrument historically used for surveillance as an extension of the "White gaze" is now used as a kind of mirror to project back to the White community and White-dominant power structures in real time the violence that the Black community knows has continued since their enslaved ancestors were taken from Africa and brought to this land. It enables the creators and curators of the content from the margins to reach the masses with raw visual images to amplify their perspective before power presents its own whitewashed version. The weapon of choice for defense is not the gun but technology of a different kind, one that aims not to kill human bodies but to capture the often-tragic interactions between White and Black bodies.

This is a book about art as a restorative and prophetic performance. The art of filmmaking is retelling and reenacting our own nonfictional, based-on-true-events stories that are often mistold or untold. It is the redramatization of our history, similar to the oral tradition that passed our stories down from generation to generation. This book intersects artist and prophet and filmmaker and cultural critic. This is not art that necessarily entertains but art that disrupts comfort, the way one might feel when staring at an abstract piece that does not cooperate with logic. It is in fact a book about reimagination. It invites the reader to imagine themselves sharing a space of lament and suffering, dancing with prophetic creativity and hope.

This is a book about the instincts to not only survive but thrive while pursuing racial justice, healing, and solidarity. The telos of the footage from video cameras is not just to stop injustice but to right wrongs: the true realization of justice. When there is true justice, the whole community is able to heal. Shalom is apparent when what was meant for destruction has turned into an opportunity for restoration. The camera is not the be-all and end-all, but it gives the African American community—as well as any marginalized, voiceless group—a chance at justice.

This is a book about the work of the Spirit. Neither the camera alone nor the person recording the events with the camera can cause sustained cultural change. Individuals are the instruments of God at work within creation. The camera is an extension of those human instruments. The Spirit is at work. Those with ears to hear, let them hear. Those with eyes to see, let them see. Social movements for justice have roles filled by individuals called to prophetic performances. But the narrator, director, and producer of the movement is the spirit of God. However, God is not limited to exclusively using the manifest church (professed followers of Christ); God may also use those whom Paul Tillich calls the latent church (where God's ultimate concerns that should drive the church are addressed in cultural forms).[8]

Finally, this book is about the dignity of Black bodies. Black lives do matter. *Matter*, here, is a verb. Black lives/bodies "signify" or point to the divine as much as any other body positioned atop the racialized social hierarchy preset by whiteness. Black bodies are symbols of resistance and resilience, essential characteristics for surviving and thriving in the liminal, unseen existence of blackness. This book is about the form of blackness subjected to perverse expressions of power wielded by whiteness. It confronts readers with many questions: Can you see yourself in Black bodies? Can you feel what Black bodies feel? Can you love Black bodies/beings/persons? For anyone struggling with the first two questions, is not the humanity in Black bodies enough?

Basketball Hall of Fame inductee Isaiah Thomas was correct when he said on an ESPN *30 for 30* documentary while defending the greatness of the 1980s Detroit Pistons, "Film don't lie." The camera's unaltered footage has the privilege and the integrity to tell the whole truth, even when the truth is not welcomed. Reflect on that truism. The assumption is that Thomas means *unedited* "film don't lie." It tells the truth.

I Was There

I was there
I saw the whole thing
The cries for mama
The knee on the neck
The blue eyes staring into mine were written on my
technological soul
I grieve with the Black mothers fathers daughters sons
and wives
I screamed on social media and got the attention of the
world
I presented the evidence of the institutional disregard for
Black lives
I then documented the movement so that your
descendants knew you did not accept the terror
When you are gone I will continue to speak on your
behalf
I will play the reruns so that the truth is not lost in the
hands of power
You will get paid royalties in the form of equity equality
justice
And reparations
I witnessed your
Death
Lament
Revolution
And rebirth
I was there
I saw the whole thing
I heard you when you said "I can't breathe"
I captured your breaths

*I choose to remember those rather than to define you by
    your deaths*
Because I was there

—Phil Allen Jr.

CHAPTER I

Unseen Violence

Blackness as the "In-Between"

I t is a cold morning in December in Southern California, and I prepare for a long run to start my day. I get dressed in the appropriate gear to make sure I stay relatively warm from start to finish. I put on my sneakers, my Nike Therma compression tights, and a long-sleeve T-shirt underneath a light sweatshirt, and then I hesitate for a moment before covering my head. Every time I put a "skull" cap (beanie) on my head, I think about how I'm perceived when I encounter people even while running. I dare not pull a hood over my head. I think twice about wearing a skull cap every time I grab one to cover my head, especially at night. I wear them anyway if the weather requires it. The fact that I must think about it is troubling to me. I remember vividly the description given to the police in 1999 as I walked to the bus stop on a cold Maryland morning. I had done nothing, yet a White man saw me as suspicious in my own neighborhood. My body was seen, but my humanity was not. His view of me seemed informed by his biases and fear.

Some days I feel invisible, while other days I feel the weight of the "gaze" of whiteness upon me. This long look, in my mind, ranges from a gaze of curiosity to one of surveillance, from fetishism to disdain. I feel the weight of having to posture myself in such a way that counters the invisibility of my humanity that my black skin seemingly overshadows in a culture founded on racialized ideology. In that hierarchy, blackness anchors it at the bottom. It is the racial code and the meanings attached to it that were imposed on African identity and upon which whiteness has stood to build its status, its prosperity, and its social security. In between racial slurs and lynched bodies, discriminatory acts caught on audio or video and anti-Black violence are part of the everyday mundane reality of microaggressions and microtraumas that describe being Black and navigating White spaces.[1]

I imagine the Underground Railroad as a space between being enslaved and "almost" free. It was in the hiddenness of this space that Harriet Tubman courageously led enslaved Africans north to "freedom." The Underground Railroad stands as a metaphor for the existential reality of blackness even today. The anxiety and fear of being caught and taken back to the perpetual "hell on earth" of Southern slavery and the simultaneous hopefulness of reaching the destination that represents freedom—both had to have been palpable. Their bodies and minds living in that tension without a reprieve until the destination was reached. The inner turmoil of resisting the temptation to turn back and the eagerness to finally get to the "promised land." It is a reality of suffering, anticipation, faith, and resiliency. Could the Underground Railroad experience be an active metaphor for that "in-between," liminal existence for African Americans that tends to be unseen by or of little concern to White Americans?

What does it mean to be Black in the United States? What does it *feel* like in one's body? Is there any difference between being Black and being White or another person of

Color? These are legitimate questions to reflect upon. But what is also important to ask is, "What does it feel like to live a reality, tell that reality, and have the narrative of that reality not believed or taken seriously?"

One evening as I spoke with a White woman in Southern California, we happened on the topic of slavery. I shared a bit of the history with her, and somehow in the midst of my sharing, she found a way to highlight one particular ex-slave who managed to buy his freedom from his owner. She spoke of his experience with a mild, relatively kind (for the times) owner as if that was the normal experience of slavery for millions of Africans. She said, "Well, at least he didn't treat him too badly." Her response shocked me, but I could also tell she honestly had no clue about the truth regarding slavery—though this does not justify her comment. Unfortunately, this is not an uncommon view of not just slavery but the entire history of the Black experience.

For far too many people, the Black experience—from slavery to Jim Crow, to mass incarceration and police brutality, to institutional racism in every sector of society in the United States—remains hovering in a type of social ether in which its reality is unfelt, unseen, and in fact, unknown. Particularly for many White Americans, this "violence of abstraction" justifies the assumption that the Black experience is only distinct from the White American experience by choice, not by design. The choice to commit crimes that impose deserved prison sentences, to not work hard enough to attain the promised American dream, or to dwell on an irrelevant past of a time that should be long forgotten.

The trauma of our past must first be seen and understood in order to appreciate the plight of blackness in the United States today. Maybe the reason blackness is not widely felt or known is because it is an *unseen* or *undiscerned* reality outside of the Black community. When I use the term *liminal*, I mean it is more than just unseen; it is an "in-between" existence. In other words, to be Black is to be in-between (seen as) human and (treated as) nonhuman. To be Black is to be in-between visible (admiration of Black bodies and culture that entertain or labor for White prosperity) and invisible (apathy toward Black suffering so as to not disturb White conscience). To render blackness invisible means to not acknowledge Black presence, Black thought, Black agency, or even Black humanity until any of these expressions of blackness are perceived to be a threat.

Blackness is the unseen space between violence and resilience. Violence should not be understood exclusively as physical, but its range of application is relevant to comprehending the extent to which blackness has been under assault in the United States for hundreds of years. The word *violent* means "to have a powerful effect."[2] The effect usually results in harm, injury, or death. Further, *violence* is related to *violation*—to treat with irreverence, profanity, or dishonor.[3] Racial violence, however, is not always noticeable. Racist laws and policies have been historically violent to the African American community. The codified and unwritten/unspoken practice of assimilation is injurious to African Americans' individual and collective identity. Unwarranted punishment—whipping, lynching, burning at the stake, dismemberment, police brutality, and so on—as a means of social control and flexing White dominance psychologically and physically is not merely harmful but destructive and dehumanizing. The ghettoization—isolation and/or segregation—is dishonoring and destructive to the community and is a root cause for social, familial, economic, and educational death. Despite the shadow of White violence that hovers over blackness, African Americans have endured it all through faith, community, activism, creativity and improvisation, and play—sports, comedy, dance, and so on.

Blackness is the unseen space of always fighting for or being stuck in the threshold of cultural change, hoping for more equity, equality, and just treatment. It is an in-between space because this progress is always incremental, since inherently anti-Black power structures have always been at play with counterresistance to and nonacceptance of Black social movements. What's worse is the fact that this space, while it is a lived reality for African Americans, is largely hidden or ignored by White Americans. One important ethic of blackness is its ability to innovate ways in which this experience is no longer hidden in order to creatively prick the collective conscience of the nation, including those within the African American community who may have been lulled to sleep by progress, Black exceptionalism/excellence, or the illusion of a postracial society.

Blackness as the "in-between" is necessarily a space of subversive and restorative practices. The health, survival, and progress of African Americans are dependent upon the capacity to marry practice with theory in what Peter Paris calls a "surrogate world."⁴ During the Jim Crow era, the areas of society where African Americans could not participate or were afforded limited participation—in voting, government, leadership, and so on—in one sense felt like an abyss where Black voices were unheard and Black humanity was unrecognized, blending in with a background of deep nothingness. In another sense, the "surrogate world" was created for and by African Americans as a space of safety, affirming Black dignity, strategizing for Black flourishing, and worshipping a God of liberation taken from the clutches of white supremacy that presented and worshipped a God of Black oppression. Women, the poor, LGBTQ+, and differently abled people are marginalized groups as well, but the intersection of these groups with a Black identity further intensifies their marginalization. Restorative practices as resources for wellness are inherently subversive because they undermine the intended destructive effects of social structures upon African Americans that are inextricably rooted in white supremacy. These practices foster resiliency and healing amid social structures that dehumanize.

Blackness as the invisible "in-between" is a dark space, but it is also a creative space. African Americans, performing those subversive practices, have creatively found ways to not only survive but thrive. The story of blackness is told through our music. Our songs enliven the various shades of our black and brown bodies to dance as a form of resistance and restoration. African Americans embody a theology and ethic of play that is most understood in the surrogate world of blackness. From the Geechee utterances of the Gullah dialect in the Lowcountry region of South Carolina—once viewed as a dialect of the uneducated—to the countless stanzas of poetry and hip-hop music, the in-between space of blackness is life-giving out of necessity. It has been appropriated to become a space of divine, creative performance. Like God created the earth out of nothing, so it has been with blackness—ex nihilo, out of nothing—*still becoming* something good. It is the ever-evolving story of this human goodness, marred by White oppression, that must be seen and heard.

"I Want the World to See What They Did to My Boy"

In 1955, Emmett Till, a fourteen-year-old African American kid from Chicago, was visiting family in Money, Mississippi. He was accused of either whistling and/or saying, "Hey baby!" to a White woman named Carolyn Bryant while he was making a purchase at a local grocery store. The young woman's husband, Roy Bryant, and brother-in-law, J. W. Milam, went in search of Till with murderous intentions to avenge the alleged dishonoring of a White woman. Bryant and Milam arrived at Till's uncle Moses Wright's home demanding that young Till come outside. They proceeded to kidnap and torture him. After beating Till, they shot him in the head, tied a metal fan with barbed wire around his neck, and threw his body into the Tallahatchie River, where he was later discovered.

Bryant and Milam were later accused of the murder and brought to trial. During the trial, Till's uncle Moses Wright testified of the abduction, and a man named Willie Reed testified that he overheard the men torturing young Till.[5] In spite of their testimonies, an all-White jury found them not guilty after an hour of deliberation. In 1956, after being acquitted of murder, the two men confessed to a journalist from *Look* magazine that they had in fact killed Till. What irony is the magazine's name, *Look*? Where did the article that contained the audacious confessions of the two men direct its readers to look? Were readers directed to "look" at the two White men with disdain or admiration for their actions? Was it simply to get readers to look at and purchase a copy of the magazine with a compelling article? Was the author asking the readers to look at or imagine Emmett

Till's disfigured body? What would have happened if Reed had a video camera to capture the torture and present as evidence? What effect would video footage have had on the jury and the judge despite the blatancy of white supremacy during the Jim Crow era?

What happened to Till was not uncommon but was indicative of the Black experience in the United States since the seventeenth century. Much of that experience, familiar to African Americans, has had its images edited from the textbooks, the history lessons, the sermons, and the stories passed down from generation to generation of non-Black, and especially White, communities—so much so that any account of history that emphasizes or merely includes the terror of the African American lived reality is challenged as some type of historical heresy proclaimed against the United States. African Americans have been telling their perspectives of this history since slavery through the voices of figures such as Frederick Douglass, Sojourner Truth, W. E. B. Du Bois, the narratives of the enslaved, and other historians. These accounts, testimonies, and perspectives challenge White-dominant narratives of US history. The de- and reconstructive work continues today. Nikole Hannah-Jones and the other contributors to *The 1619 Project* shine a light on the unseen, unheard, unfelt, and unknown reality that is "blackness" in order to reintroduce this historical narrative and this people to those whose mental and visual lenses have been veiled by whiteness. Many conservative White (and non-White) Americans see this as a threat and work tirelessly to condemn *The 1619 Project* as Marxist ideology and blackball it from school curricula and libraries. But why is it a threat?

It is not US history that is threatened, nor is it the image of the United States as the greatest nation on earth.

I suggest it is whiteness that is most threatened by the project's objective to "reframe the country's history by placing the consequences of slavery and the contributions of Black Americans at the center of our national narrative."[6] To know the United States is to know how whiteness in general, and white supremacy more specifically, has organized society around itself. To know the United States is to not turn away at the White violence and terror toward people of Color. To know the United States is to sit in the discomfort of the fallacy of white superiority that prioritizes, values, and centers whiteness—White bodies, White thought, White interests, and so on—that has socialized all of its inhabitants.

The Violent In-Between

For more than two hundred years, enslaved Africans were chained together and congested in the belly of European slave ships like cargo. Millions of Africans spent months in the traumatic liminal space uncertain of their destination or fate. In the hole of the deck on the slave ships was the smell of death that accompanied them on their travels to foreign lands. For millions of Africans who did not die on the journey to the slave ships on the West coast of Africa, life (if we can call it that) on the ships would be but a temporary existence before a life (if we can call it that) of forced free labor and brutality under White oppression in a new country became the norm. For millions of others, it would be the place where they would take their last breaths. Some would be thrown into the ocean after dying from sickness while others would choose the water in suicidal desperation, trusting that their souls would be reunited with the ancestors. Either way, they would become food for stalking sharks as shark migration patterns shifted to follow the ships headed West.[7]

The belly of the slave ships was an unseen Black reality. The Middle Passage was the space in between the homeland of Africa and the New World of the Americas and the Caribbean (British sugar islands). It was in between life and death, freedom and captivity, humanity and inhumanity, and being and nonbeing. It forced enslaved Africans at the time to have to choose one (life) or the other (death) before any human should have had to make such a choice, and in ways that no human should have to be subjected to.

Enslaved Africans were haunted by the decision to choose suicide over a life of forced servitude in a strange land. One enslaved African, whose name is unknown, tried to explain to the crew how he and his family were wrongfully enslaved. From the time he was held captive on the ship until his death, he refused to eat. He attempted suicide by cutting his own throat. The crew and doctor managed to save his life only to learn of a second attempt the next night. He chose death over going "with white men" into slavery.[8]

This unseen reality on the slave ship inspired many to fight for their freedom to the death—or the death of their White captors—through planned insurrections. While the slave ship intrinsically had a dual function in that it served as a mobile prison for the human beings of African descent but also transported cargo—textiles, firearms, gold, and ivory—one could argue for a third function: the birth of Black social movements resisting white supremacy.[9] There, the humanity and beingness of the Africans were erased by the treatment they received and the conditions they survived or died in, generally reserved for nonhumans or nonbeings. This context nurtured the individual and collective impulse to *rehumanize* themselves. They had to learn to assert agency and not be willing participants to their own annihilation "by any means necessary" and by any means available to them.

In attempts to preserve the profitable trading of human cargo, many slave traders exaggerated or blatantly lied about the conditions of the enslaved upon the vessels to their parliamentary or government officials in their respective countries. This was to combat the abolitionist propaganda spread by antislavery advocates. To be an enslaved African on those ships was to live in between the lie—that they were happy and content—and the truth; the lie, more often than not, without the benefit of eyewitness testimony, would prevail. John Riland, the son of a slaveowner in Jamaica, was the eyewitness who confirmed the abolitionist argument against the slave trade. Riland, "no friend of the slave trade . . . [wrote] one of the most detailed accounts" decrying the conditions on the slave ships.[10] This is the witness needed in the unseen space of the slave ship to help recover and restore a semblance of African humanity.

Surviving until they reached the New World did not guarantee an extended life or less trauma for the enslaved Africans. An estimated 1.5 million, or about 15 percent, died within the first year of labor on slave plantations.[11] The slave ship and the plantation are inextricably tied to one another. The plantation cannot be understood without understanding the slave ship. For one reason, the plantation was dependent upon "the shipment of labor power";[12] on the other hand, the slave ship was also used as a "factory" for the organization and exchange of cargo, including human cargo.[13] By the early eighteenth century, "the slave plantation had emerged as the most distinctive product of European capitalism, colonialism, and maritime power . . . with racial sentiment acting as the binding agent . . . and without preparedness to flout a traditional 'moral economy,' the slave plantations could not have been constructed."[14]

It is this moral economy that undergirded the institution of slavery in the new land that would come to be known as the United States. The ethic at the center of this moral economy evolved almost exclusively into the commodification of Black bodies for White profit—namely, White families in the South. The preservation of wealth drove the sanctification of the dehumanizing treatment of enslaved Africans. Millions of Africans survived the belly of the mobile prisons of slave ships only to labor from sunrise to sunset in the production of cotton, sugar, tobacco, or rice plantation fields. The moral economy of capitalism—as well as a Europeanized theology of white sovereignty—justified White violence upon Black bodies to discourage escape, insurrection, or work stoppage.

Frederick Douglass writes in his autobiography, *The Narrative of the Life of Frederick Douglass*, about the trauma of being awakened by the shrieks of his fellow enslaved, sometimes even his own family members, being whipped until they were "literally covered with blood."[15] Enslaved Africans had to endure the whip in the hands of White men and women tearing away their flesh and leaving behind life-long physical and psychological scars for any reason White people deemed necessary, whether reactively as punishment or proactively to prevent rebellion by the enslaved.

Aside from the inhumane practice of whippings, there was the torture of minimum sleep with the expectation of maximizing production or simply completing a task on time—failure to meet daily goals would lead to more whippings. Victoria Adams, a formerly enslaved woman in Columbia, South Carolina, remembers, "Da massa and missus was good to me but sometime I was bad they had to whip me. I 'members she used to whip me every time she tell me to do something and I take too long to move 'long and do it."[16]

Enslaved families never truly had a chance to be nurtured as a whole family unit, as they were always under the threat of separation. White slaveowners had complete say in whether or not one of their "properties" would be sold to another planter in any other city or state. When and how many children an enslaved woman had depended completely upon White men. Whether the child lived and had a lengthy stay on the plantation with his mother was determined by the slaveowner, even if he raped and fathered the child for his own profit and pleasure. Oftentimes the wife of the slaveowner demanded that the mulatto child he fathered be sold to another plantation.

This was the life of the enslaved: tortured, whipped and beaten, starved, deprived of rest, institutional conservatorship over every aspect of their lives assumed by not just slaveowners but by White people in general. Yet it still shocks me when I hear any White person minimize the lived reality of my enslaved African ancestors. To hear a White woman or a White male politician, on camera, confidently declare that the end of racism coincided with the end of slavery is sickening. The Civil War may have ended slavery, but it did not end white supremacy.

Reconstruction was a brief twelve-year period bookended by the Civil War and Jim Crow. It was once thought to be a reprieve for the formerly enslaved Africans from the blatant brutality of white supremacy. African "Americans" began to occupy seats in state governments. According to the Equal Justice Initiative (EJI), however, there were an estimated two thousand terror lynchings of Black bodies during Reconstruction.[17] The removal of Union military personnel by President Andrew Johnson in 1877 ended this period and ushered in the era of Jim Crow, but the same anti-Black terror continued.

Jim Crow's separate-but-equal culture disenfranchised the newly emancipated people for approximately the next ninety years. Oppression came in many forms. There were approximately fourteen million acres of land taken from African Americans by force, by fraud, or by both. African American farms decreased from nearly one million—one-seventh of all farms in the United States—to just 2 percent by 2012.[18] An estimated 4,700 African Americans—men, women, and children—were lynched by mobs of White people at will and without recourse. Lynching was not exclusive to being hung from trees but was understood in the culture of the time to include any time a mob of White people attacked African Americans for the purpose of doing harm and did not require death. If a White person claimed an African American insulted, assaulted, or committed a crime, or whatever they could conjure in their minds, they were believed no matter what African Americans testified.

Jim Crow culture, with its racial caste system, was so insidiously violent against Black people that many people believe that it originated in the South—where the open, blatant violence against African Americans was most documented—when in reality, it originated in the "free" Northern states of the Union before ever being employed in Southern states. Historian C. Vann Woodward writes in *The Strange Career of Jim Crow*, "One of the strangest things about the career of Jim Crow was that the system was born in the North and reached an advanced age before moving South in force."[19] While the North developed the policies grounded in the same ideology of the inferiority (and the questionable humanity) of people of African descent, Southern White people applied those policies with unrelenting force.

The only difference between the North and the South was the fact that the Northern states did not depend on agriculture and the plantation as their primary means to build wealth. The view of African Americans and the violence to the humanity of African Americans was the same in either region of the country. Woodward is correct when he claims, "Just as the Negro gained his emancipation and new rights through a falling out between white men, he now stood to lose his rights through the reconciliation of white men."[20] While slavery was divisive among Whites, separate-but-(not)-equal was a more agreeable set of policies and practices for White men and women to find common ground.

The slave trade isolated African American bodies to the bellies of slave ships. The plantation isolated enslaved Africans to not only the fields in which they worked from sunup to sundown but also their living quarters on the property. Jim Crow further isolated African Americans to particular areas of towns and cities without providing them the resources necessary to flourish. The ghettos of modern times are simply natural by-products of a systematic ghettoization of African Americans that has lasted over four hundred years.

We Need Surveillance

These "ghettos," or laws and policies that ghettoize, produced conditions that are inherently violent. When I use the term *ghetto* as a verb—"ghettoize"—it means "to put in or restrict to an isolated or segregated area."[21] Though it has an Italian origin, it was first used in reference to the Jews who have been forced to live in segregated parts of European and North African cities since the thirteenth century.[22] But its usage has been expanded to include the forced isolation of minority groups in European and American cities. During the suburbanization of America, which saw the migration of many White families to suburban areas, African Americans were prevented from the same opportunities.[23] With the relocation of White families, there was also the relocation of companies that could have continued to employ African Americans in urban areas. The suburbanization of America, which included the ghettoization of African Americans by default, led to high unemployment. High unemployment led to an increase in crime and, thus, overpolicing. White people did not have to commit anti-Black violence as they had in the past; the system now operated unpiloted, or with minimal piloting, to achieve that end.

The combination of the lack of resources, increase in crime, overpolicing—which includes racial profiling—and fewer quality educational resources all contributed to what Michelle Alexander calls the "New Jim Crow" of mass incarceration. She notes, "The racial dimension of mass incarceration is its most striking feature. No other country in the world imprisons so many of its racial or ethnic minorities. The United States imprisons a larger percentage of its Black population than South Africa did at the height of apartheid."[24]

The War on Drugs, as declared by President Ronald Reagan in 1982, produced quite different results than the "health epidemic" that describes the government's plan of action in response to the opioid addiction spreading through White suburban neighborhoods today. The former sanctioned anti-Black violence under the guise of stopping the expansion of crack cocaine, while the latter is an act of compassionate response to drug addiction affecting many White families. The drug use and drug trafficking in the Black community resulted in a dramatic increase in African American men, women, and teenagers in the penal population. The same activities in White communities have long been accompanied by the "benefit of the doubt" that acts as a buffer that minimizes their incarceration rate while offering recovery opportunities that are restorative rather than punitive.

For example, I once met with two young adult White Christian men at a Starbucks in the Los Angeles area for a conversation around race and racism. We sat outside in the patio area, where I answered some of the questions they had been reflecting on for some time. By the end of the conversation, I shared with them the disparities in arrests for drug use or trafficking between the African American and White communities. One of the young men admitted he understood what I was saying and began to share his experiences of privilege when he was caught by police officers in his community for drug possession. He admitted that he knew all he had to do was "dress the part" of a harmless, average White teenager, and he could likely get away with a warning. He described how he was stopped a couple of times by the police, and they found the drugs on him, but their response was a gentle warning to stop doing what he was doing. This occurred more than once for him. He was never arrested or charged with the crime. I did not have to say anything before he voiced how he knew had he been an African American, he would not have gotten a warning (much less two warnings) for selling drugs.

In the White community, there is the benefit of the doubt. In the African American community, there is the presumption of guilt. It is this instinct in US American culture, when law enforcement (and others) interacts with African Americans, that has led to filling the juvenile detention centers, prisons, and parole offices with Black bodies. This is the first phase of the violence, the "presumption of Black guilt" that leads to their high percentage of death or incarceration—often falsely. As of 2016, African Americans made up 47 percent of exonerations in the United States.[25] Alexander says, "What has changed since the collapse of Jim Crow has less to do with the basic structure of our society than with the language we use to justify it."[26] The language is ambiguous and dangerous but permits plausible deniability, or the benefit of the doubt. The chameleonic white supremacist "dialect" of Jim Crow and slavery eras is what has persisted undetected intergenerationally.

What if there was a Darnella Frazier with a smartphone who was to be the "fly on the wall" capturing the events that so many dismiss as nonegregious or as actually not occurring at all? On social media there is no shortage of videos and articles of African American men and women who are profiled, mistreated, enduring excessive force, or unnecessarily—and often wrongfully—taken in handcuffs to jail. Black bodies have been under surveillance since slavery. The camera is the device that puts the means of surveillance in the hands of African Americans for their own protection and eyewitness account, and history confirms its necessity.

Without this historical context, the indispensability of the camera has no relevance other than to the individual incidents that it may capture. The camera is capturing a narrative, not just an incident. "Blackness"—the Black experience—is historically an ongoing liminal existence in the United States. Blackness as the "in-between" is an analysis of the insidious ways that anti-Black racism undergirded by white supremacy produces an experience where to be Black is to be seen, but invisible; to be heard, but unheard and misinterpreted through racial and cultural lenses; to be African and American and living in the tension of these two identity markers—the former being one's ancestry, the latter being an imposition upon African ancestry. This chapter seeks to set the context of a history of anti-Black violence, trauma, criminalization, profiling, imprisonment, and policies that many outside of the Black community are not privy to witnessing, whether because of being shielded from this reality or choosing to ignore it.

The Black experience is analogous to an extended Israelite wilderness experience—402 years at the time of writing this, to be exact—that has forces that aim to maintain the wilderness existence in perpetuity. Those same forces have morphed from one era to the next to maintain efficacy.[27] Israel's time in the wilderness began after Moses's resistance to Pharaoh's oppression and unwillingness to free the Israelites. After ten miraculous events Yahweh performed through the servant Moses, Pharaoh relented. But soon after releasing the Israelites, Pharaoh went after them as they embarked on their journey to freedom. Fortunately, Yahweh swallowed up Pharaoh and his forces in the Red Sea after separating the waters so that the Israelites could cross without further harassment on dry land into the wilderness on their way to the Promised Land.

But that time in the wilderness consisted of being in constant survival mode for the most basic necessities, facing battles with people groups they came in contact with, and enduring persistent grumbling from those among the tribes complaining that Moses was failing as a leader. Some, apparently showing signs of either the trauma or internalized oppression, considered turning back to Egypt or betraying

Moses as a leader. One could understand the trauma of being in the wilderness with the barest of provisions and the fear that may have generated. There are stories of some enslaved Africans considering returning to the plantations in the South out of fear of being caught while they attempted to escape via the Underground Railroad. One could also understand the reality of the effects of internalized oppression that could influence some in the group to turn on one another, to either return to the place of their oppression or at least undermine the efforts of the leader to employ their own vision for leading the people. There was unlikely to be collective joy in this space. Certainly, there was collective frustration and fatigue from having to live in constant improvisation to survive and flourish.

This time in the wilderness—402 years—is made up of survival, resistance to those who traffic in oppression, infighting between groups divided on what is the best course of action to flourish, and uncertainty that makes improvisation and creativity necessary to live. The wilderness of the Israelites parallels the in-between space of blackness in the United States; a space that is often hidden, erased, or ignored. But this is now the space that is being documented for all to not only see but be invited into. What is at stake is life or death (literally and metaphorically). What is at stake is the benefit of the doubt or the presumption of guilt for Black bodies.

Conclusion

The violence of Black invisibility is often unseen because it is often subtle, adaptable, and protected by white supremacy at every level. Historically, White power structures have been gaslighting African Americans and allies who are aware of this space and join resistance movements. Whether politicians, teachers, pastors, or White parents, the narrative has been "There's nothing to see here" or "It wasn't that bad." The narrative continues today with more emphasis on casting blame on African Americans for their social conditions, school infrastructures, incarceration rates, and even deaths at the hands of law enforcement or ordinary citizens. This history makes the case for the imperative of an eyewitness that perpetually sees, documents, and publishes the truth of what happens in this in-between space. History compels the Darnella Fraziers of the African American community, and allies from non-Black communities, to be witnesses. They must be prepared to point and shoot—the camera-equipped phone—at any given time and allow the footage to speak clearly and emphatically on behalf of the Black experience in the courtrooms or the public sphere.

Anti-Black violence is most often seen when it has fully *matured.* In the liminal space of blackness, it is always *maturing.* Death and injury are the implications, but a profiling gaze, a defiling word, an assertion of authority over a Black body, and finally the drawing and firing of a gun all are distinct forms of violence that make up the maturation of anti-Black violence, some of which are seen, heard, and felt, while others are undetected. What is interesting is that violence bookends the "in-between" space as the cause of "blackness as liminality" and the response to it. Violence causes suffering and lament. Suffering and lament give birth to Black creativity and improvisation. But it is the creativity and improvisation of African Americans that arouse White violence in response to the resilience and persistence of Black agency. This story of anti-Black violence in the "in-between" must be documented.

CHAPTER 2

Unseen Violator

Unveiling Whiteness

I often wondered (and dismissed) why there is a "Black" television network, "Black" TV shows, "Black" theology, or "Black" history. I never questioned the imperative of Black perspectives for society in these areas. I was challenged, however, by the need for the qualifier "Black" when we never say "White" television networks, "White" TV shows, "White" theology, or "White" history. I realized how much all of us have been conditioned to place a racial qualifier in front of any idea, art, religious thought, and so on that originates from marginalized groups, and anything associated with the White community does not require *white* as a qualifier. It is simply assumed that what comes from the White community *is* the thing itself and what comes from other communities is a deviation from it. The standard-bearer of an entity does not need a qualifier, since all things are measured against it. Whiteness, in this way, is canonized and is hidden underneath the cloak of universality. It is as elusive and fictitious a construction as the infamous wizard in the *Wizard of Oz*, but its implications on African Americans and other people of Color are as real as life itself.

In the Sermon on the Mount, Jesus offers insight on the character of false prophets. He says, "Beware of false prophets, who come to you in sheep's clothing but inwardly are ravenous wolves."[1] Jesus's warning to his disciples and the crowds of listeners in his Sermon on the Mount should extend beyond a warning regarding false prophets. One could say this applies to all of humanity. Anyone—family, friend, employer, stranger, and so on—can have access to the sheep's wardrobe. The lesson here is that appearances and intentions are not always consonant. The wolf is willing to adapt to devour the prey. The protean capacity of the wolf can deceive a person into thinking they are safe, but the reality is, in due time the wolf must shed the sheep's gear and nakedly embody its true nature—to deceive, destroy, and annihilate in order to satisfy its cravings.

I had an enlightening interview with Andrew Heckler, writer and director of the film *Burden*. He, like many people, had a preconceived idea of what white supremacy looked like. *Burden* is a compelling, based-on-true-events film about a member of the Laurens, South Carolina, Ku Klux Klan—Mike Burden—who through the influence of his then-girlfriend left the Klan and was befriended in 1996 by an African American pastor in his town, Rev. David Kennedy. At several points prior to their friendship, Mike was assigned to assassinate the pastor who led a resistance movement to stop the establishment of a Ku Klux Klan Museum. In one scene, Mike had Kennedy in the crosshairs of his rifle from a nearby rooftop during a demonstration that turned violent. Before he had a chance to pull the trigger, he caught sight of his girlfriend's son. Seemingly in a moment of clarity, he did not shoot Kennedy. His failure to complete his assassination assignment put his own life and the well-being of his girlfriend and her son in jeopardy. With few options and homeless, they soon crossed paths with Kennedy, who initially helped them with food when he saw them panhandling outside of a local restaurant. His help would not end there. Through shared grace and choosing to witness the love of Christ, Rev. Kennedy and his family agreed to protect Mike, his girlfriend, and her son from the Klan. He invited them into their home, fed them, and gave them a safe place to sleep.

On Heckler's research visit to Lauren, South Carolina, he wanted to observe those who were either still active in the Klan or were at least known white supremacists. He was directed to visit a local diner for lunch, and he was assured he would see Klan members there. The problem was that Heckler's idea of what white supremacists looked like and how they interacted with African Americans was inaccurate. Instead of the expected divisiveness and aversion between the two, what he witnessed was a diner with White people and African Americans engaging one another and laughing as if they were longtime friends. The reality was many of them were friends from childhood. He left the diner confused and assumed there was nothing to see. The African American man who advised him to go to the diner reassured him that he had in fact seen Ku Klux Klan members in there, and they were the ones talking and laughing with African Americans. The supremacy he had imagined was unseen. It was not as palpable as he assumed it would be. The hate he anticipated was not as apparent as he had suspected. He could not see the wolf because he was distracted, even lulled to sleep, by the sheep's "clothing."

This did not surprise me at all. I grew up just a few hours away from that town in another small town in South Carolina called Georgetown. I grew up with children of known racists / white supremacists. Some were unapologetically racist in their views toward African Americans and other people of Color. Others kept their racist views cloaked in unassuming indifference or a superficial or false sense of friendship. Over twenty years after graduating from high school, I had dinner with one classmate and former little league football teammate. He confessed to me that "had someone told me that I'd be having dinner with a Black guy years after high school I would have told him he was crazy." Of all the White classmates I remember, he was not one I would have considered to have secretly held to a racist ideology. We played on teams together. We laughed and told jokes together in class. We likely got in trouble together. His supremacist sensibilities (at the very least, blatant racial prejudice) were not visible to me.

Some have commented that George Floyd changed the world. He did not ask to die with a knee on his neck. I believe what happened to Floyd was a tragic but catalytic event that caused some change in the world. What happened *to* him is what changed the consciousness of many in the world. Furthermore, I believe Darnella Frazier's courage and instincts on that day are what was world and culture changing. Her footage, much more so than the police officer's body cam footage or surveillance camera footage from across the street, captured Derek Chauvin, his posture, his demeanor, and his facial expression while his knee was on Floyd's neck. While George Floyd became the symbol of the ensuing social movement, Chauvin is a symbol of whiteness and, more specifically, white supremacy.

He was comfortable kneeling on this Black body, constricting its breathing until there was no more life inside. He was as comfortable kneeling on his neck as the European slave ship captains and crew were comfortable marching chained Africans to their mobile prisons and into the bellies of slave ships. He was as comfortable as White slaveowners were when whipping enslaved Africans publicly in front of other enslaved Africans and other White people to assert dominance. He was as comfortable as White people were hanging and burning Black bodies in front of hundreds and thousands of witnesses, who would later participate in dismembering Black bodies as keepsakes from the lynchings. He was as comfortable as the officers who wielded their batons to beat African American protesters during Bloody Sunday in Alabama or those who sprayed fire hoses against African Americans who peacefully protested during the Civil Rights Movement. Chauvin with his hand in his pocket, unbothered, undeterred, and unafraid, offered the White gaze into Frazier's camera phone as if to dare anyone to challenge his authority to violate a Black body as he so chose to do. He may or may not have known that he also offered the world a chance to peer into his soul through his eyes. It was as if he was posing for the camera to capture whiteness in its most natural and desired posture, dominance.

Making Whiteness Visible

This invisible, in-between reality of blackness does not exist by chance but by design. There have been forces at play since a European presence entered the New World that organized and structured a landscape that exploited and commodified Black bodies—four hundred years of Black enslavement, lynching, disenfranchisement, mass incarceration, and state-sanctioned murder. If one wants to *see* whiteness, they need not look any further than the oppressive and destructive structures that have shadowed blackness.

Whiteness and, more specifically, white supremacy and white sovereignty are the unseen roots beneath the American soil in which the visible trees of racism are planted. The anti-Black violence and trauma mentioned in the previous chapter are the results of a sinister worldview based on pseudoscience, heretical biblical doctrine, capitalistic aspirations, and social dominance of one group (Whites) over people of Color. I call white supremacy the "unseen violator" for several reasons: (1) it does not require obvious attitudes (malice) or actors (bigots) to be effective, as it is built into the culture and the laws of the land; (2) it has benefited from selective amnesia and omission from textbooks and other historical accounts in the White community; and (3) it is baked into society by the normalization of racist attitudes and practices. Figuratively speaking, whiteness can present itself as a wolf in sheep's clothing. What may seem normal and acceptable is ravenous by nature.

Whiteness is most notably unseen to White people. It is common knowledge that they do not see themselves in racialized terms. The notion of ethnicity is usually reserved for people of Color even though those of European ancestry are just as much an ethnic group as any other. Oppression does not register to White people unless it is in the context of class, gender, ability, age, and so on—all universal categories that are inclusive to whiteness. This reality is a product of white supremacy, white normativity, or centralizing white-ness against the experiences of particular groups of people. Whiteness is generally understood in universal, "human" terms because the two—whiteness and human—are indistinguishable according to its ideology. In this way, whiteness attempts to go unidentified, unknown, and unseen. In other words, the corrupted power of whiteness is its capacity to legitimize and normalize its status as canon for humanity. It simultaneously appears (at least to White people) to untether itself from this claim of standard-bearer for humanity and from the oppressive practices born from embodying this worldview.

The Beginning of Whiteness

I often say that racism is not the issue, but whiteness is. Before there was any society in modern times organized by race, there were the seeds of whiteness that functioned even within European nations and clans. When I use the word *whiteness*, I am drawing from New Testament scholar Love Sechrest and theologian Johnny Ramírez-Johnson, who describe "whiteness" in *Can "White" People Be Saved?* as "the phenomenon . . . which orders global systems of dominance that favor Whites and that have in turn nurtured racism, white supremacy, and patriarchy."[2] White supremacy is then defined as "the ideology that centers whiteness, and we can note how it creates and sustains institutions and practices that promote the social, political, and economic dominance of Whites and the oppression of people of Color."[3] Charles Mills calls it "the unnamed political system that made the world what it is today."[4] In this "white racial frame," whiteness is about "prizing White beauty, values, opinions, stereotypes, and culture."[5]

White sovereignty, like white supremacy, is an outflow of whiteness. I consider it to be distinct from white supremacy in that supremacy speaks of the supreme *quality* of whiteness (and the social systems and structures that reinforce this) by which all other "races" are measured. It is the standard for what it means to be human and, in the United States, what it means to be American. Sovereignty, however, speaks of the assumed *authority* of whiteness. Whiteness has assumed the authority to conquer, to name, to define, and to subjugate all other racial groups and their cultural expressions. It is supremacy that justifies this entitlement to authority, but it is sovereignty, believed to be established by God, that sanctions these attitudes and behaviors that demand obedience. Willie Jennings is right when he says, "Whiteness as a way of being in the world has been parasitically joined to a Christianity that is also a way of being in the world."[6] This union of authoritative worldviews would prove to be beneficial for Whites and destructive and manipulative for people of Color, particularly African Americans.

Whiteness innately assigns meaning to groups of people based on physical features and cultural behavior, and those meanings are intended to be unchangeable. Who these groups of people are become based on this meaning imposed upon them by White "so-called" authoritative voices. They have assumed the power and the audacity to create and control the narrative of others. This will later prove to be integral in maintaining white supremacy. Though this is based not on race per se but on culture, it turned out to be the nascent stages of a racialized society—a society that "uses race for maintaining the power and economic advantage for some while others are permanently disadvantaged and subjugated."[7]

Nell Irvin Painter, in *The History of White People*, writes in detail how those in positions of power and influence such as Julius Caesar or Roman historian Tacitus mastered defining, distinguishing, and stratifying the different European people groups. His observations determined who would be considered barbarians.[8] People who were outside of Roman rule were labeled Germani. While he spoke of them and other groups in racial terms, he was really describing cultural expressions. It did not matter. For more than 1,800 years afterward, his descriptions of the Germani served as a kind of template for theorists (and those in power) who too used cultural differences and turned them into immutable, racial identifiers that societies were organized around.[9] In other words, powerful White men used this logic to their advantage and to the disadvantage of whoever was available to them; it just so happened to be other White people at the time.

Slavery has a long history dating back to antiquity, but in medieval and more modern history prior to the African slave trade, there were mostly White bodies traded in slavery. The Irish were victims of the largest slave market in Europe during the eleventh century.[10] In the Roman empire specifically, and eventually among European nations more broadly, human beings were enslaved and used as instruments of commerce in exchange for other goods, like sugar, tobacco, or wine.[11] Why is this important? It is important because it sheds light on the multilayered motivation of white supremacy. Whiteness is first motivated by that which supports its power. Capitalism is as deeply rooted in white supremacy as the racially motivated stratification of society. Capitalism funded and continues to fund and support the whiteness "project" and its global influence and power. Capitalism and white power are mutually benefiting. Capitalism, though, continues to nurture white power at the expense of people of Color through preconfigured economic, political, legal, and social systems and structures.

Slavery did not create racism; it facilitated it. The seeds of racism were already germinating in European minds in the nascent stages of the slave trade and the formation of the US American colonies. By the time Europeans encountered Africans, the standard for beauty, intellect, civility, and even humanity was already being standardized by White bodies and aspects of White culture. Even among those identified as slaves, Africans were considered ugly and prime for "brute labor"; beauty was assigned to "luxury slaves"—White women slaves who were Circassian, Georgian, and Caucasian.[12] Whether beauty or any other human characteristic used in taxonomy, the centralization of whiteness and the exclusion or marginalization and dehumanization of other groups of Color were evident. European scientists and philosophers based their observations and conclusions on White people of the world, which means the beauty, civility, intellect, and dignity of other people groups—especially the radical "otherness" of African ancestry—were measured against the human standard of whiteness. It is from this context that Europeans entered African slavery and interacted with the descendants of those Africans they enslaved.

Slavery amplified these white supremacist ideas when it expanded enough to the south to reach the continent of Africa. Slavery was not primarily about hate or initially about race, but race became central, and White people's hatred of African people matured over time. The treatment of people of African descent was affirmed by the ideology of white supremacy and pseudoscience that claimed this inherent white superiority over all "others." This relationship evolved into racial hatred for two reasons (though likely not an exhaustive list): (1) poor Whites were adversely impacted and squeezed out of opportunities by the free labor slave-owners of large plantations received in Africans and (2) it was a response to any assertion of Black agency that resisted the institution of slavery and the racist culture of white supremacy. Whiteness was invented, and the ideology of white supremacy is its offspring, but hate was nurtured, and anti-Black violence was and continues to be its fruit.

White Supremacy, Theology, and the Dominant Narrative

Ideology remains unseen until it expresses itself in someone or some group's ethics. It is built upon and sustained by two primal features that motivate human thought: survival (enduring) and flourishing (prevailing).[13] Antonio Damasio points out that these features are built into prehuman organisms. One could argue from a theological standpoint that God has built into all of creation the instinct to survive and flourish. These instincts are evident and are foundational for ideology. They influence the feelings we have as we navigate this world, woven into the language we create around it—language is foundational to the creation of any social reality and is what grounds individual and group behavior. Our language and patterns of behavior are linked to what we value, what our norms are, and ultimately, what reveal and define our ethics. Our ethics are the fruit of our ideology, worldview, beliefs, language, and convictions. It is incredibly difficult to detach ourselves from these. It is virtually impossible, without hypocrisy, to consistently divorce our ethics from what we claim to believe or how we see the world. The two are inextricably tied.

Until the ideas and beliefs take the form of shared language and later are institutionalized/concretized by laws, rules, and practices, those ideas and beliefs are hidden. White supremacy, as ideology and in its ethics, manifests in both blatant and insidious ways, in religious and public spaces. White supremacy that is easily identified through White body agency wore the Ku Klux Klan hoods in decades past or was seen in a 2017 video in Charlottesville, Virginia, chanting, "Jews will not replace us!"[14] White supremacy, however, can be cloaked in supposedly innocent commentary boldly demanding that Black athletes in particular "shut up and dribble."[15] The former intentionally asserts itself, craving visibility. The latter clings close enough to plausible deniability to preserve its legitimacy from accusations of echoing racist rhetoric from the past.

White supremacy emerged from the network of sources that interdependently manufactured and maintained the superiority of whiteness and contributed to the validation of this dominant narrative. White supremacy is ultimately the product of the joint efforts of Enlightenment-era theology, science, education (universities), and law. According to Jeannine Fletcher Hill in *The Sin of White Supremacy*, white supremacy was justified theologically by Christian supremacist theology that claimed, "The theo-logic . . . rests on the singularity of God's plan for humanity and a sliding scale of humanity that allowed White Christians to argue themselves closer to God's favor and their non-White, non-Christian others deficient in God's eyes."[16] Its ideology found momentum in education when it was expanded through colleges founded by slaveholders where "the theology of Christian supremacy played a pivotal role as bedrock to the White racial frame."[17] Aside from theology and universities, "race science" reified the notion of white superiority and stratified society along constructed racial lines with White at the top of the hierarchy. The law then further organized society along White-dominant racial terms by turning ideology into structures and systems.[18] It is out of this context that the "royal," dominant narrative of white supremacy is formed.

I will explain more about the "royal" narrative in the next chapter. Consider it to simply be the narrative that is controlled and disseminated and finds its origin with those in power. In the case of the United States, this narrative can be under the control of the government; corporations, including news outlets; and other institutions (educational, ecclesial, etc.). It just so happens that all these entities, except for the Black church, are led predominantly by White people. Certainly, there are some exceptions (individuals and/or organizations within institutions) within each entity that align with counternarrative movements, but it is more the exception than the rule. The church, government, educational system, and judicial system are all the realms in which whiteness, with its prevailing royal narrative, has been able to camouflage and sustain itself intergenerationally.

The church in the United States was motivated by a White racial framework that benefited Whites in two ways: they were led to believe they were ordained by God as the new Israel, the new chosen ones, and Scripture was used in nefarious ways to sanction oppression and justify White prosperity. It is the latter that would emerge as the driving force behind the heretical teaching. White supremacist theology co-opted the "curse of Ham" from Genesis 9:18–27 in such a way that fits its tendency to prioritize and hierarchize groups of people over others to stratify society. Cain Hope Felder, in *Race, Racism, and the Biblical Narratives*, describes how this passage has been exploited and misinterpreted to lead people to believe that people of African descent have been cursed, destined to be subservient to the white-skinned descendants of Shem as an ugly, lesser kind of human being. Felder captures what he calls a "racist hermeneutic" from *Dake's Annotated Reference Bible*:

> All colors and types of men came into existence after the flood. *All men were white up to this point, for there was only one family line—that of Noah who was white and in the line of Christ*, being mentioned in Luke 3:36 with his son Shem. . . . [There is a] prophecy that Shem would be a chosen race and have a peculiar relationship with God [v. 26]. All divine revelation since Shem was come through his line. . . . [There is a] prophecy that Japheth would be the father of great and enlarged races [v. 27]. Government, Science and Art are mainly Japhethic. . . . His descendants constitute the leading nations of civilization.[19]

Interpretations like this were later compounded with "the prominent preaching to the slaves. . . . 'Servants, obey your masters.'"[20] This theological manipulation is the kind of insidious violence that is not physical but psychological. It is designed to co-opt the will of God to supposedly affirm the enslaved African's condition of servitude and position at the lowest level in the hierarchy to quell any thoughts and strategies of resistance. The intersection of theology and slavery was prominent given the fact that many colleges in the United States were headed by slaveholders who used the slave trade to fund their schools.[21]

The indoctrination into whiteness and white supremacy continued through education (or lack thereof) from slavery to Jim Crow to the present day. This method occurs on three fronts: (1) when African Americans are prevented from receiving education by invented obstacles or when Black schools are underfunded; (2) when information affirming the voices, value, and contributions of African Americans is omitted from textbooks and curriculums; and (3) when White voices are the dominant voices leading classrooms and the material taught reinforces, in obvious and subtle ways, white supremacy.

For example, growing up as a child in the school system in South Carolina, I do not recall seeing much information (aside from slavery, a handful of popular Black figures, and the Civil Rights Movement) in US history that brought the African American presence from the shadows at the margins. Fortunately, I was exposed to history from a Black perspective in my home. There was a sense of pride for not only the resiliency displayed by my ancestors but also the brilliance and beauty they embodied as well. I aspired to be a poet like Langston Hughes, Countee Cullen, or Maya Angelou. I wanted to dress and act and philosophize like the renaissance Black men decades before me. Without this exposure, white supremacy would have been even more fortified in my thinking than it already had been.

It is common knowledge that during slavery, the enslaved Africans were forbidden from learning how to read. Except for a few White people who secretly taught enslaved individuals and the ones among the enslaved who had the courage and skills of deception to learn on their own, the vast majority were systematically prevented from the benefits of education.

Right after the Civil War, "public education for Black children equal to that of White children was not universally opposed."[22] President Andrew Johnson changed any hope for equal education and true lasting freedom from White oppression once he removed the federal troops from the South. The schools were segregated between Whites and African Americans and so were the funds allocated to them. White supremacist ideology and its agents were determined to continue the enslavement of African Americans in some form or another because, as W. E. B. Du Bois wrote in the *Freedman's Bureau*, "the South believed an educated Negro to be a dangerous Negro."[23] The miseducation of White people and the under(funded)education of African Americans was (and still is) the perfect formula to reinforce white supremacy as a multigenerational inheritance.

All four of these entities support and even employ the language of white supremacy, which is the language of control, commodification, and commercialization of Black bodies. It is the language of violence, *unseen* violence. The normalization and uncritical acceptance of this language of white supremacy are themselves violent. Anti–white supremacy language, not just anti-racism language, is necessary to further expose and reverse the effects of white supremacy. Anti-racism language is reactionary, addressing symptoms. Anti–white supremacy language delves deeper, targeting the unseen root of the problem of racism. It is language that is deconstructive, reconstructive, and restorative to African Americans in particular, and society in general, who have all been subjected to white supremacy's violence.

White Body Trauma

The violence seen in recent history among White people toward people of Color, especially toward African Americans, did not appear out of nowhere. Over the years I've often asked the questions, Why are White people so violent? (Of course, this is a generalization based on the origin of so much violence toward people of Color; not *all* White people are violent.) How can they be so apathetic to Black suffering? Days following the release of the Floyd video, NBA basketball coach Doc Rivers, through tears, stated, "It's amazing we keep loving this country and this country doesn't love us back."[24] His grief resonated with me deeply. What if anti-Black violence by the White community is a projection of the fear and violence that live in the collective White body? That toxic combination of fear and violence coupled with animus that built up over the course of slavery and Reconstruction was the perfect cocktail for what seems to be more than a hateful but destructive ethic.

Resmaa Menakem asks a profound, thought-provoking question: "Did over ten centuries of medieval brutality, which was inflicted on white bodies by other white bodies, begin to look like culture?"[25] It is in this context that I want to consider the thinking and behavior of many White Americans, especially in response to African Americans and other people of Color. What seems like the serious remnant of the culture of hate, indifference, fear, and violence is retained trauma in the collective White body from generations past. This may add depth to understanding why actions have been taken and laws and narratives are created to maintain (whether intentionally or unintentionally is irrelevant) what Menakem names "white-body supremacy."

He calls the trauma inherited by White bodies "dirty pain," and "the efforts to manage this dirty pain in White bodies, both individually and collectively, led to the ever-greater institutionalization of White body supremacy—in science, history, economics, governance, courts, policing, education, employment, housing, medicine, psychology, and just about everything else."[26] In other words, the violence of pervasive institutional racism—the unseen or undiscerned form of racism—targeting African Americans and other people of Color is a result of the practices stemming from unseen or undiscerned pain and violence absorbed and retained in the bodies of its originators and gatekeepers.

White body trauma can at least be expressed in three ways, though this is not an exhaustive list: fear, violence, and the claim of victimhood. On January 6, 2021, a large group of protesters gathered in Washington, DC, at the summoning of then-President Donald Trump. After a series of impassioned, fiery messages by Trump and his legislative and legal loyalists, the protesters marched to the Capitol building. Before long, the protest turned into an attempt at an insurrection to stop the certification of the presidential election results. Law enforcement officers were attacked and beaten with makeshift weapons as the mob of insurrectionists illegally penetrated the Capitol building. Certainly, this group does not represent all White Americans and likely not even all conservative members of the Republican party. But they do represent a significant proportion of a historically dominant group of White people in the country who yearn, consciously or unconsciously, for days past. This was White body trauma and White body supremacy in operation. They had the audacity to storm the Capitol, attack law enforcement—whom they typically support with chants of "blue lives matter"—and yell phrases like "This is *our* house." Yet they were appalled when hundreds of them were later charged and arrested. They believed they had done nothing wrong. This is the air of entitlement of white supremacy.

Even in this incident, white supremacy is hidden to many. It is not just the fact that the majority of the people that breeched the Capitol were White or the fact that there were white supremacist groups and confederate flags present. It is the expectation of autonomy that is so pervasive in white supremacy/sovereignty thought and behavior. The idea that they could illegally enter the building with the sole purpose to stop the legitimate certification of the election—democracy in process—and then assault law enforcement officers, threaten to hang the vice president, and believe there should be no repercussions is the air of supremacy and sovereignty in action. Anything that infringes upon white autonomy is viewed as oppressive or taking away their freedom when in fact those rules apply to everyone.

This audacity is the same as that of those White Americans who stood proudly and unashamedly in front of cameras taking pictures while standing over or beneath Black bodies they had just lynched. It is reminiscent of White slaveowners and White audiences who watched Black bodies being whipped for trying to escape to freedom or for being defiant enough to talk back to a White person. In these instances, they were not only declaring that this was their land or their house, but they were also proclaiming that even Black bodies were "their property." Ownership—of bodies, spaces, and institutions—is a central theme in the ethos of white supremacists.

Politicians and ordinary citizens supporting the insurrectionists routinely compared the January 6th event with those protests of Black Lives Matter (the same protests many of them condemned) from the previous summer, as if the Black Lives Matter protests of 2020 justified the actions on January 6th.

This insurrection was fueled by the politics of fear, aided by conservative media and conspiracy theories. This rhetoric (language) and disinformation agitated existing violence in White bodies and gave further encouragement and validation for White victimhood. The latter seems to be the trend—or an excuse, depending on how one wants to interpret it. There are constant claims from many White people about reverse racism. Reverse racism, however, is impossible unless a group of Color has collective institutional power to adversely impact the lives of White Americans as a group. The only forms of reverse racism that are possible are bigotry and other forms of interpersonal prejudice or discrimination. However, these are only fractions of the broad spectrum of racism. These forms of prejudice are not supported by any kind of group supremacy or group power but, more often than not, take place in response to a history of violence at the hands of white supremacy.

It is not uncommon to hear assertions from the White community of being *victims* of affirmative action when their children do not get into a university because of the need to meet diversity quotas. They do not pause to consider facts, such as that in 2009, 75 percent of enrollees in the top 468 colleges and universities in the United States were White.[27] They also do not consider that even in studies as recent as 2020, 75 percent of full-time faculty at degree-granting institutions are White, and only 3 percent are African American men and women (the same statistic is true for Hispanic men and women).[28]

Here is why manufactured victimhood is problematic. It does precisely what white supremacy was designed to do, which is recentralize whiteness or White bodies in response to the work that racial/social justice movements do to decentralize whiteness and dismantle white power structures. It is an attempt to turn the oppressing group into the oppressed, another tactic at hiding white supremacy ("Surely the victims are not supremacists."). Those who participated in the insurrection have touted themselves as victims, and many refuse to acknowledge the physical and psychological trauma police officers sustained that day, from the violence and the deaths and suicides of fellow officers.

White victimhood insulates White Americans from being exclusively associated with the history and legacy of racism and white supremacy. Around the time that this chapter was being written, I was walking down the street in Pasadena, California. I could hear a conversation that four young White adults were having even though I had AirPods in my ears and was listening to music. I'm not sure if they were speaking at a volume hoping to get my attention or not, but I could make out that they were dismissing the notion of white privilege. They made comments criticizing the practice of grouping all White people as having privilege in the United States. Clearly, in my opinion, they did not have a deep understanding of racism and the privilege it affords the White group in contrast to African Americans—as a group—and other people of Color. Conversations like this are commonplace among White Americans. They share the tendency to defend whiteness rather than look deeply into the implications of whiteness upon all of us, including themselves. This defense is a type of buffer from having to confront or be confronted by the reality of whiteness and white supremacy.

Victimhood is expressed in the defensiveness of White Americans who show fragility in response to honest critiques of whiteness. Facts about *whiteness* are now considered attacks on White *people*. Historical data about the patriotic, White ancestors of the "great" United States that do not hold them in a positive and benevolent light are now considered false or misinformation. But this victimhood is betrayed by the sustained group power wielded by White Americans on every level and in every realm of US American society. It does not square with the degree of inherited insulation from, for example, structural and institutional anti-Black racism.

The "White" Wall of Hostility

Growing up as an African American kid, you learn quickly that a wall is not exclusive to a physical barrier, but the idea is much broader. You feel a distinct shift in the atmosphere and scenery when you go to the "other side of town." Even if there is nothing constructed to keep you from exploring that section of the city, you know there are restrictions intended to keep you separated from White folks and the resources they hoard, protect, and feel entitled to. The wall is invisible to the untrained eye, but it is there. You see it once you see the buildings change. You perceive it in the landscape and the beautification of the properties—both private and public—as you transgress the invisible boundaries. The freeway or a main thoroughfare indicates the dividing line between poor and wealthy, which is usually (though not always) synonymous with African American and White, the Black side and the White side.

These barriers are hostile. They are the residuals of Jim Crow–era written-and-unwritten or spoken-and-unspoken laws and policies that formed invisible structures to protect White bodies. The architects of these city structures were the agents of white supremacy. These walls, though not physical, are still constructed today. They are only seen, however, when a "Karen" decides to call the police because people of Color—namely, African Americans—have taken up White space, to her (or his) inconvenience or discomfort. They appear once a White person calls the police and merely suggests there is a stranger in *their* neighborhood that they've never seen before. They are noticeable when cultural expressions of blackness disrupt the supposed standard of American culture—whiteness. The response to Black presence, Black culture, or Black moral agency is often as hardened, cold, and hostile as a concrete slab that stands eight feet tall.

The apostle Paul writes in Ephesians 2 about "the wall of hostility," drawing upon the physical image of a constructed wall that separated Jews and Gentiles as part of the design of the temple. He also analogizes that wall and uses it as a symbol of the unseen wall of the Law that separated the Gentiles from both God and the people of God. A wall he insists is broken down by the body or flesh of Jesus on the cross. Theologian and Bible scholar John Stott describes the design of the temple wall:

> Of this double Gentile alienation—from God and from God's people Israel—the so-called "middle wall of partition" (verse 14, AV) or "dividing wall of hostility" (RSV) was the standing symbol. It was a notable feature of the magnificent temple built in Jerusalem by Herod the Great. The temple building itself was constructed on an elevated platform. Round it was the Court of the Priests. East of this was the Court of Israel, and further east the Court of the Women. These three courts—for the priests, the lay men, and the lay women of Israel

respectively—were all on the same elevation as the temple itself. From this level one descended five steps to a walled platform, and then on the other side of the wall fourteen more steps to another wall, beyond which was the outer court or Court of the Gentiles. This was a spacious court running right round the temple and its inner courts. From any part of it the Gentiles could look up and view the temple but were not allowed to approach it. They were cut off from it by the surrounding wall, which was a one-and-a-half metre stone barricade, on which were displayed at intervals warning notices in Greek and Latin. They read . . . not "Trespassers will be prosecuted" but "Trespassers will be executed."

This wall, with all its features—height, thickness, and signage—was intended to not only separate but intimidate Gentiles. It is this wall that Jesus destroyed. In the new economy of God, this wall has no place and no value and is no reflection of who God is and what God stands for. Jesus, with the participation of the people of God, aims to form a new humanity by reconciling all to God. This wall persists as an active metaphor today. Forms of this "wall of hostility" include ideologies, languages, laws, ethics, and social/political movements that are anti-God. The oneness that a God of hospitality and solidarity desires to see manifest cannot be fulfilled if this wall stands and functions as it has been. It is in fact a deterrent to community.

Today, to demolish the "wall," we must name it. We must recognize how we, too, participate willingly or unwillingly in its continued construction or reinforcement. There are factions, even among the White community, who are intentional in its destruction and those who are steadfast in its preservation. The latter, however, will deflect responsibility or complicity in the socially and politically constructed barriers and will deny there is a barrier in the first place. Perpetuating an illusion of a community of solidarity across the Black/White (or people of Color / White) divide without being honest about what undergirds and underscores the divide itself does an interpretive disservice to the passage aside from its intellectual offensiveness.

Conclusion

Whiteness (and more specifically, white supremacy and white sovereignty)—the "wall of hostility"—inflicts violence on African Americans but also on the true church of God and the name of *God* itself. One reason it has prevailed is because of its covert nature, which is difficult to document. Darnella Frazier's camera could not capture it in its most dormant state, only in the state when it was aroused and its agents were undisciplined enough to be caught on video being what they are and doing what they do. It is an unseen violator on Black lives and the whole of humanity. It requires actions like Frazier's to document these violations, bring them to the nation's and the world's consciousness, and inspire the alternative consciousness necessary for a new humanity disentangled from whiteness.

The camera removes the veil each time it is used to document the experience of violence and injustice—blackness as liminality—that African Americans have been decrying for centuries. No matter how adaptable whiteness may be, it cannot escape the prophetic lens of the camera. No matter how disingenuous and misleading interpretations of recorded anti-Black violence may be from many in the White community, at some point, the anthology of footage will expose whiteness. Humanity cannot sustain resistance to the truth without self-destructing. The Black Lives Matter protests during the summer of 2020 are proof that denial and ignorance to the reality of white supremacy and racism produce collective nausea, and the foreignness of White ideology must be regurgitated from the body politic to be well again.

The solution to the problem of a racist society does not lie in addressing the products—the justice system, laws and policies, policing, disparities in health care and housing, education, hiring practices, and so on—that are experienced by African Americans and other people of Color (although it is important to do so). The solution is in addressing the source, which is whiteness / white supremacy / white sovereignty. Whiteness created and continues to sustain the social reality of racism. This is not an overnight fix. This is not a generational fix, as history has proven. This may not even be a fix that is possible "on this side of heaven." But there can be spaces—in time, geographically, and institutionally—created that do not allow whiteness to thrive. This is the reason the camera is most relevant.

CHAPTER 3

Unfiltered Lies

White Framing of the Black Narrative

When I was a child growing up in Georgetown, South Carolina, the lens through which I was given to see people who looked like me was shaped by White men and women with the decision-making power to project their version of blackness over the airwaves. I spent many nights sitting either next to my grandmother on her bed or in the family room near my grandfather as he sat in his La-Z-Boy chair watching the eleven o'clock local news. The news station we tended to watch was based out of nearby Charleston. Inevitably, each night there would be news of burglaries, assaults, or other crimes committed in that city. The vast majority of the time, the criminals shown were African American men. Week after week, the faces in the mugshots looked like men or teenage boys who could have been my cousins, uncles, friends, or me. After seeing these images repeatedly on television, I began to have a fear as a young boy of visiting Charleston. My view of the city was that it was unsafe, and it was because of the behavior of "my" people. I had been conditioned to see African American men, particularly in Charleston, as threats. The news coverage systematically erased their humanity over time and replaced it with barbarism and savagery.

I was not mature enough to understand that the news media was erasing my humanity vicariously. I was seeing other African American men, but I was also seeing myself in them. I was viewing them through a window and viewing myself in a mirror tinted by the dark imagination of whiteness. Therefore, my assessment and interpretation of who they were and who I was had been distorted. It is inevitable that the messaging fed to me would be internalized, and I would live within the tension between that understanding of blackness and the one taught to me by family, African American voices in literature, clergy in the Black church, and other public figures. What seemed so normal and uneventful in terms of media presentation turned out to be artfully life-forming for me.

There is power in the cultural messaging of media (especially explicitly racialized messaging) to shape our views of people groups, including our own. Matthew W. Hughey and Emma González-Lesser insist that "there is no media message that exists asocially."[1] If this is true that media are cultural or societal products, then an inherently racialized society necessarily produces racialized messages, whether intentionally or not. How that messaging influences depends on who is behind the camera, who is directing or producing what is disseminated to the public, and what the agenda is to produce the message. In the 1980s, there was a high likelihood that the decision-makers of the news stations were predominately White and male. Whether they were conscious of and deliberate in criminalizing African Americans or their inherent racial biases kept them blind to the symbolic and literal violence they were perpetuating on blackness is of little relevance. The reality is that they were producing the destructive narratives about Black people for Black people.

The power to control the narrative is more than a trait of white supremacy; it is a strategically executed plan of white supremacy. In a hierarchical society—based on race, gender, economic status—media messaging agendas are tethered to power and domination.[2] By the narrative, I mean the story line, full of embedded meanings, about all things regarding humanity or the human experience. Monopolizing media affords White men this power to create false and misleading or one-dimensional narratives around bodies. It is the power of the dominant group's practice of "othering." The false images of African Americans meant to characterize them as an*other* kind of human or subhuman—from savages to innately sexual deviants to criminals and sex vixens—have been presented to the world for centuries. To challenge their narrative is to challenge whiteness, which causes the gate-keepers of the White narrative to "double down" on their characterizations while preserving the excellence of all things White—bodies, beauty, intellect, theology, civility, sophistication, and so on.

Beyond misrepresentation, (visual) media especially has the capacity to justify the mistreatment of those same bodies presented through the camera lens and framed in a White-dominated narrative. Roslyn Satchel is correct when she writes, "Media representation plays an integral role in the racialization process. Through priming, cueing, framing, and racially representing groups as stereotypical Others, entertainment and news content producers shape, and are shaped by, what individuals and societies think about race."[3] Unfortunately, this is not a new ethic but a time-tested one that has sufficiently sustained the racial hierarchy—its attitudes, assumptions, and stratified societal assignments and positions—that organizes US American society. One way this has been accomplished is through the entertaining, but manipulative and potentially destructive, use of films.

Visual media, particularly video, is extremely potent compared to written and audio mediums because of its ability to arrest both people's attentions and their imaginations in ways that the other mediums cannot. Theologian Ralph Watkins highlights the power of still photos during the Civil Rights Movement. He asserts, "It is the still image that makes [America] stop. You can't go to the next frame."[4] It was the storytelling through those still shots that helped narrate the truth of what happened during the movement. While this book focuses primarily on the visual media of the video camera, it is necessary to recognize photography, along with video, as crucial to the strategy of civil rights leaders—namely, Martin Luther King Jr. In his lecture, Watkins highlights photographers such as David Jackson, Charles Moore, James "Spider" Martin, and Joseph Louw who captured numerous images, from Emmett Till's disfigured body to Bloody Sunday and many moments in between, during the Civil Rights Movement.

I would add that while still photos make America stop and look, as Watkins claims, video images make America stop, look, listen, and feel the event being recorded. It is in the next frame or the frame before that even greater context is given as to what is happening and the extent of the violence. Videos present bodies, movements, demeanor, gestures, skin tones, sounds, violence, and suffering, to name a few images, beyond still shots and written or voiced descriptions. There is no need to imagine the drama as it is already produced and set before the audience. Seeing the drama as it unfolds on the screen (on television or in theaters) amplifies the effects of dramatization compared to just reading about the event, viewing a photo of it, or listening to its audio. This medium has been used to concretize beliefs, ideas, and misconceptions and to anchor convictions, as well as dispel the same about African Americans. Unfortunately, producers of the former have proven to create quite a dilemma for producers of the latter, who are attempting to counter incomplete or false narratives historically.

Birth of a Nation

It is imperative to understand at least a part of the historical context from which African Americans have been viewed today through the camera lens and why African Americans intentionally and persistently resist dehumanizing stereotypes. Arguably, *the* most influential film that created a narrative with residual effects lasting over one hundred years to the present was *The Birth of a Nation*, released in 1915 and directed by D. W. Griffith, based on the novel and play *The Clansman* (1905) by Thomas Dixon Jr. The novel—and the subsequent play and, ultimately, the film—was a direct response to emancipation and the South losing the Civil War. It portrayed Ku Klux Klansmen as heroes while it presented the formerly enslaved African Americans as anti-American. Black men were seen as a threat to "American" values and ways of life, and particularly to White women. They were falsely portrayed "as violent, brutal primitives driven by savage-like desire for sex with White women."[5]

The film can be described as a fallacy, destructive, and hypocritical. It was patently false to characterize African American men as violent when historically, since the beginning of the transatlantic slave trade, African American men and especially women have been the victims of unconsciona-ble violence at the hands of men of European descent. The lives of African Americans since 1619 have largely consisted of surviving slavery, Jim Crow, and the residual effects of both eras. It was destructive because to instill fear in the hearts of White people at the sight of or when interacting with African American men was to justify them being the targets of White violence. Even in their innocence, African Americans were likely to not be given the benefit of the doubt but would be assumed guilty based on cultural perceptions created by the images and the narrative of the film. Lastly, it is hypo-critical to say that African American men were driven by a "savage-like desire for sex with White women." It has been documented that a normal practice of White men—namely slaveowners—was the raping of African American women.[6] Whether this was motivated by profit (producing more of the enslaved), pleasure, or likely both, it was indicative of White men's behavior during those days. It could be argued that the film was a projection of the nature of whiteness onto blackness as if to deflect from the reality of who the true threat was and which group was susceptible to those threats.

What is certainly true is the fact that *The Birth of a Nation* was the product of the racist, white supremacist ideology of the author of the novel (Dixon) from which it was adapted. Dixon, a Baptist minister from North Carolina, was known as a "professional racist who made his living writing books and plays attacking the presence of African Americans in the United States."[7] He was anti-Black in every sense of the term. His hatred for African Americans was driven by a belief that "White southerners were the victims in American history."[8] The tragic brilliance of Dixon's project was that he managed to use fear and victimhood, ignoring and rejecting history and the realities of his day, to convince White Southerners in particular and White Americans in general that they are innocent victims to the African American disruptive presence and "destructive" nature.

Dixon created the image of African Americans as "incapable of suppressing their animalistic instincts and unable to resist their urges for white women."[9] His description of African Americans has stood the test of time. This is the rhetorical history that comes to mind when statements like the one where Hillary Clinton referred to African Americans as "predators" when she was First Lady are made. This is what many African Americans are reminded of when White citizens and politicians use binary language when saying things such as "We must take back *our* country," "*They* are destroying *our* country," or "Make America great again." Who constitutes the "our" in their statement? From whom and why must *they* take *their* country back? When was America great, and who would benefit most from going back to an era of supposed greatness? Racist dog-whistling is used to entice the White community out of the tide of progress and to invite them to revisit a time and reestablish a narrative that unabashedly dehumanized African Americans (and others) without challenge.

Dixon's novel and the worldview it promotes has proven to have staying power. During Jim Crow, the fear of and disdain for blackness that justified anti-Black practices were foundational for White men and women accusing African American men of crimes they were never even present to commit. It was also embedded in the culture of law enforcement to the degree that African Americans have always disproportionately been profiled, falsely arrested, imprisoned—with longer sentences—and exonerated after decades of incarceration.

Dixon, in shopping his story *The Clansman* to film companies, reconnected with an actor in one of his earlier plays, D. W. Griffith. Griffith was just as racist and anti-Black as Dixon. With views compatible to Dixon's, Griffith wanted to make a film that was special enough to warrant launching his new film company. This film and its content were so important to Griffith that he staked his career, his future, on its fruition and success. He, too, set out to make Ku Klux Klansmen the heroes who reunited the (White) nation after the Civil War while restoring White rule in the South.[10] This theme of "white savior/hero" versus the vilified African American took shape and went viral as intended.

White Hero, Black Threat, and Black Childlikeness

This practice of characterizing white-hooded, and more importantly white-skinned, Klansmen as having salvific function was not an American invention. The idea that people of European descent were God-ordained to civilize and Christianize the world was centuries old by the time *The Birth of a Nation* was released. The most blatantly deceptive strategy was in the misrepresentation of the ethnicity of Jesus. A Brown, Jewish rabbi with coarse hair was whitened and re-presented to the world as a European man, coinciding with white supremacist ideology. What arrogance it requires to take God-in-flesh and remake the historical Jesus into the image of another ethnic group. Many have posed the question, "What does it matter what 'race' he was?" To that question, I respond, "If it mattered enough to change his ethnic background, then it must have significance." If Jesus's ethnicity matters enough to change it in the first place, then it should matter enough for it to "be [presented] historically accurate."[11]

Coinciding with the Europeanization of Jesus, Western White interpretations of the Old Testament narrative around the so-called curse of Ham hold to the idea that descendants of Ham—one of three sons of Noah, with darker skin—were to be slaves according to God's will because Ham looked upon his naked, drunken father, Noah, as he slept. This act of dishonor lead to the curse of Ham. They understood and propagated the heresy of this social caste system that rendered those of African descent with darker skin subordinate to the lighter, whiter-skinned humans (even though the curse was not upon Ham's sons who later dwelled in Africa, but upon Canaan). The perpetuation of this idea, where "succeeding generations of one ethnic group [White/European] . . . construe salvation history in terms distinctly favorable to itself as opposed to others," Cain Hope Felder identifies as "sacralization."[12]

This sacralization of the text rendered African-descended people a threat beyond absolute servitude (to White people, descendants of Noah's son Japheth). Because of ambiguity in the biblical text surrounding the curse of Ham, interpreters have been led to "developing self-serving theological constructs like, for instance, the Canaanites 'deserve' subjugation."[13] An entire doctrine of race theory or theology was projected onto this text as it was misappropriated to justify racial hierarchies, systems, and bigotry. All based on the presumption that darker skin was evidence of being cursed as a descendant of Ham.

Of course, on the other hand, according to Willie Jennings, whiteness—through the European racial imagination—"was being held up as an aspect of creation with embedded facilitating powers."[14] In other words, Europeans assumed roles and agency that allowed them to assign positions within the social hierarchy based on race and reserving the position at the top for themselves (what I identify in this book as white *sovereignty*). This position is more than supremacy in quality, but it also constitutes a superintending and parental role similar to the biblical narrative's description of the spirit of God functioning at creation, with omniscience, omnipotence, and an omnipresence that warrants authority and autonomy. Whiteness is the "signifier of identities" and supervises to assure order is kept and all parties are in their assigned places according to status and identity.[15] The disruptive otherness of Black (moral) agency is then viewed as the cause of disorder and a *threat* to the whole of society's peace and flourishing as God intended.

In contrast to the curse that shadows those of African descent, Japheth's descendants were figured to have been blessed to constitute the great race.[16] Intellect, civility, sophistication, and creativity would be attributed to this race, while African-descended peoples remained in a condition of utter dependence upon White people. The salvific function of whiteness was not only to save themselves and society from the threat of blackness but also to "save" African-descended people from their own perpetual childlikeness. Creating narratives around the polarities of blackness as threatening or as childlike was a strategy employed to justify the white savior narrative.

Birth of a Nation set the precedence for using the business of filmmaking to reify the concept of white savior versus Black threat and/or Black childlikeness. In this seminal film, Silas Lynch, the newly elected, villainous mulatto lieutenant governor of South Carolina during Reconstruction, appeared to be intensely attracted to a young White woman. This was a not-so-subtle attempt at influencing White viewers to believe that whether enslaved or free, illiterate or intelligent,

African American men posed a legitimate threat to White women. This is a surefire way to arouse White Southerners specifically and White Americans more broadly. The collective white savior would be summoned.

Gone with the Wind (1939), on the other hand, portrays the happy, gullible, and unsophisticated enslaved Black characters as grounds for the reasonableness of the white savior. The film centralizes White bodies, sentiments, and concerns in its plot, while being sure to cast in supporting roles the asexual, Black woman caretaker of White children and the smiling, appropriately harmless, childlike Black man, both uneducated. These are shells of blackness, caricatures as representatives of the race.

The film *Mandingo* (1975) was described by respected film critic Roger Ebert as "betray[ing] not the slightest sign of taste . . . [and] racist trash."[17] The theme of interracial relationship/affairs between a White man and his enslaved African woman, and one between his enslaved African man and his White wife, anchors itself entirely in racist tropes. A major takeaway from the film is the sex-obsessed African man defiling the White man's wife while he, the slaveowner, satisfies his own sexual drive with the sex-driven African woman who did not meet his standard of purity. Of course, by the final scenes, White men are presented as the victims of Black violence, underscoring the twin ideas of the white savior and the Black threat.

Attentive viewers can find this theme in a lineage of films such as *Song of the South*, *The Green Mile*, or *Avatar*. Each film either shows the content, docile, slave-like African American man or insinuates the imperative function of the white savior, which benefits White and Black people. Uncle Remus was the happy slave in *Song of the South*. John

Coffey, in *The Green Mile*, was more than content to use "his magical powers to heal White authority figures and punish their enemies. . . . But he amazingly does not use his magical powers to liberate himself—or oppressed Blacks of the segregated South of the 1930s."[18] *Avatar* is considered to be, arguably, the most racist film of modern filmmaking. Ibram X. Kendi offers his commentary on the film:

> In "Avatar," the main White male character is portrayed as a complete failure unable to walk literally *and* figuratively in White society. He is sent to the "hell" of Pandora where dark enormous "natives" with braids and locs live—an undeniably symbol of a Black society. This failure in White society quickly masters the ways of the Na'vi, amazingly conquering Pandora's most unconquerable animal, amazingly out-excelling the Na'vi's best warrior, amazingly attracting the chief's desirable daughter, and most amazing of all—compelling the Na'vi's God to do something unprecedented, thereby saving the Na'vi from annihilation. *A projected failure in White society becomes almost godlike in this symbolic Black society.*[19]

Here is how the narrative created about Black childlikeness and Black threat are compatible. Black childlikeness is the opposite of threatening. It is comforting for whiteness and its inherent insecurities that influence its worldview and ethics of oppression. To normalize Black docility and contentment to entertain and serve whiteness is to amplify any form of resistance, even resiliency, that does arise from the African American community as threatening rather than as warranted expressions of Black moral agency in response to oppression. In other words, the Black childlikeness/docility narrative serves to establish what is an acceptable expression of blackness and simultaneously highlight the supposed threat of defiance among African Americans.

But what does "Black threat" look like? What about blackness is threatening? I argue that *Birth of a Nation* and films of its kind, on the surface, were about blackness as a threat to White women but as an existential threat to white supremacy. African American men as a threat to White women is a smokescreen to "arouse the base." In reality, they were seen as a threat to White men. Ironically, the film portrayed African American men and women not only as violent savages but as entertainers and at the disposal and service of White people's ambitions for preserving a prosperous existence for themselves—the spectrum of White views of Black being. Those views predictably omit blackness as sophisticated, intelligent, beautiful, and capable of accomplishing anything that White people have achieved. At the pinnacle of American achievements are those from the hands and the innovations of White men. The greatest of these achievements is the very social structure of American/White society, an ideological shrine that needed to be protected. This is a film that Woodrow Wilson affirmed in a statement: "In their determination to 'put the white South under the heel of the black South.' . . . The white men were roused by a mere instinct of *self-preservation* until at last there had sprung into existence the Ku Klux Klan, a veritable empire of the South, *to protect the Southern country.*"[20]

To betray the worldview of white supremacy by showcasing the best of—or what is potentially appealing and beautiful about—African Americans is the real threat to the superiority of whiteness. If African Americans are not beasts or subhuman and are equal in all things to White people, then the institution of slavery was morally wrong, Jim Crow separate-but-(not)-equal laws are morally wrong, and the legal, economic, and social foundation upon which the nation was built is morally wrong. If this is true, then everything about the ideology of whiteness and everything that is born from it—US American systems, unjust laws, institutions, theology, and so on—are lies and immoral.

Legitimizing White Power on Film

These films either reinforce and further normalize the existing social hierarchy, or they project a narrative onto society of what ought to be. In doing so there must necessarily be systematic amplification, even deification, of whiteness—and simultaneously, the erasure, demonization, and annihilation of blackness. Ironically, one way that blackness is erased (other than in its omission) is by how it is portrayed and *seen*. In other words, the suffering and resiliency built into the Black experience are often replaced in visual media with characterizations of docility, criminality, immorality, or a lack of intelligence. This is the handiwork of whiteness behind the camera lens. While these traits can be observed in any person among any culture, when used to define African Americans monolithically, they erase all or important aspects of blackness. It is another form of anti-Black violence and a mechanism for justifying the rightful, morally superior status of White people in society.

Though not an exhaustive list, there are three themes that can each be drawn from all or some of the abovementioned films that are used insidiously to legitimize power dynamics in America: (1) the romanticizing of the goodness and misrepresenting the suffering of whiteness (White victimhood), (2) the contentment in African American's codependency on White people (White paternalism), or (3) ultimately, blackness as an existential threat to White Americans (White fear). What these themes imply is that White is not only good but the only legitimate entity—whether in the form of people, thought, or culture—that functions for the well-being of the country. White victimhood justifies White violence and the forcefulness of its power. White paternalism speaks of benevolence and whiteness superintending all under its care. White fear, like White victimhood, justifies White violence, but as it points to the threat of all things Black—Black persons, Black culture, and Black progress—it shows the fear of loss. Black presence and progress imply loss of possessions, authority and power, and space for White people.

Dehumanizing film representations erase the humanity and dignity of African Americans while enhancing the same for White Americans. The themes in the film and television story lines aim to strip away any hint of Black dignity and center whiteness as that which must be "saved" from the diabolical presence of blackness *and* as that which saves. In doing so, Black suffering, Black resiliency, and Black spirituality are nullified in deference to a shell of blackness that, on screen, suggests either that African Americans accepted white supremacy as a benevolent ethos or that those who did not accept it were ungrateful at best, or innately dangerous at worst, and sought the demise of White Americans. This is an erasure of Black humanity and its dignity, decency, and inherent hospitality.

Television shows and news broadcasts are guilty of the same insidious practice of erasure. The problem of erasure begins prior to depictions of African Americans on screen and originates in limiting opportunities in front of and behind the camera. A UCLA study tells the "tale of two Hollywoods" in its analysis of the 2017–19 television season:

- Network heads were 92 percent White.
- Show creators are 89.7 percent (digital scripted), 89.3 percent (broadcast scripted), and 85.5 percent (cable scripted) White, respectively.
- Credited writers on digital, broadcast, and cable are 76 percent White.
- Directors for shows airing or streaming were 78 percent White.
- African American actors reached proportional representation in 2017–18 (12.9 percent) and overrepresentation in 2018–19 (14.1 percent); both in cable scripted shows/programs.
- African Americans were also overrepresented in total cast diversity for broadcast shows (18 percent) and cable shows (18.2 percent) in 2018–19.[21]

Among the storytellers and those who sign off on the shows, Black representation is only a piece of what is left of the "American" pie not already reserved for White people. There is absolutely progress in front of the camera as compared to years past, but is this something to be excited about? To finally reach the point of proportional representation is the equivalent of breaking even in business. This should be the baseline, not the goal. There is considerable work yet to be done.

If this is what occurs behind the lens, then naturally, the erasure of African Americans in their "full-bodied-ness" is expected in front of the lens. The handful of Black creatives who are in decision-making positions are largely responsible for providing opportunities for on- and offscreen talent and funding the projects that uplift blackness.[22] Erasure, through stereotypes and biases, shapes the degree to which blackness is seen, valued, and understood. Either TV show creators (and filmmakers) make space for African American storytellers to dispel historical racialized myths, or the industry will perpetuate dehumanizing and degrading narratives of African Americans.

There is no limit to the extent of white supremacy erasing people of Color from any realm of society that does not follow its narrative. It is the egregious erasure of blackness, but even more diabolical is its substitution of whiteness in place of God as that against which humanity should be measured or as the entity that is deserving of allegiance and idolatrous reverence. The *prophetic lens* in the hands of white supremacy becomes the *perverted lens*. Rather than challenging power, it legitimizes social power assumed by White people. Social power, through this lens of entertainment and documentation, subtly converts to divine power—white sovereignty.

When I was a child, my favorite superhero was Superman. No other fictitious character intrigued me more than the "man of steel." On the surface, I was in awe of the chiseled body, the suit, the cape, and most importantly, his ability to fly faster than the speed of light. I wanted the same muscles with superhuman strength, the outfit that would accentuate those muscles, a signature accessory, and I wanted the freedom to move about the world whenever and wherever I chose.

I was too young to understand the subliminal messages of a messiah-like figure from a place beyond this world that could defeat evil personified and overcome the crippling effects of kryptonite.[23] What was even more subtle was the fact that Superman—like all the other "messiahs"—was in a White body. How different is the Superman narrative from the *Birth of a Nation* narrative or even the Eurocentric interpretation of the biblical narrative? I would argue they share a similar theme—the white savior complex—told in distinct ways, certifying the salvific function of White men. Watching Superman save the planet enough times, I inevitably, but unconsciously, believed in the idea of the White messiah. Conversely, the strategy made it difficult to imagine a Black Superman, even though I yearned for one. Furthermore, it made it difficult to see a brown-skinned Jewish Jesus (physically) or a Black Jesus (ontologically and/or physically) who is the messiah figure of the Bible on whom the Christian faith is built upon. The Superman character and narrative had many farther-reaching implications than most (especially a child) understood or critically thought about enough to disrupt.

It was not until I grew older that those subliminal messages became more pronounced in my mind. The legacy of *The Birth of a Nation* was seen in the countless films that reinforced these disparities in how people viewed and valued White versus Black in terms of people, culture, and abilities. Consider how many television drama series and movies have a cast led by a White person (man or woman) with the token presence of people of Color as supporting cast members. The supporting cast is not just secondary in "status" for the promotion of the show but also secondary in terms of the ways those bodies are realistically portrayed in society.

Each film is also a reflection of the iterations of racism expressed in their eras. Post-Reconstruction white supremacy was blatant and largely accepted among White people.

There was no fear nor repercussions from within the White community of having white supremacist views, attitudes, and practices. During the latter decades of the twentieth century, especially after the civil rights era, those views were less accepted, and expressions of racism became more hidden and strategic. An argument could be made that the era and the messaging of the Superman films were more dangerous to African Americans and other people of Color. While the messaging of more recent film and television helps shape peoples' worldviews, just as *The Birth of a Nation* had, they are doing so indiscernibly.

What are the implications on race and racial justice when the camera is in the hands of White Americans who hold to whiteness, white supremacy (knowingly or unknowingly), and white sovereignty? In these hands, the camera lens predictably captures perspectives that underscore racial biases and stereotypes that depict African Americans according to a White worldview. They also reinforce white (body) supremacy. For example, consider most major films that are nominated for mainstream awards. White bodies are positioned as the lead characters surrounded by token bodies of Color. Until recent years, most positions of authority in films were portrayed by White men. Because of these depictions, there becomes the expectation of complete obedience by African Americans to White figures of authority, whether men or women. Then it should come as no surprise that many in the White community vilify African Americans seen in videos of police brutality because they "did not comply" with the officer "just doing his or her job." For instance, George Floyd not complying when told to get in the back of the police car is more egregious than Derek Chauvin kneeling on his neck until he died. Chauvin's position on this Black body is normal through the lens of White body supremacy. Floyd's noncompliance is unacceptable behavior regardless of any indication of trauma he displayed when attempting to avoid getting into the back of the car.

These viewpoints become ingrained in White culture and influence how other groups view African Americans and even how African Americans view themselves. Generation after generation of media misrepresentation of White bodies (supreme in quality and function) as well as Black bodies and Black culture (inferior and unsophisticated) have socialized audiences to accept the stereotypes and the associated behaviors as cultural facts. Once perceived as facts, to represent African Americans in a different light is often met with denial and rejection because it does not fit the White narrative that has been echoed multigenerationally.

The narrative of degradation does not allow room for a counternarrative of affirmation of blackness. When African Americans attempt to testify of their persistent unjust treatment at the hands of White Americans, particularly White law enforcement officers, it is not taken seriously or believed at all because it goes against the narrative ingrained and internalized within them. When African Americans go further and express sentiments of pride for their blackness—in body and culture—these pro-Black movements are also met with resistance, futile claims of reverse discrimination, and pro–white power rhetoric.

Fueling the Idolatry of Whiteness

The Birth of a Nation had not only social implications but spiritual and political ones as well. In classic cinematic entertainment fashion, the film dramatized the normalization of the idolatry of whiteness. Whiteness is more than complexion, ethnicity, or even ideology. It is, in Andrew T. Draper's definition, "a religious system of pagan idol worship that thrives on a mutually reinforcing circularity between the image (the ideal or the form) and the social constitution of those who worship it."[24] The "image" is *both* the ideal (white supremacy and sovereignty, or ideology) and the form (White bodies, or corporeality). The idolatrous and cultic allegiance to both has been aided by a systematization of *theology and liturgy* (erasure of African presence in the Bible; conflation of Jesus with power structures and European ethnicity), *laws and policies* (redlining; sentencing disparities), and *cultural messaging* (media). All are mechanisms used for the conflated practice of upholding whiteness and the Euro-Christianization of humanity.

One point that deserves repeating is that the most blasphemous use of this practice was in the Europeanization or "whitening" of the Jewish rabbi Jesus. Jesus did not need to have a narrative created around him that made him a hero. In the Christian faith, he is the "cornerstone," the "Way," and God incarnated. What Europeanizing Jesus did was co-opt the salvific role of Jesus and attribute it to whiteness / White people. This gave the invisible God, who is the Spirit, the *ideal* "White" *form*. To be White was godly. To be White was holy. To be White was the archetype for being human. Whiteness was understood less as an ethnic expression of humanity, but humanity was measured against and understood as *the* expression of whiteness. The more proximal one is to whiteness, the more their humanity is acknowledged and affirmed. To be other than White was to be sub- or nonhuman, a deviation from the fullness of true humanity, which is conceived in whiteness.

Whiteness, while it consciously and unconsciously self-proclaims divinity, is diabolical in its nature and purpose. It is not merely sanctioned by God, but it assumes God's role. According to Christian theology, humanity is made in the image of God.[25] But whiteness, as a nationalistic hero, the source of salvation, replaces God as the new "image" by which humanity is measured. In this white supremacist view, non-White ethnicities are considered a deviation from not only whiteness but humanity. Then it would only make sense that blackness/Africanness—positioned at the bottom of the social hierarchy as the radical other to whiteness—as the lesser human, appears to be the greatest threat to whiteness, and thus humanity.

When African Americans have historically asserted moral agency to resist white supremacy or to make progress, there has been a response of a re-creation or reemergence of the White messiah figure. This figure may be incarnated in movie stars (e.g., John Wayne), athletes (e.g., boxer Jim Jeffries as the "great white hope" versus African American great Jack Johnson), preachers (e.g., Billy Graham), or politicians (e.g., Ronald Reagan or Donald Trump). The form of the white savior, as presented in *The Birth of a Nation*, has always been preserved. The form is essential to the liturgy of whiteness. It unifies and clarifies the object of collective allegiance and the corresponding "worship." The latest iteration in the form is Donald Trump.

It is important to note that Trump is not the most dangerous nor the most destructive figure. He is merely the newest manifestation. The idolatrous belief and allegiance to whiteness are what is truly dangerous and destructive. Allegiance is not so much to Trump but to the perception or the ideal of whiteness as embodied in him as the White messiah figure. Agents of whiteness—those who embrace and adhere to its beliefs—have a vested interest in this messiah. The messiah figure, as an embodiment of whiteness, reflects White identity in its fullness that all in the community share but continue to aspire to.

As I stated earlier, not all White people subscribe to white supremacy and have consciously bought into legitimizing the White messiah figure, but all are shaped one way or another by whiteness. Those who do subscribe to this figure are comforted by the affirmation of this figure and troubled by any challenge to his or her authority. The challenge or threat is taken personally, as if it is a challenge or threat to each of them as individuals or as a collective. The challenge to the imagined supremacy and authority of the White messiah is seen in the very presence of African American bodies, thought, progress, and prosperity. Every messiah needs a nemesis. The Black body is the historical nemesis to White body supremacy as personified by the White messiah figure. This, too, is a significant part of the legacy of *The Birth of a Nation*. In fact, in the silent film, there is a caption that states, "The bringing of the African to America planted the first seed of disunion."[26]

Internalizing White Narratives

Messaging that is repeated from perceived authoritative voices is powerful in that it shapes culture even beyond the life span of the source. That influence is even greater when the messaging is internalized, particularly by marginalized, minority groups. This should not come as a surprise, as this is ultimately the goal of the dominant group in its efforts to maintain dominance. It is imperative that these groups believe the narrative that is imposed upon them. Although it is a type of violence upon the identity and dignity of their humanity, when the messaging is no longer opposed and is assumed to be fact, whether consciously or unconsciously, resistance is less likely.

Internalization of films produced by White filmmakers occurs within White people as much as it occurs with any other ethno-racial group. The internalization, however, appears differently and produces a more positive self-perception in White people. While White people do not perceive themselves as racialized persons (neither in the films nor in real life), they do internalize the status, portrayal, and response to the White characters in the films with whom they identify. African Americans, until recent years, have not been afforded the same luxury of being represented and portrayed in the strong, positive ways that White people have been, save for a few exceptions. African Americans, therefore, have hovered in the liminal, in-between space of internalizing and resisting the internalization of themselves being portrayed largely in stereotypical ways such as being subservient to White people and as thugs/criminals, sex vixens, or uneducated individuals, as well as other dehumanizing roles.

African Americans and other minorities persistently resist the prison cells of the perceptions of White majority media power brokers as they limit their representation to safe stereotypes that pose no threat to the supremacy, sovereignty, and economic dominance of White maleness. Satchel highlights the effects of the "Looking Glass Theory of Media Influences" and the impact—largely positive for White people and negative for African Americans—that film has on the development of self-image.[27] Self-image, as a consequence of internalizing film representation and portrayal, can influence a person in two ways: (1) they either live up to the stereotypes—conscious assimilation to appease or associate with White people—or (2) they underperform out of the fear of proving negative stereotypes to be true. Claude Steele calls this "'stereotype threat'—being at risk of confirming, as self-characteristic, a negative stereotype about one's group."[28]

I suggest that White people ought to internalize *in a different way* to become conscientious participants in the disruption of whiteness, especially as it is performed in films. They ought not to internalize and metabolize the illusion of white superiority as shown in the dominant characters and story lines in many films. Instead, they must begin to internalize whiteness. They must employ the same practices that African Americans and other people of Color have on their journeys to self-discovery and rewriting the narratives around their identities. White people must first feel it (whiteness), sense it in their bodies, and become aware of its disorienting effects. They must then reflect on it, wrestle with it, think critically about it, learn its origins, ways, and manifestations, and understand how they too have had their identities stolen in return for a distorted self-image and worldview.

Why is Frazier's video so important? What she captured brought many White people in front of the mirror to see what has long been invisible to them—their whiteness. This presents an opportunity for White people to internalize whiteness as a human construction out of their community rather than a universal norm for being human. Not that there have never been violent anti-Black images published before, but her recording, in disrupting the comfort of the hiddenness of whiteness for this generation, and the tranquilizing effects of white normativity, raised awareness in the White community arguably unlike any other images before. White normativity had been fostered, in one way, by the White producers behind movie cameras projecting and reifying the "binary opposition" of the images of White dominance versus Black subordination for at least a century of filmmaking.[29] It requires a deep reflection of whiteness and its implications on White peoples' collective identity, worldview, theology, and ability to fully honor the humanity in others to truly heal White people. Only then can whiteness be weakened and the humanity of its agents be restored along with the humanity of African Americans and other people of Color.

In contrast to Frazier's prophetic action, *The Birth of a Nation* promotes the "good news" of the dominant group that persists in the United States. For many White Americans of that era and subsequent decades, whiteness is evangelistic. It does not require much internalization or critical thought. It does not present any alternative consciousness that may create tension for White people. The message of the film is not offensive. It does not evoke the lament required from White people for repentance. Instead, it sets out to affirm the dominant thought among Whites, lulling its audience to social apathy to remain compliant and uncritical of the status quo.

The good news of the Old Testament, before it was co-opted by New Testament theology, was the news brought to the battlefield by a messenger declaring to the fighters that the war or the battle was over and that victory was by the strength of God. It was what Dietrich Bonhoeffer calls a message of "earthy" salvation for the people of God. The prophetic message, while it was a message of conviction for Israel to turn away from sin, also contained the "good news" of God's desire to save or restore them from adversaries or from the consequences of their own sin upon repentance. The good news in the Old Testament, however, was not necessarily a message of repentance. This is what the prophet writes in Isaiah 52:7: "How beautiful upon the mountains are the feet of him who *brings good news*, who *publishes peace*, who *brings good news of happiness*, who *publishes salvation*, who says to Zion, 'Your God reigns.'" Paul draws upon this verse in Romans 10:15 when he writes, "How beautiful are the feet of those who *preach the good news!*" It only takes the skill, discipline, and self-deception of cognitive dissonance to hear only the positive from the messenger and never discern the change that is required or to grieve and appreciate the amount of death and sacrifice it took even in the victory. The evangelistic message is about the victory. The prophetic message is about the *cost* of the victory. The evangelistic message draws the crowds and builds the churches. The prophetic message often turns them away and provokes the ire of the people. *Birth of a Nation* evangelized white supremacy, and the African American community has been using every tool available to them, including the camera—to tell the counterstory with a prophetic accent—ever since.

The Belief/Ideology That Won't Die

The film and its descendants create, preserve, and amplify stereotypes through lack of, or misrepresentation of, non-White people. They traffic in racialized cultural messaging that is controlled by the dominant White group. The sacrificial lamb in this "religion" at its greatest degree of destruction is the collective Black body—not to lose sight of the fact that all bodies of Color have experienced the degradation of this tool of white supremacy. The tool is film. The mechanism is storytelling. The result is an ideology that transcends generations, regions, and forms of resistance. Its message is simply believed. It is effective to the degree that it forms not only beliefs about people but sentiments behind those beliefs. Human cognition is inseparable from the unconscious emotional responses that go with it.[30] It plants seeds of hatred while watering the soil already impregnated with those seeds. It nurtures a climate that is unwelcoming and counterresistant to alternative views, narratives, and depictions of whiteness (e.g., critical race theory, Black Lives Matter).

White people feed off the images of themselves and African Americans portrayed in the films they view. If they see themselves as the group with a salvific role for creation and a paternalistic role—to care for and discipline—they will act accordingly. Threats in any form are not welcomed. The threats can form an unbreakable group allegiance to both beliefs, persons, and identities (e.g., conservative, evangelical Christian Republican Trump loyalists). The threat of alternative narratives further justifies one's beliefs, no matter how unsubstantiated those beliefs may be. Adrian Bardon, professor of philosophy at Wake Forest, writes,

> "System justification" theorists like psychologist John Jost have shown how situations that represent a threat to established systems trigger inflexible thinking and a desire for closure. . . . In ideologically charged situations, one's prejudices end up affecting one's factual beliefs. Insofar as you define yourself in terms of your cultural affiliations, your attachment to the social or economic

status quo, or a combination, information that threatens your belief system—say, about the negative effects of industrial production on the environment—can threaten your sense of identity itself. . . . Under the right conditions, universal human traits like in-group favoritism, existential anxiety and a desire for stability and control combine into a toxic, system-justifying identity politics.[31]

Whiteness has been so strong that largely every generation of White people has been willing to accept the degree of injustice and dehumanization that African Americans and other people of Color have had to endure (this includes active bigotry and silent complicity). This with only a minimum amount of White folks who have proven to be allies in movements against such injustice and dehumanization. Most White people accepted slavery. Most were indifferent to Jim Crow segregation with its Black Codes and lynching practices. Most today have been apathetic regarding racial profiling, police brutality, and mass incarceration all targeting African Americans disproportionately.

Conclusion

These films either reinforce and further normalize the existing social hierarchy or project onto society what ought to be. For example, Moses, performed by Charlton Heston—a White man playing the role of a Hebrew man leading other Hebrews played by White people—serves to normalize White male headship while completely erasing the presence of non-White people.

The tendency of whiteness—and by extension, its creative endeavors such as filmmaking—is to create an enemy. This enemy, whether in person(s) or thought (ideology), poses a threat to the White/American/Christian way of life. It does so by projecting this practice onto Christian theology. Anything that does not comply with whiteness is the threat. Expressions of patriotism must be approved by White voices even if the patriotism of "others" is authentic. For example, Colin Kaepernick kneeling during the national anthem is an act of patriotism. His gesture is one that honors those who fought for the freedoms we are privileged to have in this country and the values the flag represents. His choice to kneel—nonverbal speech—is one of the freedoms and privileges afforded citizens of the United States. Yet many White Americans condemn the act as unpatriotic. This sends the message that the flag is a symbol for selective freedoms, those selected and approved by the "patriotic" White majority.

Whether it is filmmaking, news coverage, or ordinary White citizens behind the camera creating enemies or affirming their own worldview, the aim is to reinforce White dominance and further subjugate people groups and any perspective that challenges white supremacy. This reality makes the camera as a tool stewarded by African Americans even more imperative.

CHAPTER 4

Uncovered Truth

A Prophetic Alternative

One of the most powerful weapons in any society is the ability to control what is perceived as truth. It is the construction of perceived truth and the dissemination of the narrative it is cloaked in that forms a society's ideals, values, and norms—its culture. Consequently, embedded within that narrative is how people groups come to be viewed and thus treated. In the hands of those in power, truth is an oppressive weapon. In the hands of the oppressed, the construction of truth from the margins is a liberating weapon. This is why Foucault says, "There can be no possible exercise of power without a certain economy of discourses of truth. . . . Power never ceases its interrogation, its inquisition, its registration of truth."[1] Truth is at the center of the societal struggles between oppression and liberation, dehumanization and dignity, and justice and injustice that exist between races and classes, or the intersection of the two. The struggle from the margins of power structures is one for an alternative story. The struggle from the center is one for the preservation of the status quo to the benefit of those in power and the disenfranchisement of those without it. The camera can be a tool in the construction of truth for both the powerful and the seemingly powerless.[2]

Greater than the need for alternative portrayals *in front of the camera* performing a counternarrative is the need for different storytellers *behind the camera*. The narrative is not necessarily changed by the performance—as it too can be misinterpreted—but it is changed with the imagination, creativity, and audacity of authors, cinematographers, directors, and producers of those stories telling the unseen and untold Black experience. This is the role of the Darnella Fraziers of the world, to capture, with urgency and seriousness, the Black experience *from within* the Black experience, in real time. She is the de facto cinematographer of the footage of George Floyd's murder that depicted a very different story than the narrative initially published by the Minneapolis Police Department.[3] Here is an excerpt of their statement regarding what is described as "a forgery in progress": "Two officers arrived and located the suspect, a male believed to be in his 40s, in his car. He was ordered to step from his car. After he got out, he physically resisted officers. Officers were able to get the suspect into handcuffs and noted he appeared to be suffering medical distress. Officers called for an ambulance. He was transported to Hennepin County Medical Center by ambulance where he died a short time later. At no time were weapons of any type used by anyone involved in this incident. . . . No officers were injured in the incident."[4]

Whoever controls the narrative controls perception. Had there been no video footage other than police body cameras and surveillance cameras from businesses in that neighborhood, history tells us it is likely there would have been no charges, arrests, and convictions. Had the Minneapolis Police Department been the only "producers" of the video footage, the outcome would have been drastically different because the narrative, which appeased established racialized perceptions, had already been published. Age-old assumptions of the Black man, the criminal to be feared, and the White police officer with his knee on this man's neck, subduing him to "save" or protect society, would have been uncritically accepted as fitting and believable.

Reframing the American Dream

I often think about the "American dream." I wonder who this idealistic life in the United States was meant for? It is the great sales pitch that lures US Americans into lives of work and the pursuit of wealth and comfort even at the cost of one's neighbors and his or her own lives. The genius and the danger of the myth of the American dream is that it convinces many Americans to accept the status quo, with its social injustices and inequities, and reject the disruptors passionate about making those wrongs right. People are vigilant to protect and preserve things *as they are*. These questions should always be raised: Who benefits from things *as they are*? Who benefits from existing social realities—institutions, systems, and the existing cultural norms? The answer is quite simple: the group in power that controls not only the institutions but also the dominant narrative that reinforces those accepted injustices, inequities, and norms.

For too many people, especially for many African Americans, the elusive American dream—while some aspects of it are attainable—is more analogous to a nightmare. By nature, nightmares evoke cries and yelps that suggest a traumatic encounter during sleep that suddenly and shockingly awakens us. These cries are guttural and sensed in the body. The irony of the American dream is that it lulls people to sleep, and after some time, the reality of pursuing it tirelessly and realizing it just may not be attainable or as satisfying as once imagined has the tendency to shock and awe individuals into craving new consciousnesses and new realities in much the same way a nightmare can violently disrupt one's sleep and awaken them.

If this dream is more elusive for many Americans or for particular groups of Americans, then can it actually be a lie? A half-truth? Could this be the social cosmetic that attempts to cover the ugly reality of being Black in the United States? If the American dream is equitably and equally available to and beneficial for all, then cries from the African American community can be dismissed simply as a collective victim's mentality. If this were true, then racism is the lie, and whoever controls the narrative around racism determines whether the truth is revealed or hidden. The truth is, the "dream" often comes at the expense of the poor and people of Color, with African Americans arguably paying the greatest cost.

One of my uncles told me a story about how my paternal grandmother, as a teenager and young adult in the 1940s, had the boldness to confront White owners of restaurants in Murrells Inlet, South Carolina, who would not serve African Americans, as was the norm in the Jim Crow South. She would encourage her siblings to join her when she entered a restaurant and sat at a table waiting for service, even though she knew they would never serve her. She would sit there for a little while, and after not receiving service, she would leave until the next time she returned to enact another "sit-in." Whether she knew it or not, what she did was prophetic in nature. She was confronting power structures, demanding changes to unfair and discriminatory practices that marginalized and oppressed people that looked like her. She moved beyond rhetoric to embody prophetic action, which she intended to challenge and hopefully change the dominant narrative of her day that comfortably existed as the status quo.

Decades later, on February 1, 1960, four North Carolina A&T State University freshmen decided to do in front of the gaze of news cameras what my grandmother had done without notice or fanfare. What they did started a national movement for change. On day one, it was the four freshmen Ezell Blair Jr. (Jibreel Khazan), Franklin McCain, Joseph McNeil, and David Richmond—known as the "A&T Four"—sitting at a whites-only lunch counter at a Woolworth's restaurant in Greensboro, North Carolina. The next day, twenty-five more students from A&T and other Greensboro colleges and universities joined them. Over the next couple of weeks, there were more statewide sit-ins. By week three of February, there were over 400 sit-ins in at least 250 major cities and towns across the country that lasted for the balance of the year. Woolworth was desegregated by the end of July 1960.⁵ A group of young, courageous men decided to confront the giant of Jim Crow and its narrative of "separate-but-equal," demanding the consciousness of a new counternarrative and energizing the formation of a countercommunity hungry for a new society. They lived out their "prophetic imagination."

This imagination envisioned the "wall(s) of hostility" coming down to make space for a new humanity, a new consciousness, and a new reality for all. This imagination can see the unseen future as it responds to both the visible and invisible barriers of the present. This imagination points humanity toward the divine telos as it navigates the now-but-not-yet. It is resilient by nature in the penultimate.

It inspires risk-taking, courage, and long-suffering, all necessary for the "new thing" God desires.

Brueggemann's Prophetic Imagination

What does it mean to be prophetic? The term is tossed around flippantly within the church and even in broader culture. To put it simply, the prophetic comes in the form of forth-telling (discerning and predicting future events) and foretelling (confronting power with truth). It can be presented in the form of rhetoric and/or embodied in actions.

Walter Brueggemann, in his book *Prophetic Imagination*, articulates how the prophetic ministry functions in a social context that conflicts with Judeo-Christian ideals. He clearly states, "The task of the prophetic ministry is to nurture, nourish, and evoke a consciousness and perception alternative to the consciousness and perception of the dominant culture around us."[6] Brueggemann uncovers the insidious nature of the dominant consciousness that he also identifies as "royal consciousness." He claims that this was the central focus for Moses, the consciousness that undergirded the "royal regime" that tended to be oppressive to its citizens.[7] The prophetic ministry offers an alternative way of thinking, and ultimately *being*, that seeks to dismantle the structures of the regime or "empire" that is founded upon this oppressive consciousness.[8]

The prophetic ministry is public theology that purposefully engages the dominant culture on behalf of those made vulnerable by the dominant ethos. Justice is at the heart of any prophetic movement. The dismantling of power structures is necessarily public. Both Moses's and Martin

Luther King Jr.'s prophetic, public ministries were not for the purpose of personal and individual reflection (although that may have occurred) but rather aimed at "the formation of a countercommunity with a counter consciousness."[9] Pharaoh in Moses's day and White Americans—namely, Southerners—in King's day were forced to respond to creative tension publicly. The tension is between the old, oppressive, and complacent royal consciousness and the disruptive alternative consciousness of agency and liberation.

To evoke this new consciousness, Brueggemann offers two essential qualifiers for prophetic ministry: *criticizing* and *energizing*.[10] Prophetic ministry *criticizes* royal consciousness and *energizes* the oppressed and marginalized "other" who will be edified by the alternative consciousness. This must be a both/and strategy. Both criticizing and energizing are necessary to dismantle and build anew. Royal consciousness is strategically and persistently managed by the royal regime (empire) that has shown resiliency in maintaining the status quo. Empire, as it pertains to a US society organized by race, cannot be disentangled from its undergirding ideology of white supremacy, which will instinctively resist the efforts of prophetic ministry.

Therefore, both criticizing and energizing go together. Criticizing says the royal consciousness is insufficient and ineffective and permits injustice and inequities. Energizing inspires hopefulness for a more just future. While there will always be injustice simply because of the human condition, the alternative community is never content with injustice and is proactively in pursuit of justice and equity. The alternative consciousness is bookended by these practices. In this new society, shalom is normalized. This is the prophetic alternative, "an alternative to a social world void of criticism and energy."[11]

When I was playing basketball in college, I had a great freshman season and a disappointing sophomore season. During the summer after my sophomore year, while in the gym shooting around, a friend came up to me and wanted to offer his critique on why my jump shot was not as accurate as it was the previous season. I was skeptical to hear what he had to say, but as he shared his criticism, he gave me the truth about the form on my jump shot, and it turned out he was right. Once I accepted what he said was true, no longer deceiving myself that the form of my jump shot was good enough, I made the corrections and applied what he told me. His criticism, as challenging as it may have been for me to hear, was necessary for my success. Every shot I took, I was conscious of his critique, until awareness of those details became engrained in me, and my subsequent execution became natural. The next season turned out to be the best season of my college basketball career.

Years later, as I transitioned into a career in Christian ministry, I had a life-changing conversation with my mentor. He tended to be brutally honest with me. It was a trait in him I respected and needed. The context of the conversation escapes me, but one statement left an indelible mark on me. He said, "You're prideful." Surprised at this assessment, I responded, "No I'm not." He replied, "Yes you are." There was a pause in the conversation. Not an awkward silence, but a moment of reflection he made space for. After thinking about his statement, I humbly, but reluctantly, agreed. Here is why this conversation was life-altering, even prophetic for me; he criticized me, and then he energized me with encouragement. He continued by affirming for me that while I was not naturally humble, due to being supremely confident in myself, I try to practice humility. There is a distinction. He assured me that I was not to be ashamed, nor feel defeated, by his criticism. He encouraged me by pointing out that he noticed that I tried to live a life dependent on Jesus and interdependent on others, even though I am a naturally self-initiating and self-sufficient individual. The former was initially hard to receive, but the latter was energizing for me and gave me hope that I did not have to be crippled by the constructive criticism of my pride.

Rarely would an individual, group, or institution invite criticism. To avoid it would be safe. To criticize means to find fault or make a judgment. When Frazier pressed the record button on her phone, she was producing critical content of a more-than-centuries-old, state-sanctioned practice of anti-Black policing that is tragically woven into the American fabric—the nightmare part of the American dream. She was sounding the alarm. She was pointing the finger. She was saying to all who would dare take notice, "Look y'all; they're doing it again!" Her content would cause the collective global gasp from the bad dream that the truth about policing African Americans revealed. A new consciousness that contradicts the dominant consciousness was both born in some and heightened in others.

When Moses was sent to confront Pharaoh and demanded the liberation of the Israelites, he was confronting the royal regime and challenging the royal consciousness. In a modern-day US context, the royal regime is analogous to the White group, and whiteness / white supremacy is the royal consciousness. White supremacy, like royal consciousness, insists uncritically that the status quo is beneficial for everyone.[12] The new consciousness, instead, critiques the status quo, energizes those oppressed under such a regime, and offers an alternative way of thinking and being that serves to ultimately dismantle the dominant consciousness.[13] The status quo is a dangerous proposition that even King recognized White segregationists of his day were dedicated to maintaining.[14] It is dangerous in that it is a space for the normalization of attitudes and deeds that goes unchallenged and breeds apathy in its citizens. Its advocates are "unable to be seriously energized to new promises from God."[15]

However, there will certainly be energy invested in resisting the critique and disruption of royal consciousness. Brueggemann claims that the royal consciousness will naturally respond with counterresistance, as it "cannot tolerate serious and fundamental criticism."[16] Richard Delgado and Jean Stefancic in *Norms and Narratives* were right in saying, "For most persons . . . society's dominant narratives will seem unexceptional and 'true'—demanding no particular improvement or expansion. . . . Divergent new narratives, ones that could jar and change us, always spark resistance; we reject precisely those narratives that could save us from history's judgment."[17] In other words, the royal consciousness that oppressed the Israelites and the white supremacy that has done the same to African Americans and people of Color in modern history both thrive in societies that slumber. However, the prophetic ministry cannot sleep by nature. It haunts the dominant group, proclaims the truths, and asks the questions that arouse the collective conscience of the people.

In *The Construction of Whiteness*, Sandha Bery helps us understand what I mean by "haunts" when she draws upon Avery F. Gordon's definition of the concept: "Haunting is the animated state in which a repressed or unresolved social violence is making itself known . . . and [its] impact is felt in everyday life, especially when [it is] supposedly over and done with."[18] Gordon continues, "Haunting is a socio-political-psychological state that produces a 'something-to-be-done'; that is, when whites can no longer repress and contain the haunting specters of slavery [for example], they are compelled to account for them in the present."[19] This is where the tension lies. While some may want to account for the haunting past, others further suppress that past at their own peril, and at the peril of society. Unfortunately, death at the hands of the dominant consciousness is an option for some.

The critique of the royal consciousness of white supremacy must lead to the complete deconstruction of all forms of white supremacy (*if* that is possible) and to the construction of an alternative consciousness (this *is* possible), as the two cannot coexist. I agree with Brueggemann when he uses the cross as "the ultimate metaphor of prophetic criticism because it means the end of the old consciousness that brings death on everyone."[20] In other words, it is the finality (or its prospects) of the dominance of the royal consciousness of white supremacy that invites the energy to conceive and give birth to the counterconsciousness.

I don't believe the cross is understood that way by many in the church today. For some, the cross is nothing more than a symbol of Jesus's sacrifice on behalf of humanity for salvation. One must be willing to take sacraments like communion much more seriously and be willing to consider what it means to enter into the experience of the death of sin—active sin, personal sin, or complicity in social or institutional sin. For instance, if Christians framed communion in terms of trauma and resiliency embodied in Jesus, it may carry more weight for them. He was traumatized. The community was traumatized vicariously because of what they witnessed together. That kind of trauma was not easily forgotten by early Christians. It was a felt experience that would have likely "haunted" them.

The cross should not be a trigger for a traumatizing event, but it should remind us of the resiliency of the man, Jesus, as he gave of himself (upon the cross) willingly as an instrument of the prophetic criticism of sin and death, but also of those power structures that create a social context of sin and death. The most vulnerable in society being the most susceptible to the latter. The cross, and all that it means relative to trauma and suffering, is also the symbol of resiliency that inspires hopefulness of a new reality.

Energizing Alternative Consciousness

Cultural criticism alone is insufficient. It is not enough to simply point out the flaws of a society, a group, or an individual. Prophetic criticism, however, does more than announce judgment and expose flaws that need to change; it also points toward the alternative consciousness, ethic, and community that reflects the diligent pursuit of the shalom of God. But the alternative requires social energy and momentum. This also underscores the camera's relevance. Its footage, when published, evokes the indignation and passion required to fuel the alternative.

Brueggemann asserts, "Prophetic ministry has to do not primarily with addressing specific *public crises* but with addressing, in season and out of season, the *dominant crisis* that is enduring and resilient."[21] Systemic racism—in this case, expressed in anti-Black policing policies and practices captured by both King and Frazier—in the United States has proven to be the dominant, enduring crisis that has plagued the nation and left no one untouched by its traumatizing effects. It is baked into the fabric of US American history. When the content of the camera confronts and criticizes white supremacy, it has the potential to energize a movement for justice (e.g., Emmett Till's open-casket photo catalyzing the Civil Rights Movement).

Immediately following George Floyd's murder, studies showed that the video seemingly aroused the collective conscience of White people in the United States. As if the videos documenting the previous killings and beatings of unarmed Black people were not enough, Floyd's death is thought to have triggered a longer-lasting shift in White people's awareness and opinion on racism. Nolan McCaskill of *Politico* writes, "Public opinion on race relations and police misconduct has shifted dramatically since the killing of George Floyd in Minneapolis, with Americans significantly more likely to say they believe in systemic racism."[22] The Floyd video had a profound impact on the nation and energized a multiethnic response of protest and social unrest for change.[23] Following Floyd's murder, 60 percent of White Americans now believe racism is a big problem, compared to 21 percent believing the same according to a 2011 CNN / Kaiser Foundation Poll.[24]

When making an even more specific inquiry as to how much of a problem systemic racism is in law enforcement following the killings of unarmed Black people, the same increase is seen. McCaskill continues, "In a Washington Post/Schar School (George Mason University) poll . . . 69 percent of respondents—including 68 percent of whites—said Floyd's killing was part of a broader problem within law enforcement. That represents a large increase from a December 2014 ABC News/Washington Post poll, when only 43 percent of all respondents and 35 percent of whites said then-recent police killings of unarmed Black men were signs of a broader problem."[25] Certainly, there have since been gestures by White individuals, institutions, and even corporations that have suggested significant change is occurring in how racism, especially anti-Black racism, is viewed in the United States. But this sudden change in consciousness was short-lived. After the initial shock, outrage, and grief fades, unless the countercommunity is active and effective, the masses are lulled back to the familiarity of the status quo with the belief that, because they felt something they had not felt before about racism, enough has been done for societal transformation.[26] This will always be the case if change is measured or determined by the royal regime's satisfaction with its efforts. The newly formed countercommunity must continue to press the dominant group—in this case, the White community, the wealthy, and governing officials. The prophetic imagination finds its home among those with new energy and new consciousness, not among the dominant group who is limited to a cerebral or an intellectual understanding of the crisis by choice or by default from social distance. The countercommunity responds with an embodied understanding of the effects of racism.

For Brueggemann, prophetic energizing points to the past and the future. A consumer culture, one that satiates individuals and institutions to the point of social lethargy, tends to erase identities and faith traditions, dim hopes for the future, and mandate an urgency of the "now"—including an eternal now.[27] At stake is the memory of a past (ancestry, heritage, events) that grounds us and a future hope (liberation) that drives us. Prophetic energizing fights the inertness of such a culture that requires little to no social action by invoking memories that affirm the identity and dignity of the oppressed and by casting an alternative redemptive vision for the "beloved community" God is actively forming.

As the past is uncovered for some and recovered for others, it evokes both a sense of pride for historical achievements of ancestors and indignation for the atrocities they were subjected to in the name of the royal regime of white supremacy. In retrospect, the resiliency of those who have endured injustices in the past is as deserving of equal recognition as their trauma. This history lesson is empowering to active participants and those who are reluctant to participate in the prophetic ministry for racial justice. Ironically, this memory is critical for nurturing and maintaining a sense of hope for the future. The progress one observes from remembering is meant not to foster apathy but to recognize that there is movement, despite its apparent glacial pace. By remembering individuals and groups of the past, there is the opportunity to reignite (or ignite for the first time) passion in the present to right wrongs or to build upon the work of predecessors.

In prophetic ministry, memory is necessarily linked to a vision for the future. The prophet passionately reminds the people of God of the lineage of immorality, injustice, and oppression experienced by the most vulnerable among them and then points them to the redeemed future that God desires for them. Amid the exile to Babylon, the prophet Jeremiah declares the word of the Lord to the Israelites in Jeremiah 29:11: "I know the plans I have for you, declares the Lord, plans for welfare and not for evil, to give you a future and a hope." It is important to note that when God causes things to happen for Israel, it does not suggest passivity on the people's part. What is expected is their participation on varying levels.

This prophetic vision requires repentance by the people that they might then be co-laborers in God's redemptive work. God's redemptive work is the steady, unrelenting work of justice, equity, and the liberation of all humanity. Without remembering the past—identities, traditions, and shortcomings—and envisioning the future, prophetic energy is compromised. When prophetic energy is compromised, the risk is collective regression toward a vision akin to "mak[ing] America great again" (MAGA). MAGA was the campaign slogan for then-presidential candidate Donald Trump. He coined the phrase and inspired what some would consider a cultlike following with these words and the attitude and policies that came with it. MAGA became more than a tagline; it became the ethos of a faction of society with divisive, dangerous, and tragic implications.

Evidence of this backlash is seen in the rise in white supremacist hate groups (a significantly loyal portion of Trump's base) contributing to the increase in domestic terrorism. The momentum began following the election of Barack Obama in 2008.[28] Consider the presence of an African American occupying the highest office in the land to be a type of prophetic event achieved by the collective (Obama received 53 percent of the vote). Many White people were confronted with a radical shift in the direction of the country, reminded of the change in demographics, and threatened by the greater share of power and influence of African Americans and other people of Color. Obama's presence, the Black vote, and this level of progress infringe upon white autonomy, and everyone witnessing this political and cultural shift must think differently, alternatively about the present and what it says to us about the future.

While the backlash found momentum with the election of the first African American president in the history of the United States, the violence has continued to increase even after Obama left office after serving two terms. According to the Center for Strategic International Studies, since 2015, right-wing and left-wing extremist groups have been responsible for plotting and executing acts of domestic terrorism. Not to excuse the egregious acts committed by those on the left, but right-wing extremist groups have accounted for 80 percent of the terrorist acts (267 of 333) and 82 percent of deaths due to domestic terrorism (91 of 110) in this period; of those, "more than twenty-five percent of right-wing incidents and just under half of deaths in those incidents were caused by people who show support for white supremacy or claim to belong to groups espousing that ideology."[29] The energy that the prophetic ministry—or by extension, prophetic embodiment (Obama as president)—generates for the formation of an alternative consciousness and countercommunity will be matched or challenged by the energy generated by the dominant group to halt any lasting cultural change that would diminish their dominance. The data suggests this is a fight that continues into the near future. FBI director Christopher Wray told the Senate Judiciary Committee on March 2, 2021, "The problem of domestic terrorism has been metastasizing across the country for a long time now, and it's not going away anytime soon."[30]

The prophetic energy cannot be restricted to impassioned rhetoric. It is not an intellectual nor an oratorical exercise. This type of permanent cultural change must include embodied agency in some way. Frazier's video is the corridor by which those insulated from the violence of all forms of racism—but namely, police brutality toward African Americans—can experience in their bodies a reality foreign to them. The countercommunity lives along the proverbial "Damascus Road."

The apostle Paul, by his own admission, was a Pharisee in his early career, prior to becoming a leading voice for the "Way." Saul—as he was known before his name change—persecuted and imprisoned Christians. He witnessed and approved the execution of Stephen, a follower of Jesus. He was convinced of the theology and doctrine he was taught that shaped his worldview and fostered his convictions. There was likely no intellectual argument a person could have made that would have convinced Saul of the errors of his ways. He fit comfortably in the violent space of the dominant group/narrative within the Jewish community (although they, too, were marginalized in the broader Roman context). It would require more than prophetic speech. Saul needed to experience something in his body to transform his thinking. He needed to *feel* the message from the energy of the countercommunity. He was then given the gift of an embodied experience with the leader of that countercommunity, Jesus.

Saul, soon to be identified as Paul after his conversion, encountered Jesus on the road to Damascus. This was not just an audible experience but one that would physically bring him to his knees and take his sight. His peers traveling with him only heard a voice but did not see what he saw (more about this in chapter 9) or felt what he felt. He did not regain his sight until God sent Ananias to him to lay hands on him. Saul would never be the same. In fact, he not only joined the countercommunity, but he also became a leader within that community.

Effective prophetic activity confronts the royal regime, criticizes the royal narrative, and affects not just the intellect and emotions (through rhetoric), but it is sensed in the body as well. Prophetic energy is meant to be felt. George Floyd's cries for his mother, the anxiety he displayed when they attempted to put him in the back of the police car, and the posture and "unbothered" facial expression of Derek Chauvin while kneeling on Floyd's neck was felt by all who watched, even if they could not intellectually comprehend the tragic event. The video footage from the business across the street could not fully capture all of this. The police body cam footage recorded the sounds but not the full drama produced by Frazier's perspective. Her presence, position, and proximity were critical to capturing the whole drama as it unfolded and became the catalyst for the energy needed to spark collective indignation and social movement.

The prophetic ministry is fueled by passion. When you trace the etymology of the word *passion* to its Latin roots, it lands on the idea of suffering. The suffering of Jesus is often described as the "passion of Christ." Even film and stage productions depicting the final days of Jesus and his suffering use the term *passion* of Christ rather than *suffering* of Christ. What we see in still shots and videos of anti-Black violence (or recent anti-Asian violence) should evoke passion. It should cause a degree of suffering in our own bodies as witnesses to human suffering. This is not to be confused with the ephemeral nature of emotionalism. Passion is the energizing force for follow-through and commitment to real change. It is "kryptonite" to the royal regime / royal consciousness / white supremacy. Brueggemann is correct when he writes, "Where passion disappears there will not be any serious humanizing energy. . . . Passion as the capacity and readiness to care, to suffer, to die, and to feel is the enemy of imperial reality. Imperial economics is designed to keep people satiated so that they do not notice. Its politics is intended to block out the cries of the denied ones. Its religion is to be an opiate so that no one discerns misery alive in the heart of God."[31]

Never had there been such a global response to racial injustice like what followed the murders of Ahmaud Arbery, Breonna Taylor, and George Floyd. The video of the Floyd murder was the proverbial "straw that broke the camel's back." It provided the content that was inherently a critique of US American society, but it was also the catalyst for energizing movements and legislative reform nationally and locally. The multiethnic, multigenerational, and multinational global movement reflected the energy that was fostered by video images. The tool at the center of seismic shifts in collective consciousness is the camera. It is the repeated, courageous, prophetic use of the camera at the most crucial moments shining light on oppressive practices, once hidden, that will move society toward the vision of an alternative countercommunity. There must be continued exposure of the violence. Although the images can be traumatizing, every video posted is significant to keep the energy. Without them, apathy will likely set in. Just as God sent prophet after prophet to the people of Israel on behalf of the vulnerable among them, so must an embodied prophetic ministry continue today, undeterred by counterresistance or recurring apathy.

The Camera as Prophetic Tool

How is the camera considered a prophetic tool? The camera is not prophetic on its own. It is a tool of the modern-day prophet as seen in the imagination of Martin Luther King Jr. In this case, it functions prophetically as an extension of Black moral agency to expose, "testify" to, and resist racial injustice. Its use does not guarantee justice, as was the case with the police officers captured on video violently and unjustifiably beating Rodney King in 1991. The camera, however, provides a kind of revelation—revealed truth or fact—about the African American experience once unknown or unacknowledged by White Americans. It collects the "data" to make a multigenerational case for what African Americans have been talking, protesting, singing, and creating art about for generations.

While its use is creative and improvisational like art, its content is more scientific. The camera is used to document—the use of documentary evidence to substantiate a claim—and provide the content (empirical data) that cannot be disputed (although it often is disputed with creative, biased interpretations by the dominant/royal regime). The dominant, royal regime, trafficking in royal consciousness, "has created a subjective consciousness concerned only with self-satisfaction."[32]

The camera can be used to challenge that consciousness, making an objective claim with its footage that cannot be disputed but also causes the viewer to *see* the other. The tension for the viewer of the content lies in the hardening of the conscience to protect the prevailing consciousness, or to empathize and sympathize with the victims. The content may be misinterpreted and twisted to fit a narrative, but it cannot be outright denied, as is the strategy of the royal regime. The religion of the royal regime, Brueggemann says, "provided a God who was so present to the regime and to the dominant consciousness that there was no chance of over-againstness; and where there was no over-againstness, there was no chance of newness."[33] The camera's content should force the individual and the collective to ask the question, "Is God against the repeated anti-Black violence seen in this footage?" Or does God share the royal narrative that "there is no *there* there?" These are questions that are necessary because liberation for a group and the whole society is at stake. This prophetic performance, with camera in hand, is the over-againstness that challenges the heresy of the royal religion Brueggemann describes. The content of this prophetic tool challenges this supposed god that white supremacy has appropriated.

The camera can serve to disrupt the normalization of anti-Black violence at the hands of white supremacy in action. The camera is not just a lens to see through or to use to gaze at subjects, but it is a mirror. People are forced to see themselves. Whiteness is forced to see itself. The content projects back to adherents of the royal consciousness—and the rest of the public—to show them their own actions. To deny, ignore, or minimize the content is to deny, ignore, or minimize truth, which is to choose and normalize bondage. There is no liberation for society without acknowledgment, lament, and a collective antiracist response to the camera's content. It is the history of anti-Black violence that white supremacy attempts to escape. Thus, the maintenance of normalizing this behavior is in the best interest of white supremacy, but it is to the detriment of everyone, including White people. The content of the camera, however, before it liberates society, serves to *haunt* the royal consciousness of white supremacy.

Prophetic ministry cannot choose between criticizing and energizing and expect to maximize effectiveness. To choose between criticizing and energizing as if they are mutually exclusive is to undermine and do a disservice to the prophetic ministry.[34] The camera cannot be used exclusively to criticize "the system" without catalyzing action. It must both arrest the masses and stir the masses. It must be used to direct our energy to lament the darkness of evil and passionately pursue a future with a new, more just reality. The evidence presented by the camera fuels a range of passions, from rage to lament to hopefulness that moves the collective toward a counternarrative that invites the opportunity for a counterconsciousness that can lead to a countercommunity. This use of the camera is an extension of Black moral agency and meets Brueggemann's energizing criteria for the prophetic.

Though it was a still photo, the camera produced the image of a disfigured Emmett Till that many understand to be the catalyst for the Civil Rights Movement. Although Rosa Parks's decision to not move from her seat in the "White's only" section on a Montgomery, Alabama, bus sparked immediate action by the movement's leaders, even she is quoted as being influenced by the image she saw in that photo.[35] Photographer David Jackson captured the gruesome result of the murder of this young Black teen that led to both mourning and prophetic fire in the African American community to resist the status quo, anti-Black violence publicly. The photo by Jackson of Mamie Till standing over her son's open casket filled with immense grief should have spoken to the hearts of every mother, whether Black or White, that saw it. Young Till, in that image, no longer has a voice to cry out to his mother in the way that George Floyd cried out for his. Could Jackson have been attempting to energize White mothers by speaking to their humanity through Mamie Till's grief? His images did more than make a statement about what happened to Till; they brought the nation face-to-face with the evil itself. He invited them in and made them look. The camera is not only a tool for prophetic ministry, but it is also a sign. The significance of the camera is that it does not merely point people *to* the crisis; it confronts them *with* the crisis in a "quasi-firsthand" way. In this confrontation is an invitation to engage the crisis even if on behalf of others. It is a sign in the same way the cross is a sign. The cross for some means identifying with the Christian faith, but it is a sign of the passion of Christ, who was gruesomely nailed to a cross. The staff in Moses's hand was not just a tool but a sign of God's power present with Moses as he acted as an agent, or deputy, for Yahweh. Samson's uncut hair for many Christian readers represents the source of his strength or a visual representation of his Nazirite covenant. In fact, Sampson's uncut hair is not the source of his power, but it points to the source: Yahweh. The power is from God, not Sampson's hair. Human agency is resourced by God with tools that serve as signs or symbols that point to a person, place, thing, or idea beyond itself orienting people toward the power and sovereignty of God. They then would have to reconcile their understanding of the character of this God with the content of the camera. They would have to turn to this God either for justifying the violence or eradicating it and bringing about radical social change.

Darnella Frazier did not have to say a word to participate in the prophetic. Her refusal to stop recording and walk away, leaving the officers to "do what they do," was inherently confrontational. She not only confronted individual officers, but she also confronted a system of policing in real time that disproportionately takes the life of her people.

Her presence may not have saved Floyd's life, but it may have saved lives in the future, as a countercommunity of resistors was birthed from what she captured and published. Her actions have inspired a reimagination of policing with stronger accountability. Are we able to see her presence—and others like her—with a prophetic imagination needed to persist in radical societal change? Remember, there was a time just a generation or two before her when, had she been on the scene of a similar event, it would have been a risk to her life. She certainly would not have been able to openly record police officers kneeling on the neck of an African American man until he no longer had breath in his body. She may not have even had the courage to stand there and record.

Brueggemann asserts that the task of prophetic ministry is to nurture, nourish, and evoke alternative perception and consciousness to that of the dominant culture. It remains to be seen whether the instincts of Frazier indeed nurtured and nourished a sustained alternative consciousness. The protests that followed the viral video of George Floyd's murder were at the very least conceived and birthed by the instinctive but prophetic actions of Frazier. It is not just the response to the tragedy that must be sustained, but a continued active prophetic ministry is imperative to nurture and nourish the alternative social reality conceived by her actions.

To *nurture* means "to rear or to raise like a child."[36] Similarly, to *nourish* denotes feeding and promoting growth and development.[37] Prophetic ministry needs the conception, birth, and sustained nurturing and developing of alternative consciousness to create a new community, or in the apostle Paul's words, a "new humanity." The video recording and its subsequent release create social responsibility much like parents who conceive a child, give birth, and then have the responsibility of raising that child to adulthood. The prophetic ministry is not just an event, but it constitutes a personal and communal liturgy (activism) that evokes repentance (change of mind and consciousness) and maturity toward an alternative reality, especially in spaces dominated by the royal regime of white supremacy.

Simply put, the camera conceives, but prophetic responsibility requires collective, multiethnic labor and nurturing so that the alternative consciousness matures. The Civil Rights Movement is an appropriate example. Although organizing was already underway behind the scenes, and the image of Till's body conceived the energy for the movement, Rosa Parks refusing to give up her seat in a White's only section of a bus gave birth to the movement, and the Montgomery Bus Boycott that lasted 281 days nurtured that energy so that it did not dissipate after facing counterresistance from White power structures. Over the course of the next decade, there were many demonstrations and countless images shot and recorded by television and photographer cameras that nourished the prophetic ministry of the Civil Rights Movement. Those images still impact Black social movements today as evidence for criticizing and energizing the culture of anti-Black racism at the hands of whiteness / white supremacy.

Black Bodies in White Spaces

All spaces are White spaces, including culturally Black spaces. Black neighborhoods are themselves constructed by laws and policies authored by White legislative officials. *Whiteness* and *land occupation/ownership* have been synonymous from the European practice of colonialism (globally) to Jim

Crow–era policies and practices of redlining (nationally and locally). Lines of demarcation for White citizens are discerned in freeways and thoroughfares that divide cities, conditions of physical structures, and disparities in care and beautification of public and private property. Those lines are erased for White bodies that don symbols of authority—badges, weapons, titles, or last names. Where there is the presence of White bodies and the symbols of authority, space occupied by people of Color is converted to White space by default. It is the creativity and resiliency of the African American community that turns this space into home.

Black bodies must be armed in these explicitly and implicitly designated "White" spaces. In many Black communities where crime is high, young African American men arm themselves with guns and other weapons for protection. In these implicitly designated "White" spaces of Black neighborhoods, and the explicitly designated "White" spaces of White neighborhoods, African Americans must at least be armed with another kind of weapon for protection—the camera. When African Americans encounter White people (or other people of Color) with or without symbols of authority, they must arm themselves with an instrument that does not represent a tool of aggression and violence, which might give justification for use of deadly force, but that captures, documents, publishes and exposes the aggression and violence they might be subject to.

This section may seem odd in this chapter, but I include it here because, in the sense that I am discussing the camera's use, I am discussing how it records a repeated drama, the drama of Black bodies in White spaces. It is the dramatic but senseless conflict of skin tone, physical distinctions, and culture on a superficial level. On a deeper level, it is the conflict between the erroneous notion of "divine" authority assumed by White bodies—who assume ownership and sovereignty over space—and the agency of Black bodies occupying the same space. It is an ontological conflict occurring that is dislocating for Black bodies and reorienting for White bodies. Whiteness is forced to acknowledge a different way of being human, while blackness either suffocates or finds ways to breathe (though breathing has never been natural or healthy for us) in this space.

Perspectives from the margins naturally conflict with perspectives from those in power and are necessarily sensitive to any form of injustice or inequity. Black presence, for example, embodies a counterperspective to White spaces. Black culture is the expression of that counterperspective. Black bodies see, hear, feel, and express themselves in ways that White bodies cannot due to having to navigate and be on the alert for the many forms of racism. These Black bodies must move in ways that affirm their humanity, movements that White bodies do not have to consider. Black bodies dance, walk with swag, dress, and don crowns upon their heads of afros, cornrows, braids, and twists. They laugh with and at one another through comedy to experience joy despite surrounding oppression in the neighborhood, the workplace, or school. These expressions of Black culture seek to affirm self- and collective worth and are resources for wellness and healing. Therefore, the narratives from the African American perspective are resistant to the biased, marginalizing, and exploitative narrative of groups in power.

Multiethnic churches, generally homogeneous in culture, are still considered White spaces from an African American perspective. These spaces tend to exploit Black bodies in token ways, as superficial efforts toward diversity and church growth ministry. Brueggemann criticizes the contemporary American church as being too enculturated into "the American ethos of consumerism."[38] The American church space, especially the White or multiethnic church, is in crisis. It has been lulled to sleep by American consumerism in one sense and radicalized in another sense by nationalistic viewpoints. Either way, this way of managing the church space is historically entangled at the roots with white supremacy. The African American perspective rightfully threatens this worldview while offering hope to those on the receiving end of perpetual injustice. African Americans who are socially conscious and courageous bring a sensitivity to social/racial injustice and to a space that has proven to be unconcerned about these issues.

In these White liturgical spaces, relationships tend to be transactional, as individualism is at the heart of its doctrines. The doctrines of individual salvation, discipleship, maturity, and blessings of conservative evangelical spaces contrast with the communal, justice-oriented, and prophetic characteristics of Black Christianity (although there are some Black churches that mirror White Evangelicalism). In these spaces, Black bodies continue to be co-opted, exploited, and tokenized. Those Black bodies are welcomed as long as the full expressions of blackness—dance, music, call-and-response, and so on—are abandoned or limited to the periphery. This, too, is violent in the most disguised and unassuming ways that cannot be easily recorded by the camera.

Black bodies present in White spaces are a prophetic disruption to whiteness, its comfort, its worldview, or even its theology.[39] De facto segregation, partly due to the legacy of redlining practices, insulated White communities from Black ones, and minimum interaction was necessary even in many areas of the country today. Where African Americans closed the gap and began to move into suburban White neighborhoods, "White flight" or White people trying to intimidate them away looked to reestablish that gap.[40] It is not a disruption that intends to unnecessarily compound violence, as such an ethic is not productive, effective, or moral. It is the disruption by the revelation of the "radical otherness" that fully expressed blackness poses to whiteness. Black bodies that are not noticeably assimilated to White culture speak an unfamiliar language of truth that undermines the mis- and disinformation produced by whiteness.

Black bodies are reminders of the egalitarian breadth of the image of God, while White spaces define the terrain of the authoritarian depth and death of white supremacy. African Americans must enter White spaces with the same level of alertness and caution as Moses had when he entered hostile Egypt under Pharaoh's rule. The nervous systems—the body's alarm system—of Black bodies are on high alert in White spaces. These bodies remember the transatlantic travels of their ancestors, the plantation labor, the ropes and tree limbs of the Jim Crow South, and the pavement under their feet marching for justice and equality. This is an all-too-familiar space. But these Black bodies, under the eye of the recording camera, present a new ontological narrative, a prophetic narrative of being (Black). Black bodies occupying White spaces is the narrative of poetry (creativity, improvisation, and rhythm) inserted in a space dominated by prose (predictability, familiarity, commonplace). In this space is the increased potential to be misunderstood, misinterpreted, or missed altogether. Meaning is lost or discarded, and energy is expended to recover meaning in meaningless location.

Conclusion

The prophetic imagination, as it concerns confronting white supremacy, is not an abstract idea, but it is embodied in Black bodies, the tools (the camera), the narratives from the margins they produce, and the alternative communities that are formed by those narratives. The prophetic ministry creates a necessary disturbance, prompting conflict with the dominant narrative disrupting the royal regime of white supremacy. The camera, as a cultural artifact and a prophetic tool, is indispensable for achieving justice and liberation by its capacity to critique the royal regime of whiteness and energize an alternative community consisting of those on the margins and allies from the center.

The camera is not necessarily a religious instrument, but its purpose, content, and publication of the content in the hands of conscious individuals exposing injustice make it a prophetic tool. The camera's content emphatically declares that the dominant depiction of history is insufficient at best, inaccurate at worst, and depicts God as a god who is oblivious to or unconcerned about the violence (physical, psychological, emotional, and spiritual) upon African Americans. The camera compels us to choose a side. Either a person, community, or organization is complicit with the violence of power structures, or they are resistant to it. The prophetic lens erases the middle ground and forces us to choose whether we are for or against, as there is no safe, neutral position.

CHAPTER 5

King and the Cameraman

I wonder how successful the Civil Rights Movement would have been without the news cameras that were present to capture the violence and then broadcast it to the rest of the nation and world so they could witness the violence that African Americans in the South were experiencing all along. Were Martin Luther King Jr.'s charisma and oratorical skills along with community-organizing and the marches and demonstrations enough to convince Americans in the North and West that there was a decades-long continuation of a human rights crisis in the South? In the hands of D. W. Griffith, the camera has oppressive implications, dramatizing a story that justifies racist attitudes and behaviors. In the hands of activists, it is subversive propaganda that has potentially liberative consequences.

King knew the power of shining a light upon White violence against Black people for a mostly disinterested or skeptical audience outside of the South.¹ After a brutal reception by police officers during a march in Selma, Alabama, in 1965, King spoke these words: "We are here to say to the White men that we no longer will let them use clubs on us in the dark corners. We're going to make them do it in the glaring light of television."² In that moment, King was not just a pastor, rhetorician, and prophet but a filmmaker. He did not create the violence, but he staged the drama and positioned himself and the demonstrators strategically to allow the camera to capture it as it was already going to unfold. King would trouble the conscience of Americans with intentions of awakening them to Black people's realities, once camouflaged, in the South that warranted more than awareness, but intervention. What King understood, and what has become clear for the Black community today, is that for the collective conscience of the dominant White community to be moved to action, it requires more than the dissemination of information and even passionate rhetoric, but visual, unedited imagery capturing the violence of anti-Black racism in action.

White supremacy is audaciously unapologetic and unashamed of its doctrine and ethos of anti-Black hate. Before and during the era of the Civil Rights Movement, many White people could be seen in photos standing in front of burnt, dismembered, and lynched Black bodies without any evidence of shame or remorse. The brutality had been so normalized that the inhumanity of their participation and celebration went unnoticed by some and unchallenged by many others in the White community, even among well-meaning White people (moderates, as King would call them) who did not actively participate in the violence. In other words, they were unmoved and unbothered. The many published pictures of the images of unaffected White bodies surrounding a dead Black body serve as evidence that White people at the time welcomed the attention. At the very least, they were not afraid of it and made little effort to hide.

King used the air of superiority and invincibility of Southern Whites to his advantage in order to author a more truthful and indicting narrative to white supremacy and its offspring, racism. The violence did not end when the cameras were turned on and zoomed in to capture not only batons and fire hoses directed at protesting African Americans and allies but also emotions seen in body language, gestures, and facial expressions. They did not fear the camera. Publicized White violence ordinarily served to put fear in the hearts of African Americans and anyone sympathetic to their cause. But King had the prophetic foresight to discern that times were changing. He hoped and believed that people—from the president of the United States, Congress, clergy, and many others—would respond as the Movement and the African American community needed them to respond, in solidarity.

This was reality television at its best and worst. As the cameras documented the events, chronicling the violence and trauma, they also captured resistance and resiliency. The nation was compelled to witness the worst of itself, yet the footage was catalytic in awakening a collective conscience and expediting social progress. The polarity of themes recognized here does not suggest an erasure of suffering to see the progress. Nor does it insist on the dismissal of Black resiliency while acknowledging Black suffering. Events like "Bloody Sunday" were both catastrophic and catalytic, as that dreadful day "galvanized the forces for voting rights and increased their support."[3] A new narrative was being authored—with King as the primary visionary, narrator, director, and producer—that included the whole story of blackness caught in the web of savagery spun by white supremacy. He was being trusted by the African American community to reauthor a truthful version of the racial injustice they have had to endure at the hands of White Americans in the South.

Martin Luther King Jr.'s method of nonviolent direct action did not target White persons per se as much as it targeted White consciences, which he hoped would begin to struggle with the reality of racism.[4] This inner collective struggle is catalyzed by creative tension that confronts the barbarity of anti-Black violence and anti-Black laws that undergird anti-Black social structures. What the camera did for King—and later Black filmmakers, activists, and witnesses to anti-Black violence, as was the case in the George Floyd murder—is force White America to see itself, its own *violent* performance, unedited and not disseminated or mediated in ways in which the culture of racial violence could be reasonably denied or explained away as they "wait for the details."

Since White America could not see themselves in Black victims of racial violence, the images in the video forced them to have to see themselves in the White perpetrators. What he did was put White violence on display. He gave it the platform to expose itself to the broader public. White supremacy cannot hide its violence or its oppressive nature, even for the camera. The video camera is an instrument for the improvisational tendency of Black moral agency to creatively discover ways to not only survive white supremacy but confront it and dare to create an alternative narrative and hope for an alternative consciousness. King claims there is no progress or societal change without the tension of exposing injustice: "Actually, we who engage in nonviolent direct action are not the creators of tension. We merely bring to the surface hidden tension that is already alive. *We bring it out in the open where it can be seen and dealt with . . . injustice must likewise be exposed*, with all of the tension its exposing creates, to the light of human conscience and the air of national opinion before it can be cured."[5]

The violence from Southern White people even fueled the motivations of reporters and television networks from the North. Media outlets in the South were usually quick to move on to the next story, and people would forget about what happened. Reporters and television networks from outside the South continued to document and broadcast the violence (whether to increase their viewership and ratings or because of moral responsibility is questionable). In response to an interview given to King in Montgomery, Alabama, Whites attacked local television transmitters, knocking the interview offline.[6] At every front, White Southerners tried to undermine any momentum the King-led Civil Rights Movement garnered. At each point of White counterresistance was a display of violence often caught by the persistent eye of the camera.

Creative Tension

King was unapologetic about his intent to generate creative tension with the methods chosen in the movement. He understood that for far too long, White Americans had been comfortable with things as they were. African Americans could not afford to continue to accept the status quo. The Black collective conscience did not need to be aroused (with the exception of a small minority). Their lived experience rendered them fully aware of the trauma they faced daily. It was the collective conscience of White Americans, beginning with the moderate Whites in the South claiming to be allies, who needed to be unsettled enough to be actively antiracist. He spoke and preached around the world, but it was not until the violence was dramatized on television that White apathy was interrupted on a broader scale. Many White people had not been privy to the violence that African Americans experienced until the demonstrations were televised and unveiled to the nation the relentless nature of the dogs, fire hoses, and police batons used against African Americans of all ages, without exception.[7]

The camera was crucial to King's nonviolent direct action. It is nonthreatening in that it does not cause bodily harm. It is powerfully threatening in that it exposes the violence that perpetrators of anti-Black racism intend to inflict by capturing, documenting, and publishing the drama of the crisis.[8] King advocates for tension in his method of resistance. If tension, when constructive rather than destructive, can cause growth, then it follows that the camera, as a tool for constructive tension, should be credited as being valuable for societal ethical progress and growth.[9] Progress or growth may look like change in individual perspectives, policy reform, or multiethnic and multigenerational movements of solidarity, much like what we witnessed in the summer of 2020 after George Floyd's murder.

King wanted to create tension so that White leaders both locally and in the federal government would negotiate with the African American community about necessary changes. He also knew that if they could persuade the masses to support the cause, then they could apply pressure on officials to not block the proposed changes. This tension was created without the camera, but the camera amplified it and projected it on television screens across the country. One could say the creative tension is an invitation. It is an invitation for White people to negotiate and an invitation for White people and others—including apathetic African Americans ("honorary" Whites)—to participate in prophetic anti-racism work.

This is not to say that there was no tension prior to nonviolent direct action. There was what King called the "hidden tension" between White people and African Americans. He describes this tension as a boil that will persist as long as it is covered up.[10] Likewise, injustice would persist in much the same way if it, too, was not exposed. He set the stage with marches and demonstrations that would certainly draw out unapologetically racist White people who would play their roles for the camera. King's strategy was exposure. He was the star of an ensemble cast of courageous protagonists in a story featuring the prophetic embodiment of an alternative community in its infancy. Not that the African American community itself was in its infancy, nor was the alternative consciousness in its nascent stages, but the realization of the community with the consciousness that would soon grow beyond the exclusivity of the Black community was emerging. With the technology of television news cameras, the nation was about to be invited into this community that exists for lasting social change.

Unfortunately, the camera in Black hands has also been the justification for unarmed African Americans being wrongfully shot and/or killed by law enforcement officers. Could it be that subconsciously, the camera poses a greater threat than it appears? While there may be a fear of Black bodies, especially Black male bodies, there seems to be an added fear of those hands around smartphones with cameras "shooting" first. The fear may well be the potential shots from a gun that is mistaken for the phone, but it is also the shots of a video documenting the character of the individual police officer specifically, the culture of anti-Black policing in general, and the ever-presence of whiteness hovering over Black bodies asserting its dominance.

Clearly, creative tension can be dangerous. It is not designed to produce immediate peaceful circumstances. It has the potential for volatility. It is creative, though, because it does not instigate tension; it inventively confronts the violent nature of white supremacy. The refusal of African Americans and allies to acquiesce to the status quo culture that white supremacy established compels its agents to counterresist. The tension is in the conflict between ideologies, cultures, and races. The tension is most profoundly seen in whiteness versus blackness, Pharaoh versus Moses, the prophetic versus the royal regime, and power from the center versus power emerging and asserting itself from the margins.

To King, the greatest asset to the Movement was the predictable behavior of characters like Birmingham police commissioner Eugene "Bull" Conner. As valuable and necessary as King's leadership, vision, and oratorical skills and the resiliency of the African American community were, it was the deep-seated hatred of White people like "Bull" Conner that benefited the Movement, although that trait was simultaneously the cause of great pain and suffering.

The tension created by King and the Movement compelled people to choose which side of the conflict they stood on. King hoped to put pressure on White moderates to either participate in the work of God or become allies "of the forces of social stagnation."[11] Allies from Northern states (i.e., journalists, liberals, the federal government) and segregationist sympathizers from the South and beyond were moved to fight for or against the alternative consciousness brewing amid the Movement.

There was creative tension within the Black community as well. Malcolm X and supporters of the Nation of Islam did not agree with King's strategy of nonviolent direct action.

The Black Nationalist faction of the African American community preferred to respond to violence "by any means necessary," including armed self-defense in the pursuit of self-determination. This was antithetical to King's vision. King believed that violence only compounded violence, while nonviolent demonstrations had proven to be a unifying force, bringing Whites to join the Movement.[12] What King and Malcolm X did have in common, however, was their savvy and strategic use of the camera during the struggle against White individuals and White power structures.

Malcolm X used the camera to combat the negative coverage of the White news media. In contrast to King, Malcolm wanted to capture the positive aspects of the Nation of Islam, its "fruit," to inspire African Americans who were "disillusioned with the mainstream civil rights movement" to support and ultimately join him.[13] Malcolm targeted the Black community, while King's audience was much broader, hoping to get the attention of Whites, the federal government, and anyone who would be motivated to help the Movement to end segregation and curtail racism. Malcolm understood the efforts of the White media who saw him much differently and less favorably than King. He carefully crafted and presented his own image and the collective image of the Nation of Islam to counter the narrative created by White and even mainstream Black media.[14]

Considering the framework for the prophetic ministry and its twin tasks of criticizing and energizing, an argument can be made for the prophet Malcolm X that he fits in as an energizing force for an alternative consciousness. In this sense, King and Malcolm needed each other even in the use of visual media as a prophetic tool. Certainly, there were aspects of both strategies that were both criticizing and energizing. King was the master at using the camera to criticize the perpetual violence of White racism. Malcolm was a genius at capturing the counternarrative through pictures of the positivity of the Nation of Islam that White media strategically failed at documenting and publishing.

King and Malcolm constituted the fullness of the prophetic ministry together even though they opposed each other's methods. They were two sides of the same prophetic coin. They chose different methods, but contrary to popular opinion, they were fond of each other and respected each other as fellow justice fighters for the African American cause of liberation.[15] Malcolm, after leaving the Nation of Islam, began to shift and integrate himself more in the mainstream Civil Rights Movement, as King began to shift toward Malcolm (one can only imagine the impact of that relationship had they both not been assassinated). Consider this: the camera is such a powerful and indispensable tool that it became a point of intersection for two prophets, two methods, and two philosophies—integrationism and nationalism—fighting for justice from the margins. James Cone writes about the two men, "Martin and Malcolm illuminate the two roads to freedom that meet in the African Americans' search for identity in the land of their birth."[16] Those two roads meet at the crossroads of the prophetic ministry, and the camera (with its content) serves as a signpost, guiding all who dare to travel the road for justice and park in the tension created at that intersection.

The Journalist as Ally

By the time the Civil Rights Movement began in the 1950s, television news broadcasts were relatively new. This platform was only about ten years in the making, dating back to the 1940s. It could be said that television and the Movement grew up together. Many of the networks' journalists, particularly those from the North, not only saw firsthand what was happening in the South and reported it; they had their own experiences of violence from White Southerners. Whether they intended to or not, they were allies to the African American community. They played a crucial role in telling the hidden narrative that many White Americans were content to keep concealed from the nation and that African Americans wanted exposed. The presence of news journalists and their cameras during the Movement was mutually beneficial for television and for King's strategy to expose anti-Black violence and inequities and the inherent injustice of segregation.

Television was critical in puncturing the collective conscience hardened by apathy or ignorance. The Civil Rights Movement provided the platform that transformed television into a news medium with serious social and political implications.[17] Coverage of the Movement was very much like what we see today on twenty-four-hour news stations, covering events like the O. J. Simpson trial in 1995 or the "January 6" Capitol insurrection attempt. In other words, coverage was constant, captivating the country's attention, and had serious racial dynamics and implications. Coverage of the Movement was the first of its kind. Peter J. Boyer, a writer for the *New York Times*, says the Movement was "the first running story of national importance that television fully covered." He goes on to say, "Television brought home to the nation the civil rights struggle in vivid images that were difficult to ignore."[18]

In 1955, during the Emmett Till murder trial, John Chancellor, a reporter for NBC, was interviewing African

Americans and White people to get their reactions to the acquittal of Roy Bryant and his half brother, J. W. Milam, by an all-White jury. He noticed a mob of White men, who were unhappy with him being there in Mississippi asking questions. Knowing he could not get away from them as they approached him, he turned around with his tape recorder, pretending it was a camera, and pointed it at them.[19] He said, "All right, come on. The whole world is going to know what you're doing to me." They did not realize it was not a camera, but the thought of being recorded and broadcasted to the world scared them enough to leave him alone.[20] This was/is the cost of even the appearance of allyship.

The first major event broadcasted on the news for a national audience to witness took place on September 4, 1957, in Little Rock, Arkansas, as African American students courageously integrated Central High School. The cast was present. There was the Arkansas National Guard, news reporters, angry White students and parents, and nine African American students. Elizabeth Eckford found herself alone as she departed the bus. The night before, she had not gotten the message that there was a change in the location where the nine African American students would all meet. She tried to find a welcoming face among the crowd of White racists screaming obscenities and threats at her. The iconic picture of her amid a sea of hate-filled Whites is just a Google search away. This event would be forever etched in the collective memory as a pivotal moment in the fight for equality and justice. It would also be a pivotal moment for television. One reporter from the *New York Times*, Eugene J. Roberts Jr., who covered the South said, "It was the civil rights story that made him realize the force of television news. Police dogs look like police dogs in newspaper and magazine photos, but on television the dogs snarled."[21]

Journalists, as extensions of the news networks they represented, were threats to the "White" way of life in the South. They brought unsolicited attention to the creative tension that King and the Movement generated. They served to protect demonstrators from police officers who tried to reserve their violence for when they figured the cameras were absent or turned off. The cameras provided an up-close, three-dimensional alternative to the normally two-dimensional photos that print journalism uses. It was profoundly important for the news cameras from the national television networks to be present while journalists covered the marches because the "local [newspapers] and southern television and radio stations largely ignored what was happening."[22]

White Southerners were unapologetic and unashamed in their disdain for the apparent allyship of the journalists and news stations represented covering the marches and demonstrations. They gave racially offensive nicknames to the out-of-town television networks: "NBC was Nigger Broadcasting Network, ABC was Afro Broadcasting Network, and CBS was the Coon (or Communist) Broadcasting System."[23] Journalists were beaten or shot and killed. When riots broke out, some reporters found refuge hiding in homes, churches, or even funeral homes in African American neighborhoods.[24]

The idea of journalists as allies provided more than a model for the potential to transform society with the images they captured during the Movement; it also serves as a template for the solidarity needed from the White community to fight and make significant progress against white supremacy. Progress toward a new society with a new consciousness requires White people to betray whiteness and choose humanity. As journalists covering the Movement show, there is inherent risk even to one's life when siding with justice. The royal regime of white supremacy demands loyalty. Justice demands morality. Love requires self-sacrifice. Some White allies with the camera chose morality and self-sacrifice. They took on the spirit of the Movement. They could only hope that their attitudes and actions, though precarious, would go "viral." What they produced through the lens of the camera pierced the armor of the collective White conscience hardened by white supremacy.

Collective Conscience

King knew that no cultural change could occur without fostering an alternative consciousness. The dominant consciousness was one that accepted, denied, or turned a blind eye to the violence of White racism in any region of the country, but especially in the South. He was fully aware that White America, those with the most access and those most proximal to power, would not simply make an intellectual decision to resist the same power structure from which they benefited. They had to be coerced, and the coercion could not be by physical means, nor through simply educating. White Americans needed to see themselves in such a way that it would cause deep moral reflection that would bear heavily on their collective conscience.

Why was King so intent on influencing collective conscience? What happens when collective conscience is aroused is that there is a demand for change toward an alternative consciousness that has been envisioned, declared, and embodied. White conscience seemed to have been insulated by the hardened coatings of apathy, cognitive dissonance, or willful ignorance. White Americans were, and have been, guilty of apathy, largely because of not being the recipients of racist bigotry, laws, and policies, or a power structure designed to disenfranchise them. The lack of interest or concern from the White community is because they do not *feel* the trauma of racism. Even those who may experience the oppression of classism have a baseline of opportunity that African Americans at large are not afforded simply because of nonmembership into whiteness.

Cognitive dissonance may be the most perplexing collective trait of the White community to grasp. Joy DeGruy explains White cognitive dissonance being in effect long before the civil rights era in this way in *Post-Traumatic Slave Syndrome*: "The difference between the actions of Europeans (i.e. enslaving, raping, and killing) and their beliefs about themselves (i.e. 'We are good Christians') was so great and the cognitive dissonance so painful that they were obliged to go to great lengths in order to survive their own horrific behavior. Chattel slavery and genocide of the Native American population were so un-Christian that the only way they could make their actions acceptable, and so resolve the dissonance, was to relegate their victims to a subhuman level."[25] This is what King sought to disrupt in order to arouse a sleeping majority. In this playbook, White people no longer explicitly subscribed to the subhuman status once assigned to African Americans—although they treated them that way—but they rendered them an existential threat to the "American" (i.e., "White") way of life. Strong convictions stemming from the belief in the threat justify the treatment of targeting Black bodies from de jure (and de facto) segregation to brutality to murder.

There are many Whites who were close enough to know what was happening in the South, even if they themselves were not participants, but they chose willful ignorance as a defense for their unavailability and unwillingness to stand in solidarity with the African American community. Willful ignorance does not mean one has no knowledge of the events, but it does mean there is an intentional turning away from those events to convince oneself that all is not as bad as reported. They choose to remain ignorant of the *extent* of what was happening. This is distinct from cognitive dissonance in that cognitive dissonance may suggest full knowledge and participation while claiming to believe the contrary, especially what one believes about themselves or the group they belong to. Willful ignorance—because of fear, cowardice, or fragility—is the unwillingness to know (or see) the full picture. Often, willful ignorance was aided by segregationist journalism that continued the strategy of fostering racist ideologies to its loyal audience (sounds a lot like the strategies of news networks on the "right" today).

I recently had a conversation through private messaging on social media with a pastor who served on staff at an evangelical church where I sometimes preached as a guest speaker. He was displeased with a post I shared of juxtaposed images of a slave patroller on a horse apparently whipping an enslaved African American and the image of a border patrol officer on a horse reaching out to grab a Haitian man seeking asylum while his reins came near the man's body looking much like a whip. In our debate that turned into a dialogue about appropriate actions that lead to a resolution, he dismissed the notion that it is relevant to keep bringing up history. He wanted to know what he (White people) needed to do *now* to move us forward. I mentioned it is important that White people know how we got here before trying to fix the problem and risk compounding the trauma. His statements in our conversation implied he preferred to remain willfully ignorant of the layers and dynamics of anti-Black racism throughout history at the hands of White people.

His desire for solutions to the issues around racism is valid. His choice to evade the historical realities and see looking forward as the appropriate response is naive at best, manipulative at worst. The most dangerous manipulation, in this case, is self-manipulation. He risks perpetuating the problem and potentially triggering African Americans with an apparent savior complex (he certainly would not believe he has this complex). I say savior complex because of the impulse to want to immediately and simplistically "fix" a four-hundred-plus-year-old nuanced problem. For White people to choose to remain ignorant of the past is counterproductive and counterintuitive. It is counterproductive for the reason just mentioned. To just want to come in and "save the day" with solutions to the deeply felt trauma of racism that they do not experience directly (though it is possible to experience a degree of trauma vicariously through visual images and hearing testimonies) is to risk retraumatizing others. It also risks forcing the suppression of emotions and trauma that need visibility and expression for individual and collective healing. It is counterintuitive because to resolve any social or ethical dilemma, context is imperative. Without it, the path to resolution and cultural transformation is darkened by ignorance and may lead to repeating the wrongs of history.

In many cases, the strategies of the Movement and the use of video footage and still shots to document the violence they endured worked as planned. In other instances, however, the hardened hearts and seared consciences of many White people were reinforced as they fought to maintain a strong grasp on oppressive power. King knew that the battle was not between persons, but between forces—good versus evil.[26] Just as human goodness could be evoked by strategies targeting collective conscience, human sinfulness could also be aroused, and the battle between their respective human agents ensues. A desperate and likely deadly conflict for power is waged. The royal regime clings to a morbid use of power while King and the Movement offer an equally powerful alternative that is liberating and life-giving, even to agents of the dominant consciousness.[27]

They must first be awakened and willing to identify and name the ungodly and deathly reality they not only permit through silent complicity but perpetuate through active participation. Charles Moore, a White photographer who had been inspired by King's speeches, found himself in the middle of ongoing battles of this war. He literally positioned himself in the middle of a violent altercation between a White mob/police and African American demonstrators. He aimed and shot, as one behind enemy lines, at a police dog still in the hands of a White officer attacking an African American young man.[28] The dog was an extension of the racist White man with a badge on his chest that gave him cover or power to commit such violence. Interestingly, Moore, because of his white skin, was safe enough to stand in the center of the chaos largely unharmed. He used what power he did have—his skin and his camera—for liberating purposes. He himself was free, his conscience in sync with the "arc of the universe's" divinely influenced bend toward justice.[29]

The power of King's intent to reach consciences rather than personalities alone is that the work can continue to reach consciences generations later. Without a doubt, there is still the arousal of a counterresistance to the alternative consciousness by heirs of the dominant group. The images have transgenerational effects. They may be hidden from many, but they do not—indeed, cannot—die with persons of a generation.

Conclusion

Whether White people were guilty of apathy, cognitive dissonance, or willful ignorance, King knew he needed national visibility to expose the evil African Americans faced in the South: "The civil rights revolution in the South began when a man and the eye of the television film camera came together, giving the camera a focal point for events breaking from state to state, and the man, Martin Luther King, Jr., high exposure on television sets from coast to coast."[30] King needed the television networks, their journalists, and especially their cameramen or women on the scene. It was not uncommon for a demonstration to be canceled if news outlets were not present or if agitators and White mobs were not there to provide the violence.

The violent nature of African Americans depicted by J. D. Griffith in *Birth of a Nation* was intended to intimidate and reiterate fear of African Americans and justify White violence. King essentially appropriated White violence to make his case for a moral reckoning and the end of segregation. His strategy was dangerously brilliant. The Movement was impactful because of the drama of the collective prophetic embodiment of African Americans courageously confronting white supremacy in the eye of the camera. This action provided the template for future social movements to take advantage of video cameras documenting anti-Black violence to provide an eyewitness to support multigenerational claims of the systemic bigotry, discriminatory actions, and systemic and systematic inequities of white supremacy.

King's strategy meant the differences between success and failure, between awakening the hearts and minds of the nation and permitting them to remain asleep, and between empowering Black agency and weakening it. He took an instrument used generally to entertain or for surveillance and appropriated it for a documentary-like drama that interrupted the comfort of escape television often provided. He used it to invite the audience into the harsh reality of the Black experience, to sit and not turn away, but see, grieve, and act in resistance to what the status quo allowed. He offered everyone an opportunity to be citizens of an emerging community with an alternative consciousness to that of the royal regime with its oppressive narrative about African Americans and other people of Color.

CHAPTER 6

—

The Democratization
of the Camera

A popular edict I heard as a child from my parents and grandparents was "Do as I say, not as I do." This statement meant we were supposed to obey instructions uncritically, and there was no room for negotiations. The power dynamics in our household and most households were hierarchical and fixed. While I understand the hierarchy of parents rightfully having power and the idea that children must listen, obey, and learn from them, as children mature, there should be more flexibility (as appropriate for their ages) that allows for the children to have a voice and in some ways assert agency. For example, if parents begin to allow the children to have a say in what the family should have for dinner as opposed to only having whatever Mom or Dad decides to cook; or when children are young, parents generally enroll them in activities and camps, essentially deciding what activities they will or will not be involved in. As the children get older, they are generally allowed to have a say in some of those decisions, choosing which activities *they* are interested in participating in. After all, is this not one of the purposes of parenting, to raise children and prepare them to become wise, mature, and responsible decision-making adults? To some degree, there should be room for more flexibility in the power dynamics (not that children become the parents), a democratization of power and agency shared among family members who love, trust, and value one another.

Frederick Douglass left us with a timeless truth about progress and reform. In a speech he made on the West India emancipation in Canandaigua, New York, on August 3, 1857, he reminds his audience of the necessity of struggling for change. His message was not only for his audience 165 years ago, but it is also relevant for us today.

> Let me give you a word of the philosophy of reform. The whole history of the progress of human liberty shows that all concessions yet made to her august claims, have been born of earnest struggle. The conflict has been exciting, agitating, all-absorbing, and for the time being, putting all other tumults to silence. It must do this or it does nothing. If there is no struggle there is no progress. Those who profess to favor freedom and yet deprecate agitation, are men who want crops without plowing up the ground, they want rain without thunder and lightning. They want the ocean without the awful roar of its many waters. This struggle may be a moral one, or it may be a physical one, and it may be both moral and physical, but it must be a struggle. *Power concedes nothing without a demand. It never did and it never will.*[1]

I want to keep your attention on the final two sentences. Martin Luther King Jr. echoed these same sentiments in "Letter from Birmingham City Jail" when talking about White power structures of his day. One can argue that anyone in power in any context—family, sports, war, politics, and so on—is subject to this same tragic flaw. Those with state power, royal regime membership, however, have the resources available to them to not only sustain their positions of power (at least for a period), but they have the capacity to adversely affect the lives of communities on a local, regional, national, or global scale. Their apparatus of power is expansive.

The struggle is always about power. Power is not only the ability to act or do, but it is also the ability or agency to *cause* something to happen. The struggle for African Americans is a struggle to democratize power, to equitably distribute power among the people and demonopolize power from the royal regime of whiteness. The camera phone, social media platforms, and news outlets all form the apparatuses for perspectives and power originating at the margins. In the case of racial violence, together they create the conflict of power between the African American community and any group that has participated consciously or not in the perpetuation of anti-Black racism. Power may not relinquish power, but it is forced to acknowledge and engage an emerging power that is not completely dependent upon the state, the wealthy class, or corporations—synonymous with whiteness—and their apparatuses of power.

A persistent fight for African Americans since gaining the right to be citizens and to have full participation in democracy has been the fight for the right to vote without inventive ways by White power structures strategizing to prevent that privilege. When power is concentrated within a particular class or race of people, it means those on the margins in terms of class and/or race face the existential reality of marginalization and degrees of oppression with transgenerational effects. Whether by creativity and innovation or by prophetic confrontation, power dynamics in this context must be disrupted and decentralized. What is certain is that those in power will never relinquish it willingly because to be without a monopoly on power is disorienting. To reorient to a new reality of decentralized power that invites competition, critique, or legitimate accountability is to render those in power vulnerable and threatened. Anything or anyone who does not acquiesce is perceived to pose an existential threat. The response of the gatekeepers of White power structures is to fight for the preservation of the monopoly, which is a battle for sustaining a way of life, worldview, ideology, and identity.

The dominant worldview, ideology, and identity, when left unchecked, constitute the prevailing consciousness of the dominant group and shape the consciousness of many on the margins. What is at stake is creative potential and power for those on the margins trapped in the assimilation vortex. In this case, that vortex is whiteness. It will require the improvisation of the oppressed—prophetic performance—to interrupt the dominant consciousness, energize the margins, and affirm the alternative consciousness of an already-existing and ever-maturing alternative community.

Democratization, by definition, is to make democratic or to uphold the nature of democracy. Democracy denotes "power vested in the people."[2] Furthermore, it gives voice to common people with the purpose of leveling the playing field from power being concentrated with the privileged class or group. In other words, to democratize is to divest power from a select few—elite, ruling, dominant, governing classes—to include equal and equitable shares of power among the marginalized and disenfranchised. For power to be shared across classes, there must be equitable access to resources, but there must first be acknowledged respect from the oppressor or dominant class/group toward the oppressed or marginalized. Alexis de Tocqueville in his classic *Democracy in America* offers insightful observations about democracy and the United States. From his observations about power dynamics, he writes, "When the ranks of society are unequal, and men unlike each other in condition, there are some individuals invested with all the power of superior intelligence, learning, and enlightenment, whilst the multitude is sunk in ignorance and prejudice. Men living at these aristocratic periods are therefore naturally induced to shape their opinions by the superior standard of a person or a class of persons, whilst *they are averse to recognize the infallibility of the mass of the people.*"[3] What Tocqueville recognized is inherent, unconscious bias from the aristocrats (royal regime) as they measure all others against themselves while dismissing the value of agency and wisdom from outside of their exclusive group. This practice insidiously secures and monopolizes power in a vacuum of insularity. The "superior standard" by which the dominant group shapes their opinions in a racialized context in the United States is whiteness. Whiteness instinctively protects itself and shuns the possibility of equal voice and equitable space for agency (power) of people of Color. According to the racial hierarchy, the least degree of equality and equity in this "democratic" monopoly is afforded to African Americans.

True democratization of power requires democratization of resources. Democratization of resources implies equitable access not only to resources but also to the decision-making table where determinations are made about how and where those resources are allocated and employed. When a group does not have access to the decision-making table, they must create another table, formed by the components of their own power apparatus. In this case, Frazier and others employed the camera phone, social media, news outlets, or all the above in grassroots fashion. In doing so, they invited all to the de-hierarchized table in true democratic form. The monopolized power of law enforcement, the judicial system, and the wealthy class must compete with the collective power of the people.

It's important to note that even within the apparatus of power from the margins, there continues to be a struggle. Social media outlets and news outlets are just as easily connected to networks of power and function on their behalf, as seen in the use of Facebook and certain news networks to spread disinformation. Social media algorithms can undermine a video's capacity to go viral. Accounts can be suspended or removed based on complaints from those who simply do not like the videos or information posted. This means the apparatus itself must be diversified. This is part of the conflict, the struggle articulated by Douglass. Strategies of those on the margins must be as agile, flexible, and unrelenting as the strategies of power structures.

The struggle for power and with power (structures) is the struggle for control of the narrative, which is controlling what is truth. Whoever controls the narrative of supposed truth dictates norms, beliefs, values, and so on for society. Michel Foucault writes, "We are subjected to the production of truth through power, and we cannot exercise power except through the production of truth."[4] This intersection must be taken seriously if there is any effective strategy at dismantling social structures and truly transforming society into the alternative consciousness and community of the prophetic imagination. While ideologies must be factors to consider, Foucault insists that the focus should be on a method of analyzing the nature of power—the "apparatuses of knowledge [production]"—and "the study of the techniques and tactics of domination" is where the focus should be placed.[5] In other words, understanding the dynamics of power on a granular level (root) rather than grappling alone with the structures (fruit) it has produced is imperative in any decentralizing or demonopolizing of oppressive social structures.

If Foucault is right, then the democratized truth production of the camera and social media is an existential threat to the power held by the royal regime of whiteness. Its very existence depends on having the initial and concluding say on what is right, true, or just. This self-proclaimed sovereignty of truth has stifled the imagination of the people subjected to it ("White" people) and validated its dominance. Though it is diabolical, it has claimed status and function reserved for the divine.

The Camera as a Demonopolizing Weapon

Whoever controls the narrative around an event has a monopoly on truth unless there is more compelling evidence to suggest otherwise. Whoever owns the most influential television news stations, newspapers, and websites, whoever writes and publishes the textbooks in schools, and whoever produces the biggest films and most-watched television shows have monopolizing power over narrative. This privileged position is one that shapes culture and, when necessary, shifts culture. Control of the narrative potentially has destructive implications for the voiceless and powerless (and at times, others who are or were once in positions of power). The narrative created by the royal regime can be weaponized to destroy people's reputations, relationships, earning potential, essentially, their lives.

"Cancel culture" from the politically right or left is often fueled by these narratives created by power structures. Oppressive narratives are also weaponized against entire groups of people without merit. Groups on the margins often must exert as much energy disproving false narratives as they do in just surviving and thriving in a society filled with social inequities. They must navigate these "social landmines" while they try to heal from injustices and inequities built into society and then live well within those same social structures.

For example, a popular misconception is that working-class African Americans who need government assistance are lazy and seek handouts rather than trying to "work hard," as is the American way. The truth is, most do work hard, while a fraction of the community—as in any community, including the White community—may look to take advantage of the system. Those who create and disseminate the narrative nefariously attempt to hide the reality of social inequities through discriminatory laws, policies, and practices targeting African Americans, other people of Color, and even the working class (which includes poor Whites). It seems like there should be cameras strategically installed in places to document the hardworking African Americans who also endure racist workplace culture and their unseen experiences—persistent microaggressions—that come with seeking, maintaining, and being well in places of employment.

The camera, weaponized against African Americans, highlights crime, violence, drug use, gang activity, and the like. The images that underscored the narrative put forth by the dominant group support the ire directed at the community and justify treatment according to stereotypes. For instance, the drug problem in the United States knows no boundaries. The drug epidemics of the 1980s that ravaged the African American community did not receive the same type of media coverage as the opioid epidemic that plagues suburban White communities at the time of the writing of this book. The images and corresponding language—"war on drugs" for the crack epidemic versus "public health crisis" for the opioid epidemic—frame the problems very differently. What should not be overlooked is the racial framing of the crises. This framing led to a response of disdain and "othering" of African Americans affected by crack versus empathy and compassion toward predominately White families impacted by opioid addiction. The former was deserving of the punitive response of incarceration or neglect while the latter was entitled to grace, empathy, and health care resources to prevent and help restore individuals, families, and communities.

This is also true for gun violence. For decades, African American families have had to endure the tragic results of gun violence in certain communities in cities across the country. The media puts the images of gang violence, drug deals gone bad, and robberies and shootings on display, perpetuating the same narrative of the "dangerous Black man" falsely dramatized decades earlier by the film *Birth of a Nation*. It was not until mass shootings occurred by the dozens annually in suburban White communities that gun violence became a problem worth addressing (at least among liberals). Once again, the images and the narrative depict the whole African American community as depraved and claim the problem is "theirs." The narrative and images of the mass shootings, particularly in schools, portray only the shooter as a danger to society (if he or she is White), and that portrayal is associated with mental illness, not the morality of the individual and his or her entire community. The narrative begins to tell the story, but the images (still shots and video footage) broadcasted across television often enough will cement the narratives in the minds of viewers.

The camera, as a tool in this power struggle, is but one part of a two-step demonopolizing strategy. Social media is the second step. Images caught on the camera are of little use if they are not published on a platform that distributes them without restrictions from those in power. Billions of people globally, and hundreds of millions of people in the United States, have access to social media. They can choose to criticize the images, participate in their viral potential by sharing them on their platforms, or simply view them or remove them from their feeds. Whatever their choice is, there is minimal interference from the royal regime. Where algorithms and human beings monitor and regulate the dissemination of the videos, there are ways to manipulate and avoid some of these regulations or access other platforms such as personal blogs or websites.

Just as blackness is less hidden because of the camera and social media, so are the mechanisms and agents of whiteness / the royal regime / the dominant group no longer able to operate in the shadows. But social media is a two-edged sword. It can be a space, in the hands of power, that spreads propaganda and even hate to thwart racial progress. It has also become a platform where hate groups gather and recruitment of potential members occurs. With the continued democratization of power even on social media, there are fewer places on social media that provide shadows for oppressive and hate-motivated power to flourish. The struggle for power extends to this platform. Justice-seekers must be vigilant and alert in all forums because power is at stake.

Social Media: Virtual Town Square

The camera, along with social media, erodes power that traditionally has been largely in the possession of the state, corporations, or wealthy White influential individuals who all generally benefit from, or are unscathed by, the social status quo. The camera documents the unseen-ness and in-betweenness of the Black experience, and social media is the platform that allows for its widespread viewing. The camera is the mechanism for storytelling, and social media offers democratized access to the story for viewing, commentary, and criticism and provides a voice for demanding a moral and ethical social response. In the twenty-first century, the alternative racial consciousness may thrive at the intersection of the camera and social media. This is not to say the social media platform is not another battlefield in the war for a stronghold on power. It is in fact another battlefield. It is, however, a battlefield that is democratized and invites more intellectual, cultural, and socioeconomic perspectives that can potentially weaken the once monopolized power of the royal regime.

Posting comments, pictures, and videos on social media today is common practice. It is social and cultural liturgy in the sense that it is a daily practice or habit for individuals to post celebrations, achievements, vacations, or even selfies for friends and the broader public to witness. J. K. Smith claims in his book *Desiring the Kingdom* that humans are liturgical beings (*Homo liturgicus*). What he means is that "humans are those animals that are religious not because we are primarily believing animals but because we are liturgical animals—embodied, practicing creatures whose love/desire is aimed at something ultimate."[6] It is debatable what the "something ultimate" is regarding posting on social media. It may simply be the human instincts and desire to use technology to extend our ability to be social beings with those whom we would otherwise have little or no contact. For African Americans, the practice/liturgy of posting on social media is pedagogical and a form of activism. In Frazier's case specifically, there is "something ultimate." For her, it was to simply tell the truth of an event that competes with the false narrative published by the Minneapolis Police Department. It was also to amplify truth-telling that arouses the masses to radical resistance to injustice and accountability for representatives of the royal regime. The "something ultimate" is justice.

Whenever the prophet says, "The Lord says," the prophet is publishing God's message to the people. It tends to be a message that compels just action that causes social transformation or abstaining from some unjust act. The prophet also brought a message that demanded changing legislation and policies that perpetuate inequities, exploiting the vulnerable while protecting those in closer proximity to power and resources. This is the potential for the social media platform. While it can be a cesspool of opinions that appear toxic, it is also a space for publishing messages in line with God's will for the formation of a just society. This was Frazier's "something ultimate," whether she was conscious of this or not. This was the implication of her actions.

Social media also serves as a virtual town square. The town square, the city gate in biblical times, or the barbershop and hair salon in the Black community today all serve a similar purpose. They were/are the places of public debate, exchange of ideas, encouragement, criticism, or receiving wise counsel. Also, in the Black community, there is usually a tree or some informal outside gathering location that serves the same purposes. Once ideas, insights, revelations, news, television episodes, or social events are "published" in the places that are symbols of the town square, they are discussed, debated, and disseminated throughout the community to further engage. This is the power of social media. Its viral capacity demands a tremendous amount of responsibility because of its power to influence perception, tap into emotions, and move the masses to action.

While an unchecked social media platform can do much harm, especially to the most vulnerable in society, it is also the space in which activists are able to inspire, inform, organize, and galvanize support for a needed social movement. Responsibly using Facebook, Twitter, or Instagram, to name a few, may be where many people enter the conversation on racial/social injustice. It is common for people to follow their favorite voices, whether they are pastors, celebrities, scholars, and so on who engage intelligently and thoughtfully about serious and complicated issues. Just as one can get lost in the conversation happening in the barbershop or be "under the tree" for hours learning from the "old heads" (the elders), the same can occur virtually as one scrolls through various threads on social media platforms. There are countless toxic interactions, but there are also accounts that disengage the toxicity and consistently offer healthy engagement to glean from.

The responsibility required when posting on social media is clearly seen in the spread of misinformation and conspiracy theories about everything, from Covid-19, vaccinations, political agendas, and much more. Former president Donald Trump and his loyal followers used social media to stir up his base with false claims of voter fraud in the 2020 presidential election (although there was no evidence of widespread voter fraud that would have remotely changed the outcome of the election he lost). Conspiracy theories, often originating from the former president's own social media pages, spread rampantly and began to anger those who pledged allegiance to him. They used that momentum on social media to summon thousands to Washington, DC, on January 6, 2021, the day Congress would certify the election results. The mob of Republican voters—many of whom were members of far-right-wing militia groups such as the Proud Boys, the Oathkeepers, the Three Percenters, as well as Nazis and other white supremacist groups from around the country—stormed the Capitol. This is what power without wise and mature responsible use of social media can result in. It is the antithesis of the prophetic use of social media. Irresponsibility with social media likely results in destructive or oppressive ends.

Just as the prophet speaking the convicting, prophetic message from the Lord faces risk, there is also a risk for the ordinary citizen who witnesses, records, and posts anti-Black tragedies on social media. There is certainly much support from the African American community and allies, but there is also backlash—vitriol and threats from the largely White, conservative, and Christian "blue lives matter" contingent. The risk that Frazier took on started the moment she began to film. There was the risk of absorbing the trauma of the event. There was the inherent risk of interacting with police officers whose nervous systems were on high alert. Lastly, there was the risk of obscene and threatening comments on social media, as well as in person, from rogue or racist police officers or citizens who are sympathizers of law enforcement ("blue lives"). This is the prophetic risk, whether a person is conscious of their participation in prophetic acts or not. Embodying and performing the prophetic imagination is inherently dangerous for the individual, but it is eternally necessary and rewarding for humanity, especially for the disenfranchised and oppressed.

Moses knew the risk more than anyone of prophetic confrontation with Pharaoh. The prophets, too, understood both the responsibility and the risk in speaking God's piercing revelation to the people, particularly to power—the leadership of Israel. Jeremiah, for example, endured great persecution for his truth-telling in contrast to the comforting messages that false prophets proclaimed to the leaders and the people. In Jeremiah 26, the prophet Jeremiah prophesies to all the people who came to worship at the house of the Lord. The revelation he was given was that if the people—citizens, priests, and the prophets—do not listen and walk in the law that God had set before them and listen to the words of the prophets, the Lord would make the house like Shiloh and make Jerusalem a curse, and all nations would witness.[7]

This "word from the Lord" angered the people, the priests, and the prophets. When they heard this, they "laid hold of him" and said he would die![8] They rejected what Jeremiah declared and sentenced him to death because he "prophesied against [the] city."[9] He received death threats because of the people's obstinance. But this was not the first time Jeremiah spoke this "hard" word to them. He had already prophesied and warned the people earlier, as described in Jeremiah 7. In that passage, he includes the mandate for social justice. He says, "For if you truly amend your ways and your deeds, if you truly execute justice one with another, if you do not oppress the sojourner [immigrant], the fatherless, or the widow, or shed innocent blood [unarmed African American] in this place, and if you do not go after other gods [idolatry of symbols and ideologies] to your own harm, then I will let you dwell in this place."[10]

They would rather defy God because of stubborn allegiance to the city than turn from their ways and be a more just and equitable society reflecting their God. This defiance led to their exile from Jerusalem to Babylon. Hananiah, whether he was a false prophet (although he identified as a prophet in Jeremiah 28:1) or a true prophet prophesying falsely, declared a rather comforting message, that God would bring them back to Jerusalem out of exile in just two years. Jeremiah cleverly responded to this false prophecy by saying that if this peace you claim comes to pass, then this is how they will know that the Lord has sent the word.[11] After receiving this nonthreatening response, Hananiah removed the yoke around Jeremiah's neck that was part of his punishment for his *prophetic imagination*. He then reveals a hard word for the people, but it would be the truth. He tells them they will remain in exile for seventy years; Israel would indeed remain in exile for seventy years before returning to Jerusalem.

The danger of the prophetic performance, whether in rhetoric (like Jeremiah) or other creative ways of confronting injustice (like the way the camera and social media have been used by African Americans and allies), is that the masses who side with existing power structures—the royal regime of white supremacy—will likely respond with the violence of words or actions. Just like the people of God more than two thousand years ago, many evangelical American Christians today either are unable or unwilling to recognize the prophetic ministry that originates from the margins, or they reject it altogether. In rejecting the ministry, they are rejecting both the agent and the justice of God.

Divine Democracy

Imagine a world where the only people with access to the Bible were leaders in the Christian or Catholic churches. Of course, this was a reality about 600 years ago. Imagine the power concentrated within this exclusive group that they could wield over Christians. It is not just tremendous power to influence; it is absolute power to deceive and control. One of the most consequential inventions in world history is that of the Gutenberg press in 1440. This is not because it produced the first printed text—the oldest known printed text originated in China during the first millennium CE—but because of its ability to make copies of the Bible (the Gutenberg Bible was first printed in 1452) so that it could be disseminated to many readers.[12]

This invention undermined the autonomy that the Catholic church leadership—namely, the pope—had in terms of access to the word of God. Essentially, this invention led to the democratization of the Bible. It presented the layman and laywoman with the opportunity to discover on their own and nurture their relationship with God through reading and meditation on Scripture. Whether intentional or not, this invention, leading to the opening of hundreds of printing shops throughout Europe, was subversive in its disruption of the exclusive access to authoritative writings that the Christian power structure at the time maintained.[13]

This could be viewed as mere chance, a result of techno-logical innovation and cultural ideas, or it could be understood as divine providence when viewed considering God-initiated patterns described in the biblical narrative. God tends to disrupt the status quo maintained and enjoyed by the royal regime (even within the church context) and democratize resources to those on the margins for more equitable access to those resources and a more just societal playing field. Moses, after being deputized by Yahweh to lead the Israelites out of the oppressive conditions in the land of Egypt, read aloud the Ten Commandments, as revealed to him by Yahweh, to the Israelites in the wilderness. The commandments were inscribed on stone tablets, and Moses was to steward them. Yahweh instructed Moses to "set limits around the mountain and consecrate it" and prevent the people from "break[ing] through to come up to the Lord."[14] This appears to be mutual, given that even the people, out of fear of Yahweh, preferred for Moses to speak to God and convey the message to them. In other words, they welcomed Moses's mediation and autonomy over divine revelation.[15]

Jeremiah offers another paradigm for not only under-standing Yahweh but living in relationship with Yahweh. The Law, which had been traditionally accepted as written on the stones of Moses and later in the Book of the Law, would now be written (a work of the Spirit) on the hearts of all the individuals that make up the people of God.[16] This is a divine act of democratizing access to the Law. God decides to relocate the Law so that it is infinitely more proximal to individual and group consciousness. No longer would the people of God have to go to the Law. Instead, the Law has come to them, irrespective of a person's standing in society. This is the power of divine democratization. It brings those on the margins closer to the source of power, equity, and community. In this case, to be intimate with God's Law is to be in community with the divine, and ideally, this engagement is done in community with others.

God does not stop with democratizing the Law, but he also does the same with the Holy Spirit at Pentecost in Acts 2. The Spirit in the Old Testament would come upon kings, prophets, priests, judges, or select individuals that Yahweh had chosen to perform specific tasks. This changed at Pentecost, fulfilling Old Testament prophesies such as Isaiah 44:3, "I will pour my Spirit upon your offspring, and my blessing on your descendants," or Joel 2:28, "And it shall come to pass afterward, that I will pour out my Spirit on all flesh." Access to intimacy or immersion in the Spirit was now made equitable among those who believed in and followed Jesus. The Spirit descended and fell upon all the believers that were present in sustained, passionate prayer. The evidence of the Spirit upon the group was in glossolalia, the speaking of languages unknown to the disciples as witnesses heard praises to God in their own languages. God displayed the sovereign power to communicate with each individual and each community of Jews. Each could hear God, prophesy on behalf of God, or translate God's messages to others by the Spirit. It was no longer a privileged role of the priest or the prophet but the inclusive role of all believers.

In both examples, God was investing power in the people via access to and intimacy with the Spirit and the Law. This is the essence of divine democratization; it is equitable redistribution of power, of God's self. God is not only drawing those existentially distal to the Law or the Spirit closer to God's self, but God also moves nearer to them. Democratization involves relocation. It is a practice that relocates those in power and the powerless. The aim of democratization is to close the gap of power. Individual, communal, and cultural change occurs when people and groups are proximal to God as the source of power and one another.

When God heard the cries of the Israelites suffering oppression under Pharaoh in Egypt, God sent Moses *to* them. Moses relocated from the land of Midian to Egypt to confront Pharaoh. Moses did not go without community or resources. God sent him with his brother, Aaron, and his sister, Miriam, and God invested supernatural power in the willing vessel that Moses proved to be. As God democratized power by investing God's self in the people, there is no greater investment than God taking on flesh and locating God's self among the people. Jesus is "the image of the invisible God."[17] God could well have chosen to maintain the religious power structures of Israel as they historically were—access to God being via priests and prophets. God chose to abandon (to a degree) a relationship with humanity in "the mystery and invisibility of the Spirit."[18] Instead, God taking on the flesh of humanity to walk *with* humanity and suffer *for* and *as* humanity is further democratization of God's self. The woman at the well had intimate access to God-in-flesh. The man by the pool of Bethesda had unmediated access to God-in-flesh. The disciples learned organically from God-in-flesh. God is most clearly revealed through Jesus. God makes the truth known through Jesus and through the Spirit.

In God's economy, democratization initiated by God is synonymous with the prophetic. To reiterate, democratization involves the relocation of resources and power to the margins and of those on the margins toward power. Divine democratization disrupts the monopoly of power structures, disorients individuals and communities in power who are the gatekeepers of those structures, and disseminates resources, power, and knowledge more equitably.

A Protective Eye

The presence of cameras indicates active surveillance. The watchful eye of the camera is there to deter crime, catch criminals in the act, or aid in the investigation to apprehend them. Businesses install cameras inside and outside facilities to keep a watchful eye over the property. Cities have cameras on street corners (as well as access to cameras on private buildings) to document traffic violations, criminal activity, or interactions between citizens or between law enforcement and citizens. For African Americans, however, interaction with either White citizens or police officers has required the camera's surveillance as a means for protection. It has essentially become a tool for countersurveillance.

Consider the earlier chapter on blackness as a liminal, unseen existence. It is a space of unsafety, anxiety, and trauma. It is also a space of creativity and improvisation. The camera sits at this intersection. The camera is necessary for protection and yet has been used creatively to document the often-hidden activities of this liminal space. Cameras installed alongside businesses captured George Floyd's murder just as Darnella Frazier did. However, they did not capture the cries he made for his mother. They did not show his face as life left his body. They did not record Chauvin's eyes. He was not intimate with them the way he was with Frazier's phone. To protect this Black man, she met unsafety, anxiety, and trauma with courage, resiliency, creativity, and improvisation in ways that the cameras installed for surveillance to protect the local businesses could not.

The cameras installed by the royal regime around cities were not meant to protect the people from crimes of state-sanctioned violence but meant to be a watchful eye *for* the state. The body cameras that police officers wear on their uniforms, when they are turned on, are meant to protect law enforcement officers from false accusations, not necessarily to protect (Black) citizens from law enforcement. Officers appear to continue to use excessive force, at times to the point of unnecessary death, assuming they will receive the benefit of the doubt wrapped in the legal jargon of "qualified immunity."

Sometimes the surveillance cameras installed by those in power backfire in a culture with apparatuses and devices that democratize power. In June of 2021, Keith Pool, the first African American police officer of the Sheffield Lake, Ohio, police department found a Ku Klux Klan note placed on his raincoat on his desk by Police Chief Anthony Campo. The incident was caught by surveillance video cameras in the office. Pool later shared on CNN that this was not the first time he had been targeted by Campo. After leaving the note and thinking it was funny, Campo made a make-shift KKK hat and told Pool he had to wear it on his next call. Pool insists that nothing was done regarding the other incidents of bigotry against him and other officers of Color.[19] Had it not been for the video footage, the status quo of bigotry from the captain would certainly have continued. What is striking is the audacity of Campo to commit this brazen act of white supremacy, couched in a failed attempt at humor, knowing there was a camera recording him. It was not until the video was leaked and went viral that any actions were taken against Campo. This is the power of devices such as video footage *with* social media platforms. This is democracy, power on the side of the masses.

In some cases, pulling out one's camera phone to *shoot* a video is a more effective weapon of protection than pulling out a gun to shoot bullets. When birdwatcher Christian Cooper, an African American man, asked "Central Park Karen" Amy Cooper, a White woman, to put her dog on a leash, Amy Cooper warned him that she would call the cops and tell them there was an African American man threatening her life. She said this while Christian Cooper was literally pointing his camera at her and had already begun recording. He was protecting himself, given the history of White people (especially White women) making false accusations, receiving the benefit of the doubt, and African Americans (especially African American men) being viewed as guilty until proven innocent. While Amy Cooper had created or believed a narrative about Christian Cooper in her head, assuming he had ulterior motives to attack her, he was the one who was the most in danger had he not been armed with his camera phone.

Christian Cooper was in danger of the layers of violence that come with racial profiling. First, Amy Cooper profiled him, assuming he had criminal intent. Second, history teaches that without evidence on his phone, he would have likely been in danger of racial profiling and potentially excessive force and arrest by police officers had he resisted in the least. History has also proven that Amy Cooper, a White woman, would have been trusted with the truth over the word of an African American man.

Racial profiling, as it relates to law enforcement, is defined in a Department of Justice (DOJ) report in 2000 as "[reliance] upon race, ethnicity, or national origin rather than behavior that leads police to identify a person as being engaged in criminal activity."[20] This definition is a good start, but it does not account for bias, particularly unconscious bias. An officer need only misinterpret behavior through his or her own distorted, biased lens to conceal or justify their prejudice. Today, it is as simple as a police officer saying, "He [or she] *fit the description*." This claim has become a reliable justification for profiling an African American "driving while Black," "walking while Black," or "jogging while Black."

The DOJ, in this attempt at defining racial profiling, does not account for the hiddenness and stealth-like performance of whiteness and its capacity to dominate and oppress African Americans through insidious anti-Black attitudes and behavior. Was Amy Cooper aware of this intuitively? If Christian Cooper was not equipped with his smartphone, at best, he would have been warned about his threats to Amy Cooper. At worst, he would have encountered overpolicing, and any form of resistance—be it verbal or physical, even in body language—could very well have led to him being arrested or worse. This is the reality of blackness as a liminal, unseen existence. Racial profiling in the in-between is a constant threat. The democratization of the camera functions to balance power dynamics, so African Americans have a chance to protect themselves against the violence of White misperceptions, White lies, the White gaze, and White people with tools of authority and force—badges, batons, tasers, and guns.

Conclusion

Earthly power—governments, monarchies, dictatorships—has the tendency to distance itself, monopolize power and resources, and function in insularity and exclusivity. Its nature is to marginalize some while centering select others. The gap between power and those on the margins in this binary model is the space that buffers those in power while they create and publish their dominant narrative. It is in fact a barrier that preserves a narrative that often manipulates, controls, and maintains the status quo. The democratization of the camera, thus the democratization of power, is imperative, though it does not come without its risks.

Democratization, while not perfect, is a subversive ethic as it relates to power. Technology has proven to be a tool for the royal regime to expand its influence and power, but more importantly, it has been used to the advantage of the masses demanding more equitable access to opportunity, resources, and the power to subvert the dominant narrative of royal (White) consciousness. The partnership between the camera and social media is potent enough to transform society with narratives from the margins. Roxane Gay is correct when she claims, "Social media is something of a double-edged sword. At its best, social media offers unprecedented opportunities for marginalized people to speak and bring much-needed attention to the issues they face. At its worst, social media offers 'everyone' an unprecedented opportunity to share in collective outrage without reflection."[21]

The best and the worst of democratization of the camera and social media is the tension we must endure for the sake of weakening the stronghold that the royal regime of white supremacy and institutions that traffic in its ideology have on the whole of society. The tension is what we must navigate for the sake of exposing the violence in ways that the gatekeepers of White power structures have been unwilling to do. It is in the context of this practice of democratization that the moral, political, legal, economic, and physical struggle that Frederick Douglass speaks of occurs. While power concedes nothing without a demand, that demand must circulate and be heard and seen by the masses to amplify the potency of the social movement making the demands in the first place. The camera, for African Americans, provides the visual imagery that for some confirms reality and for others conforms them to an alternative consciousness for liberation, justice, and solidarity against seen and unseen anti-Black violence.

CHAPTER 7

When the Bystander
Aims and Shoots

Darnella Frazier, like King, found herself at the center of a power struggle. She entered the battle between good versus evil, White versus Black, and individual versus institution. The royal regime of white supremacy is always vigilant in asserting its power against the vulnerable to preserve its position as the center or the pinnacle of society. Perhaps, as an agent of divine democracy, she was equipped with an indispensable tool (some might say weapon) that amplified the power of her agency. Had it not been for Frazier, walking by like other bystanders present, witnessing, recording, and publishing Floyd's murder, there would likely not have been an arrest, a trial, and the conviction of Derek Chauvin. Unfortunately, the surveillance cameras set up along the sides of businesses on that street corner did not do enough to influence the Minneapolis Police Department into issuing a truthful initial statement to the public regarding the incident. It took improvisation in the moment with pleas for Officer Chauvin to relent and the readiness of Frazier to point and shoot up close and personal—in Spike Lee, *Do the Right Thing*-style—to do the moment justice.

I am convinced of God's readiness to employ anyone who is available at a given moment to be used in the prophetic ministry. This is the improvisational nature of the prophetic imagination. It does not require humanity to manufacture the moment but to merely have the discernment, willingness, courage, and resiliency to be present in the moment and participate. God provides the resources or God takes the resources available in the moment and transforms them into tools that, despite the trauma of capturing and publishing violence, can potentially solidify justice, spark revolution and change, and become extensions of prophetic performance.

Feidin Santana exhibited the same resilience and presence of mind as Frazier did after witnessing Walter Scott's murder by North Charleston, South Carolina, police officer Michael Slager on April 4, 2015. Slager ultimately shot Scott in the back while Scott was running away from him. Slager, never attempting to chase after Scott at that point, shot him as if he were hunting an animal trying to escape the crosshairs of his gun. Slager initially lied by saying he had no choice but to use deadly force against Scott, who "charged at him after stealing his taser."[1] He was not aware that he was being filmed from a distance. Santana, who happened to be running late for work that morning, witnessed and recorded the deadly encounter from sixty yards away. He said he came forth with the video after he learned that Scott died and Slager's story conveniently did not include the part where he shot Scott as he was running away.[2]

Just as the cameramen from national news networks were allies of King and the Civil Rights Movement, the engaged bystander can be the ally for the victim and the victim's family in the event the victim does not survive the violence perpetrated against them, as in the cases of George Floyd and Walter Scott. Bystanders become the voice for the dead. Whether by happenstance or by God's providence, the bystander is present to document events that would otherwise be manipulated by those in power (e.g., the Minneapolis Police Department's initial statement and Slager's lie about being attacked by Scott). They did not necessarily ask for or seek this responsibility, trauma, and potential backlash or praise. They were simply present. Prophetic work requires the presence of those from the margins who have the instincts and courage to act as disruptors of the activities of power—the royal regime of white supremacy.

Prophetic ministry begins with presence. So does love. More than just physical presence, both require consciousness, seeing, and hearing others. We live in an era where people are not fully present with one another. I have observed couples and entire families sitting together at a restaurant, and everyone is preoccupied with their phones, and not a word is spoken for much of the time they are there. This phenomenon of present-but-absent undermines our collective ability to see one another's suffering, hear one another's cries, feel one another's trauma but also to be inspired and empowered by one another's resiliency. It blinds us to the social ills around us and limits our capacity to share in lament and joy. In other words, individual and collective agency are handicapped by the invitation to insularity by technology. Rather than being mastered by technology in this way, we must master technology and co-opt its innovation as a tool for the prophetic ministry. Opportunities abound for technology such as the camera phone to enhance the impact of our agency to affect social change.

Agency

How audacious is whiteness that it dares to determine the degree to which African Americans have agency—if any? In fact, since Europeans came into significant contact with Africans at the beginning of the slave trade, they have hardly recognized the humanity of people of African descent. Hatred, however, was not an initial sentiment of Europeans toward Africans. They simply viewed them as subhuman beings who could provide free labor in the new lands to the West that the various European countries had conquered. They saw them in similar ways as they did poor Whites, prisoners, and the homeless in Europe. The only distinction is that they recognized the humanity inherent in their whiteness. They allowed room for their agency.

What is agency? Agency is the "ability to act, to do, and to have the freedom to impose that action or will in any given situation."[3] Without agency, we are merely tools, instruments under the absolute control of another person's will and agency. A person is reduced to being an extension of another. Subsequently, their identity is subsumed by this "other," and their own humanity cannot be recognized without its validation or consent. This has historically been the tragic reality of the effects of whiteness on blackness—the erasure of identity, value, and human agency of African Americans is to be replaced with White identity while value and agency are determined by whiteness.

The democratization of the camera, power reinvested to include the marginalized and oppressed in society, is a way of reclaiming agency. The conscious person armed with a camera has the ability—for the sake of historical accuracy, accountability, and protection of Black people—to present a truthful narrative countering the oppressive, often false narrative of the royal regime of whiteness. There was a time in US history that Frazier and others would not have had the freedom to exercise agency to this degree. They would not have been allowed by law or culture to either possess such technology or use that technology, especially in ways that benefited African Americans, threatened White people, or prevented whiteness from operating with impunity. To do so would mean to challenge the absolute authority (white sovereignty) or superiority (white supremacy) of White persons.

This is in fact what the presence of Black bodies witnessing, with camera in hand, the annihilation of another Black body is doing, challenging white sovereignty and supremacy. Remember, the democratization of the camera is also the democratization of power. Whiteness has long enjoyed absolute power and absolute freedom in the United States. Black moral agency, with the help of White allies and allies of Color—abolitionists, Freedom Riders, White People for Black Lives, and other brave politicians, celebrities, and activists—has eroded "white absolutism." Not only has it eroded it, but Black moral agency in recent years has exposed it even more.

A glimpse in history will reveal that Black moral agency has been one of the triggers for whiteness exerting its energies of oppression via violent acts, unjust legislation, fearmongering rhetoric, and trafficking in anti-Black narratives to discredit groups, organizations, and individuals within the Black community. Today, it has become increasingly more difficult for whiteness to win these battles when it is having to react to the frequency of video footage at the hands of ordinary citizens being released to the public. The only strategy left is to limit the exposure of the footage, misinterpret the footage, or further discredit the person filming for an audience that is receptive to these deceptive tactics.

The fight for African Americans is the fight for the free, unobstructed expression of moral agency. If there is any progress that has been made since the end of slavery, it is there. If there is any target area for counterresistance, it is there, Black moral agency. The technology of the camera is a gift and a curse, depending on whose hands that technology is in or under whose supervision. As a curse, it can cause the destruction of bodies, property, reputation, or community. As a gift, it has democratized power and redistributed it to the masses to even the social playing field. It has been weaponized as a gift and a curse. The weaponization from African Americans on the margins, for the most part, protects and holds those in power accountable. It is the tool that is used to speak truth to power.

This Is Us

King David is referred to as a "man after [God's] own heart."[4] While this may be true to characterize the totality of David's life, this does not mean David was immune to sin and rebellion against the will and ways of Yahweh: It was the time of year when kings were out to battle. David sent Joab, his nephew and commander of his army, to lead the army in a battle they ultimately won against the Ammonites. David remained in Jerusalem. While David walked the roof of his house, he saw a beautiful woman named Bathsheba bathing on her roof. Using his power, he inquired about her and then sent for her that he might have sex with her. The first problem—other than the objectification of this woman—was that

Bathsheba was married to Uriah from the king's army. David impregnated Bathsheba during their intimate encounter. He then attempted to bring Uriah from the battlefield so that Uriah could spend time with his wife and be intimate with her. This was likely so David could cover up the pregnancy. Uriah, an honorable man, did not go to be with his wife because he did not want to pleasure himself while Joab and the other servants and fighters slept in the fields. Further taking advantage of the power he wielded, David then successfully had Uriah set up for certain death in battle by placing him at the "forefront of the hardest fighting."[5] In all, David committed adultery, tried to hide the pregnancy, and then had a man killed in battle to hide the affair.

There is no indication in Scripture that David repented of his multiple sins involving Bathsheba before he was confronted. One day, the Lord sent Nathan the prophet to David, in essence, to speak truth to power. Nathan told David a parable. He told a parable in a way that David supposed he was speaking of someone else. Nathan's parable went this way:

> There were two men in a certain city, the one rich and the other poor. The rich man had very many flocks and herds, but the poor man had nothing but one little ewe lamb, which he had bought. And he brought it up, and it grew up with him and with his children. It used to eat of his morsel and drink from his cup and lie in his arms, and it was like a daughter to him. Now there came a traveler to the rich man, and he was unwilling to take one of his own flock or herd to prepare for the guest who had come to him, but he took the poor man's lamb and prepared it for the man who had come to him.[6]

David was enraged at what he heard and told Nathan the man who had done this deserved to die. I imagine Nathan's response today would be said this way: "I'm talkin' 'bout you. This is you!"

Nathan painted a picture with the parable he told. He was essentially holding a mirror up for David to see himself. The parable was potent enough to pierce David's self-constructed insulation of denial. For more than nine months, from the time of his child's conception to Nathan's prophetic confrontation after the child was born, David had shown no remorse, at least none indicated in Scripture. It was not until he was able to see himself in the parable that he acknowledged his sin. God would show David mercy, but not without the tragic consequences of the death of his and Bathsheba's child.

When George Floyd was lying facedown with Derek Chauvin's knee on his neck and two other officers atop his lower body, Darnella Frazier had the presence of mind to begin recording the unfolding tragedy with the video capability of her cell phone. Typical for this generation, she knew to then turn to social media and publish the footage for the world to see. Keep in mind, she did this amid experiencing her own trauma, witnessing a man's life being taken by those with authority who swore to *protect* and *serve* the community. Frazier unknowingly embodied the role of Nathan, the prophet, with her actions as she confronted power to reveal the error of its ways when she recorded the murder and had the audacity to post the video on social media.

The camera in the hands of bystanders is like a mirror held in front of the nation's collective face in real time, raw and unapologetic. In the context of racial violence, that face is "White" America. For clarity, "White" is not exclusive to those of European ancestry—although they are the primary agents—but includes even persons of Color ("honorary" Whites) who uncritically and/or intentionally embrace, defend, and are agents of white ideology/supremacy/sovereignty. The footage paints a picture that far too many White people do not want to admit is a reality. But for African Americans, the images of Floyd or Scott were not surprises. This *is* America.

The Moment

There was a television show called *America's Funniest Home Videos* that showed a lighter side of using the camera to capture a family's funny moments. Sometimes those moments went beyond the immediate family and included neighbors and strangers. The footage was often impromptu. The comedy in the videos was generally unplanned, which is what makes them so funny. The surprise of the moment is part of why they make you laugh as an audience and why the people recording and participating in the video were laughing just as intensely as the television audience would be while watching. There is something profound, even sacred, when the "moment" is not lost to history without documentation. By the "moment," I mean the instances of both profundity and subtleness that are catalytic and transformational, or worthy of remembrance and celebration, respectively. It ranges from the moment the planes flew into the World Trade Center buildings, the buildings collapsing, and the look of shock and awe on the faces of our neighbors on that day to the moment you first held the hand of a loved one.

I recall watching a video of my niece Delaney when she was just about two years old. I recorded her with my phone doing tumbles in my grandparents' home. She was having such a great time entertaining all of us who were watching her and laughing. Just to the right side of the video was my maternal grandmother. She had since passed away by the time I was rewatching the video. While there was a moment of sadness seeing her and knowing I could not speak with her anymore, it quickly turned into a pleasant moment for me, because for the first time since she passed away, I was able to hear her voice and see her move and laugh. In that sense, the camera was a "prophetic" tool in another way, as the scene spoke to me (revelation) and reminded me of why and for whom I do the work that I do—racial justice and solidarity—to inspire the next generation and to honor those who went before me who lived sacrificially so that I am afforded the opportunities I have today.

Still shots are valuable because they become artifacts of times and eras. They can evoke memories, pleasant or unpleasant, as they mark moments in individual or collective history. They tell part of the larger story and happenings unnarrated, except according to the imagination of the viewer. Video footage expands that drama and adds layers to the moment that pictures are incapable of providing. Still shots say, "Look. Something happened here." Video says, "Look. This happened!" Video images add dimensions that indicate duration, depth of joy or suffering, reference points of provocation, and the intensity of the drama documented.

The moment after Rodney King was pulled over in Lake View Terrace, California, a suburb just north of Los Angeles proper, he was beaten by several police officers who assumed they were safe under the dark and stillness of the night to use brutal, unnecessary force.

Still shots from the video recording reveal images of more than a dozen police officers swinging batons, kicking his body, or standing around watching. One image captures an officer with his baton in hand at the beginning stage of a full swing before connecting with King's body lying in a protective fetal position. Another image shows an officer's foot apparently landing on King's back as he was being kicked. What the images say is that something violent happened in that moment. It does not convey how long the beating went on, how many strikes King received, or how hard the blows were against his body like the video footage does.

The importance of a bystander recording undetected across the street from the balcony of his apartment is that it provides unedited truth on behalf of the victim. The still shots leave room for creative analysis and interpretation. Those sworn to protect and serve have reasons to cover up the beating and alter the truth to protect and serve themselves. The bystander, as a witness, testifies for King. His character may have been assassinated. They may have exaggerated the extent of his condition at the time of the encounter for the purpose of sanctioning the abuse of their authority. What they could not do was say the content of the camera did not tell the truth.

The bystander who courageously stands in solidarity with the victim—especially African Americans victimized by state-sanctioned violence—by their mere presence in the moment shares in the experience. The perpetrator asks that the bystander do nothing, while the victim needs the bystander to share the burden, actively engage, and remember with them.[7] By sharing in this way, they validate the value of Black life. They say, "I see you. I won't leave you." They take the burden of the victim's suffering upon themselves, they invite future viewers to join in communal lament and indignation, and they compel society to not turn away from injustice and participate in God's redemptive work and embrace the prophetic God-consciousness of an alternative community.

Because of this invitation, the bystander participates in sacred work by recording these moments. I say sacred because, figuratively speaking, the camera shined a light on actions of darkness against the sacredness of human life in the tradition of the prophets. Sometimes the sacred work is messy. The suffering of Christ before and upon the cross just before his death was the sacred work of God that had to be included. The plagues that preceded Moses and the Israelites' liberation from Pharaoh's oppressive royal regime were part of God's sacred liberative work that needed to be executed and told. The Babylonian invasion of Jerusalem that led to Israel's seventy years of exile was God's sacred work. Each event of death and suffering was recorded in the prophetic literature, and each is associated with God's activities of liberation for Israel, specifically, and humanity, in general. The liberation occurs by God showing the people who they really are, with intentions of disciplining them, motivating them to repentance, and ultimately restoring them to freedom from the very sins that held them in bondage as a society.

In this sense, is the bystander truly a bystander by the purist definition of the word? A bystander, according to *Merriam-Webster*, is someone "who is present but not taking part in a situation or event; a chance spectator."[8] To the human eye or according to human understanding, this may appear to be true. From a divine standpoint, however, the individual is not there by chance, and he or she is certainly not uninvolved. Darnella Frazier is sharing in the suffering of George Floyd, and by documenting and publishing the event, she shared in telling the story, the counternarrative, of his final moments.

Instead of seeing Frazier and Santana as bystanders in the literal sense of the term, we may consider them to be "withstanders." The word *withstand* means to resist or oppose, to be against. Used in this way it can take on two meanings. In one sense, they stood with the victims. They did not choose to leave or keep walking or driving by, nor were they in a present-but-absent distracted state. In another sense, they were resisting and opposing the police officers' actions. By using their phones to document the murders and then make them public, they displayed resistance. But they are also withstanders in the sense that they hold up under the weight and burden of watching and recording and the responsibility to publicize the tragedy. In these ways, they are "withstanders" rather than bystanders. *Bystanders* suggests passivity, while *withstanders* implies intentionality and agency.

In moments when withstanders find themselves playing crucial roles as eyewitnesses, they are not only using resources available to them; they *are* a resource. They are purveyors of truth. They provide the eyes and ears that testify on behalf of the voiceless—the accused, the victimized, or the murdered—against the narrative of the machine that is the royal regime of whiteness. They are not "standing by" in a passive sense, but they are "standing in," "standing for," and indeed "standing with" the victims of anti-Black violence.

Behind Enemy Lines

The liminal, in-betweenness of the Black experience too often feels like living behind enemy lines. The sense of the shadow of constant surveillance is real. What makes the experience an "in-between" existential reality is that Black bodies are seen and criminalized or vilified, but Black humanity is unseen or often unacknowledged. The cameras set up for surveillance on the sides of buildings and homes seemingly keep watchful eyes on those Black bodies. Certainly, the cameras catch criminals of all shades involved in criminal activity; their presence is symbolic of a history of overpolicing African Americans, which leads to overcharging, oversentencing, and overpopulating prisons and graves with Black bodies.

In 2012, Trayvon Martin, a seventeen-year-old African American, was murdered by George Zimmerman, a White man who volunteered for his neighborhood watch group.[9] Zimmerman was told by the 911 dispatcher not to follow Martin, but he did so anyway. In the altercation between Zimmerman and Martin, Zimmerman fired a shot, and Martin lost his life. The case received national attention. When Zimmerman was tried for the murder, he was acquitted, as his actions were framed under Florida's "Stand Your Ground" law. Even though he was armed and profiled—and against the advice of the 911 dispatcher, pursued an unarmed African American teenager—he was successfully able to argue self-defense. The question that comes to mind is, "What if there was video footage?" It seems Trayvon Martin needed an objective, unbiased eyewitness to affirm it was murder and validate the value of his life.

There was another case of tragic anti-Black violence in Mississippi that did not garner as much attention. Deryl Dedmon, a nineteen-year-old White man, about eight months prior (June 2011) to Trayvon Martin's death at the hands of George Zimmerman, took the life of James Craig Anderson, a forty-seven-year-old African American man. Dedmon and friends of his decided they wanted to hunt for a vulnerable African American man to attack in the urban area of Jackson, Mississippi.[10] Dedmon and his friends found Anderson, ran him down with his truck, and then backed over him again until he died. Unlike the Martin and Zimmerman altercation, which was left to the imagination from the audio from the 911 call Zimmerman made, Anderson's murder was caught on camera. Gloria Browne-Marshall is correct when she suggests, "If the motel surveillance camera had not captured Dedmon's assault on James Anderson, there would have been scant evidence."[11] Without the lens of the camera capturing the violence, Dedmon's membership in whiteness likely privileges him with the benefit of the doubt, much like Zimmerman.

His actions after running over and killing Anderson suggest that Dedmon was fully aware of his privilege. According to police officers, "Dedmon bragged that he ran over Anderson and used a racial slur to describe him."[12] It seems he was unconcerned about the consequences of or the repercussions for his actions. During sentencing, he displayed a change of heart (maybe because of the reality of his imprisonment) as he told Anderson's family he was "young . . . dumb . . . ignorant" and that he "was not raised the way he acted that night. [He] was raised in a godly house."[13] He insisted he was a changed man, that God had changed him. While this may be true, would he have been remorseful if he hadn't gotten caught? Would he have been caught if it had not been for the motel camera documenting his and his friends' intentional, racially motivated attack on an African American man described by his family as a *true* man of God?

In 2020, under the cloak of darkness, someone, who was presumably White, took the time to hang a piece of rope tied in a noose in Bubba Wallace's garage stall before a race. Wallace is the only current African American race car driver in NASCAR's top series. It is worth noting that this occurred just thirteen days after Wallace, on national television, called for banning the confederate flag at all NASCAR racing events. His challenge angered many racing fans. An FBI investigation found that of the 29 racetracks and 1,684 garage stalls, there were eleven pull-down ropes tied in a knot, but only one was tied in a noose.[14] As a teenager, Wallace began his career with great success on the track among his peers, but the success did not come without the challenges that haunt blackness. Because of his success, he was often accused of cheating. His car was carefully inspected after wins. They—White men—needed to *see* for themselves that he had not cheated.

The FBI determined that the noose had been in that stall for a year, and since there was no way to know Wallace would be assigned to that stall, it was not considered a hate crime.[15] Conservative voices anchored themselves to that finding as if it were the gospel. There was no withstander to witness who hung the noose in the stall that Wallace "just so happened" to be assigned in 2020. Conveniently, there was no camera to be a witness. Was the camera needed to see who tied and hung the knot? Or would it have been better served if the camera revealed who made sure Wallace was assigned to that garage stall where the noose was hung a year earlier, behind enemy lines?

The Weight (of the Camera)

The withstander to anti-Black violence occupies that liminal, unseen space as well. By witnessing murder or brutality, they experience trauma vicariously and directly. They do not experience the pain of the victim, but they themselves are in pain because of what they witness up close. Witnessing dehumanizing acts, especially those that lead to the loss of life, is a dehumanizing experience itself. Yet the withstander in that moment is compelled to act in a contrasting humanizing way. They find themselves at the intersection of trauma and liberation. The weight of the withstander's role elicits for us reflections on the weight of the prophetic ministry—moreover, the weight of the camera.

The weight of the prophetic ministry should not be taken for granted. The prophet(s) see the sins of society—injustice, oppression, exploitation, and so on—and yet he or she never loses sight of God's vision of hope for restoration. They operate out of a double consciousness that remembers and projects, is present and forward-looking, grieves and hopes, and acknowledges trauma yet yearns for and anticipates liberation. One aspect of the prophet's consciousness does not overshadow the other in these polarities, but they are in constant tension with each other. The prophet(s) cannot unsee either vision—the sin or the hope. In fact, the two are in conversation with one another. It is the hope that fuels the passion and urgency for confronting the sin. It is the sin that stirs the soul and compels the prophet(s) to action.

The moral weight of the prophetic ministry is transmitted to the weight, or weightiness, of responsibility that comes with the camera. The camera captures the sin/trauma (which seems to overshadow the hope) and has the capacity to fuel hope by igniting righteous indignation at its content. The responsibility is to steward the camera, its authenticity, and its truth-telling with integrity because liberation is at stake: liberation for the African American community but also liberation for the White community and ultimately for the nation. Liberation is in the fostering, embrace, and ethics of the alternative consciousness conceived by the prophetic ministry. In the moment, the withstander with the camera may discern the weight but may not have the language to name or the foresight to understand the trajectory of their actions. This will come with reflection.

The weightiness of the camera is that its images demand something of *us*. It demands that all of us engage in the newness of an alternative consciousness and be hopeful citizens of an alternative community. The question is how many among us are willing to share the weight of the camera? What segment of society will be content with morality that has atrophied and conscience that has been seared? The withstander forces the masses to answer questions like these. Whether he or she is aware that these are the reflections influenced by their actions or not, this is what their actions will evoke in every human whose eyes and heart are available to witness their work.

The weight of the camera summons us to participate in democracy. If democracy is synonymous with shared power among the people for the preservation of justice and equality, then can we truly participate in democracy while abstaining from the work of justice? Participation in democracy is more than voting to put representatives in positions of power within the existing power structures. It is taking part in the prophetic ministry, responding to and echoing prophetic criticism while embodying and energizing a new consciousness. It is carrying the weight with the withstander who finds themselves with the burden they did not necessarily ask for. This is truly the exercise of the power of the people.

The weight of the camera in the hands of the withstander reminds of the weight of the cross in the hands of Simon of Cyrene. Simon was a witness to the suffering of Jesus as Jesus was led to the location of his crucifixion. He was commanded to carry Jesus's cross, as Jesus was struggling do so on his own. He did not ask for this responsibility. He did not plan on inserting himself in this tragic chapter of Jesus's narrative. He did not, however, shy away from it either. The suffering of the Messiah was a shared experience. Bearing the weight of the instrument that finalized that suffering was a shared experience. The symbol of the cross and the symbol of the camera (like the symbol of the lynching tree) have both come to orient us toward unwarranted violence upon bodies of Color.[16] They both call society to participate in the work of liberation and justice on behalf of those bodies of Color even if death has not been averted. Simon of Cyrene (an African man), Frazier, Santana, and other "withstanders" did not prevent the deaths of these men of Color, but their participation models an alternative consciousness, one that does not turn away from injustice, but one that is willing to embody solidarity in suffering as well as solidarity in the exercise of power. As democracy is a shared experience of the people, so is the prophetic ministry a shared experience of the people for sustained societal change.

Conclusion

The withstander often plays a critical role in the saga of anti-Black violence in the United States. *Bystander* is an inappropriate term if one considers God's providence as having a legitimate hand in the orchestration of justice (hence my preference for *withstander*). The persons who are present with the presence of mind to record these events or the mere presence of the camera affixed onto a hotel building as key witnesses are often the difference between justice and injustice or between closed or open wounds.

Recently, there have been times when withstanders interrupt legitimate police work by not maintaining proper distance as arrests are made. The latest trends in overpolicing that leave behind the carnage of Black (and Brown) bodies have compelled citizens who do not trust law enforcement to be more intrusive to ensure officers know they are being watched and that the video will go public if there appears to be the use of excessive force. Today, readiness to use the camera is always necessary, but how one uses the camera requires wisdom. In these cases, it is fair to say the use of the camera by withstanders can be unwise and irresponsible interruptions of decent police officers doing the work the right way. This is not to cloud the countless times "withstanders" do show the intuition, courage, and long-suffering required to bring darkness to light.

What is so remarkable about Frazier's prophetic participation is the resiliency she displayed. It is no easy task to witness trauma, to be traumatized directly and vicariously, and still document the trauma in real time. She, like any withstander that happens upon violence, finds herself at the center of what could be momentous in the formation of an alternative consciousness that confronts the consciousness and ethic of the state / royal regime / power structures—in the case of anti-Black violence, "White" power structures.

CHAPTER 8

Dramatizing Blackness

Black Filmmakers Retelling the Narrative

As I wrote earlier, I understand the imperative for a television network like Black Entertainment Television (BET). As a teenager and young adult, BET was showing *all* of the Black experience. There was no shortage of Black music videos, talk shows, and sports events (I once played in a college basketball game for North Carolina A&T State University that aired on BET in the early 1990s.) There was Black excellence in sports, music, news, and comedy, and there was no shortage of scholars in various fields being given a platform on BET. First and foremost, African Americans consistently saw themselves in this light day after day. Equally as important is that others, especially White people if they chose to, could see the wholeness of blackness on display. The typical White narrative around blackness unravels when BET and other Black networks like TV One interrupt those thin, monolithic narratives and introduce a thicker, more accurate, and rich presentation of who Black people are and what blackness means.

The narrative around blackness on mainstream television and film is not always what the story line is around Black bodies and Black culture. Often, the narrative around blackness is implied by the absence of Black bodies representing beauty, intelligence, sophistication, civility, and success. The pre-dominance of whiteness centered as setting the standard for, and even monopolizing, these categories explicitly validates whiteness and diminishes blackness. Kristal Brent Zook reiterates this reality in her book *I See Black People*: "Film and television is a mirror for the audience to see themselves. African Americans do not get to see themselves depicted in ways that are not narrated and controlled by White people."[1]

As a child, I hardly remember seeing men and women who looked like me portrayed in the same way that White people were consistently portrayed, with a few token excep-tions. The women considered to be the most beautiful were blond-haired and blue-eyed. The most intelligent and suc-cessful men were White men with chiseled jawlines and thin-ner lips and noses. White people, especially White men, were the most composed and sophisticated, while White women were elegant, regal, and virtuous. What I and others viewed on television and in movies said as much about Black skin tones, Black hair, Black attitude, Black speech, Black body language, and Black presence by omission as it did about the predominance of whiteness on the screen.

During the 1980s, in light of the continued lack of Black presence on both the big and small screens, there was still the call from the Black community for inclusion in front of and behind the cameras. With the exceptions of exploiting blackness or for the purposes of tokenism, the status quo continued to prevail. Actor Eddie Murphy, however, used his star power to break from the tokenism in his classic 1988 "rom-com" *Coming to America* to centralize African American characters and culture. Filmmaker John Landis, on the CNN series *The Eighties*, says, "Up until that point, Hollywood movies that featured or starred a black artist, their color was always a plot point. In *Coming to America* their color has nothing to do with the plot." Murphy "flipped the script" in *Coming to America.*[2] The only White/Jewish person in a major role in the cast was played by Eddie Murphy himself. That was an ironic and interesting twist of events from the days of blackface in *Birth of a Nation*.

Hollywood filmmaking was not the only industry guilty of the erasure—or at best, tokenism—of African American presence in front of the camera. The music industry had its own demons to exorcise as well. By the late '80s and into the 1990s, it was not difficult to see music videos by African American artists represented on MTV. In the early 1980s, however, this was not the case. Rick James and David Bowie both took MTV to task for excluding Black music and artists on its shows.[3] In fact, as the music industry made the transition, via MTV, to featuring music videos, Michael Jackson, arguably the most celebrated music artist of the '80s, could not get his videos played on MTV. CBS, Jackson's record label, had to threaten to remove all their artists from MTV's video rotation if MTV did not play Jackson's videos.[4]

The continued centering of White bodies and the simultaneous erasure of Black presence in film and television imitates reality. Erasure is violence. The term "erase" is defined by words and phrases such as "to rub or scrape out," "to obliterate," or "to refuse to recognize." Metaphorically, to erase involves friction between an active object (power) imposing its force and weight upon a passive object. Whiteness imposes its weight and rubs out blackness in media representations by mischaracterizing African Americans, stereotyping based on misperceptions and misinterpretations of Black culture, or rendering them invisible or subordinate to White characters in front of the camera. As noted earlier, one can argue that the erasure begins with the absence of conscious African Americans behind the camera directing, producing, and writing films and television shows that present blackness in its fullness, including its resiliency and its beauty.

The impact of the violence of erasure is deepened when it is internalized by African Americans. That is, when they begin to absorb and believe the narrative incessantly presented to them by White filmmakers. Blackness is not only questioned from within, but some have also chosen to distance themselves from their culture after internalizing media messages. Media messaging then becomes a tool for assimilation—the insidious, intentional stripping of identities of Color, preserving and prizing whiteness. For example, the movie poster for the 2009 film *Couples Retreat* was altered for marketing to its international audience. The original poster showed all four couples who starred in the film, including the token African American couple. The UK version of the poster "erased" the lone African American couple from the poster, leaving the three White couples.[5] The excuse given was that they decided to "simplify" the poster and use the most recognizable actors. But the message received was that African Americans were a liability to the marketing of the film. To remove them only said that they do not bring the same value to the international marketing strategy as White couples do. Frequent practices like this often lead to African Americans internalizing and believing the messaging about *disparities in value* between blackness and whiteness.

Erasure is the fruit of royal consciousness. Beyond tokenism, paternalism, or a confluence of the two, it is unrealistic to expect those formed by the royal regime, whose white supremacist sensibilities are not malicious, intentional, or at the surface of their conscience, to be the disruptors. It requires an alternative, prophetic consciousness—born from the margins or from the belly of suffering, oppression, and marginalization—to assert a new lens for a new narrative on film and television. Alternative consciousness on film and television needs native tongues to tell new stories. These are the stories that counter the stereotypes, racist tropes, and erasure of all things Black to reauthor the narrative around the Black experience. This is the imperative of the dramatization of blackness. It is Black filmmakers telling the fullness of Black stories. It is Black actors embodying the range of the Black experience, from its painful to its inspiring and liberative aspects. The dramatization of blackness captures its liminal, unseen reality that has historically been limited on the big or small screen.

Two award-winning filmmakers that retell Black stories around the truth rather than projections of whiteness are Spike Lee and Ava DuVernay. Long before Lee and DuVernay, however, was one Oscar Micheaux, a filmmaking predecessor and pioneer. His work provided a template for the impact that African American filmmakers can have on catalyzing a counterconsciousness for the humanity and value of blackness. He became the progenitor of a lineage of filmmakers who wrote and dramatized the fullness of the Black experience that whiteness had attempted to erase. Filmmakers such as Gordon Parks, Kathleen Collins, John Singleton, Spike Lee, and Ava DuVernay, to name a few, continued the legacy of filmmaking as a prophetic tool to retell and reenact the Black narrative to the world.

Pioneers of Black Filmmaking

Oscar Micheaux

Often overshadowed by narratives originating from White filmmakers, African American filmmakers have been telling and retelling Black stories for about one hundred years. The period after the Civil War was one that included an increase in defining African Americans as black beasts, primitive, docile, or the comic fool through media—newspapers and magazines.[6] Newspapers and magazines were foundational to White American films' derogatory attitudes about blackness, as they nurtured the White racist imagination before films reified them. I will refer to these efforts as the tragic *damning of blackness* through media. This is the context for the significance of Black voices creating media to tell the more truthful and full narrative of blackness. This is the beginning of the beautiful *dramatization of blackness* through film.

Beginning in 1918, the son of former slaves who was not formally educated, "Oscar Micheaux, wrote, directed, edited produced, and distributed over forty films nationally and internationally."[7] He was the only African American filmmaker whose career spanned and survived "World War I, the great migration, the Red Summer of 1919, a recession, the Harlem Renaissance, and 1930's depression years."[8]

Micheaux changed the game not only behind the camera with his presence and creativity as a writer, director, or producer, but he also changed it by putting different players, African Americans, in front of the camera. Renowned African American thespian "Paul Robeson, received his first role from Micheaux in 1924."[9] Through African American characters in his films playing the roles of doctors, businessmen, detectives, and lawyers, he invited the rest of the country to peer through a window into Black life and perspective on the topic of race.[10] It was the counternarrative in Micheaux's prophetic creativity that was necessary in attempting to create an alternative consciousness to the dominant consciousness formed by blatant dehumanizing media stereotypes of his day.

Micheaux's stories about African Americans and the roles he wrote for them, especially in his debut film *The Homesteader*, were influenced by his own life, a story that most White people likely did not see as achievable by African Americans. His mother was an educator, and his father owned eighty acres of farmland in Metropolis, Illinois. While Micheaux lacked formal education, he more than made up for it in talent, work ethic, ambition, and determination. He left Metropolis at seventeen and went from being a laborer to finding employment with the Pullman Car Company to purchasing land in South Dakota from the earnings he saved.

This is the narrative that Micheaux and other African American actors and filmmakers at the time wanted to tell about Black potential and reality "as counter-propaganda."[11] With the success of *The Homesteader*, African Americans were excited not only to see themselves on the screen in a new, more dignified light but also to see more of them behind the scenes creating these stories about their diverse realities. Unfortunately, Micheaux's prediction that White people would show up to view his film did not prove to be true. Real cultural and societal change required White people to view these films, since they were the group in power exacting violence on African Americans fueled by false perceptions created by White media.

Filmmakers with the courage to affect society by functioning in prophetic creativity must not shy away from controversy. Controversy is necessarily associated with prophetic ministry and, ironically, either conceives or nurtures and nourishes alternative consciousness. It offers a pathway out of the consciousness of the status quo. Micheaux's second film, *Within Our Gates*, was an example of this in 1920. He levied criticism and protest of white supremacy against African Americans and the "Uncle Tom" syndrome within the African American community.[12] He made films that recognized the dignity and the progress of the (Black) race. What is most interesting about certain films Micheaux made, and some films of later generations, is that the controversy lies in the fact that they told the truth. All of it.

Gordon Parks

Gordon Parks used the camera as both a photographer and a filmmaker. He captured images of blackness in all its beauty despite the surrounding reality of oppressive conditions created by white supremacy. He froze the beauty of the in-betweenness of the Black experience in his photography. Considered to be the first major African American director in Hollywood, he brought the world the iconic film *Shaft*.[13] This film spawned the blaxploitation genre. An argument can be made that, just as the word suggests, the films in this genre exploited Black people by playing on stereotypes. What Parks did, however, was cast Black actors in lead roles rather than supporting roles.[14] John Shaft was the action *hero*, not the sidekick. African Americans could see themselves, and White people could see Black characters as the "good" guy or woman rather than the threat. Metro-Goldwyn-Mayer (MGM) originally envisioned an all-White cast for the film in 1971.[15] Parks's vision prevailed.

His films were a continuation of the work he tried to do in his photography. He captured the urban underworld in his photographs, yet he still fought with whiteness and its tendency to erase, at least partially, what the Black perspective offered the world. For example, he tried to show the full range of the life of Harlem gang leader Leonard "Red" Jackson of the Midtowners for *Life* magazine. He was privy to some of the fights, diplomatic meetings with other gang leaders, and his personal life with his mother and brother at home.[16] His editors at the magazine selected images and cropped others that had a more dramatic effect and likely played into the ideas that most people, especially White people, had about Black youth in urban areas. They erased the humanity of Jackson that Parks wanted to convey.[17] This is why films like *Shaft* were so important, despite the "blaxploitation" criticism it received. It introduced the world to a different view of African Americans and a different vision of White people in relation to African Americans, inverting or disassembling the normal racial hierarchy. The hero was African American, and many of the villains were White.

Parks unapologetically brought his "Black" context to his work and intended on projecting Black sentiment and experience to the world. In response to his *Life* magazine editors' claims that he could not be objective, he writes in *Half Past Autumn*, "I was black, and my sentiments lay in the heart of black fury sweeping the country."[18] It is likely that fury, which he undoubtedly felt in his own being, that inspired his photography career. He would then arm himself with the camera. In a 1999 interview, Parks said, "I saw that the camera could be a weapon against racism, against poverty, and against all sorts of social wrongs. I knew at that point I had to have a camera."[19]

Kathleen Collins

Kathleen Collins may well be considered a womanist film-maker. Certainly, she was one of the first African American women to produce feature-length films—*The Cruz Brothers and Miss Malloy* (1979) and *Losing Ground* (1982). She began making films, along with producing plays, at a time when "nobody would give any money to a black woman to direct a film."[20] When asked about the importance of Blacks and women making films that address issues of race and gender, she replied, "I think you have an even greater obligation to deal with your own obsessions."[21] She lived a life and integrated into her filmmaking the importance of changing the narrative around how African American people, especially women, are viewed and treated. Collins "changed the face and content of the black womanist film" and "challenged stereotypes and explored the interlocking oppression of gender, race, and class."[22]

What is important about Collins's short career (she passed away in 1988, succumbing to breast cancer) is that in her mere presence as a filmmaker in a predominately White and male space, she embodied the counternarrative to the erasure of blackness (and womanhood) by White men with the camera and power to do so. She was a pioneer for the African American women who would come after her to make films and continue to "change the game."

John Singleton

One of the most iconic filmmakers of my generation is John Singleton. Singleton wrote and directed the award-winning, critically acclaimed film *Boyz n the Hood*, in which he was nominated for the Academy Award for Best Director, drawing from his own life and the lives and experiences of people he knew personally. This film and others, such as *Poetic Justice, Higher Learning, Baby Boy,* and *Rosewood,* explicitly are Black stories by a Black filmmaker dramatizing the Black experience in ways that filmmakers outside of the community are unable to accomplish. Like Micheaux years before him, he tells "all of it." *Boyz n the Hood* tells the story of a young man and his friends growing up in South Central Los Angeles trying to survive the violence of gang culture and overpolicing by law enforcement. Rather than play on stereotypes, Singleton narrates the reality of African American youth while managing to humanize them in the film. He shows a Black father present in his son's life and passionate about raising him to live beyond the reality of his "'hood." He puts Black love on display, as he does in *Poetic Justice,* in ways that have largely been missing or minimized by White filmmakers.

Singleton boldly educates (not merely entertains) and shocks the viewers of his film *Rosewood* on the little-known, tragic events around the massacre in the mostly African American town of Rosewood, Florida, in 1923. In an era when so much negative attention is given to riots or violence over the past fifty years that had largely Black participation—in Detroit, Chicago, and Los Angeles, to name a few cities—many forget about the massacres during the twentieth century that were initiated by White people against African American bodies, not just buildings. *Rosewood* invited the nation to remember and grieve. It altered the notion of which group has largely been a threat to liberty and justice for all. Ironically, this massacre and others like it—in New York (1900); Atlanta (1906); Springfield, Illinois (1908); East St. Louis (1917); Washington, DC, Charleston,

South Carolina, and Long View, Texas, during the Red Summer of 1919; and Tulsa, Oklahoma (1921)—were designed to assert white supremacy to intimidate and squelch any semblance of Black upward mobility that seemingly infringed upon the White monopoly. Singleton's films, in true Black filmmaking form, retold the aspects of blackness and American life that were historically erased or misrepresented by White filmmakers. He shined a light on the diversity of Black life because, as Ice Cube's character in *Boyz n the Hood* said of White people, "either they don't know, don't show, or don't care about what's going on in the 'hood."

Spike Lee—Do the Right Thing

Spike Lee is one of, if not *the*, most important filmmaker of his generation. His films were groundbreaking, not just in content or story line, but because of his style. For the sake of this work, I want to focus on one film in particular, *Do the Right Thing*, because it is eerily relevant, even thirty-three years after its release. In Spike Lee's own words at the thirtieth anniversary screening at the Toronto Film Festival (TIFF) when asked about the film's relevance today, "Well, shit hasn't changed."[23] This film encapsulates Lee's prophetic ability in storytelling and signature use of the camera to fulfill the twin tasks of the prophetic ministry: to criticize the dominant group and consciousness and energize toward an alternative community and consciousness.

It would be fair to use the popular phrase often said about art—especially filmmaking—"art imitates life," to describe the work that Lee does in this film. Lee is imitating in the sense that he is reproducing, simulating, or using real life as a model. Because this fictitious film with fictitious characters is so closely related to real-life African Americans getting killed at the hands of the police—still a traumatic reality over thirty years later—it could almost be considered nonfiction, based on true events. The racial tension depicted in the film, the White business owner in Black neighborhoods, and police brutality are just a few themes in *Do the Right Thing* that are prevalent today, indicating that the right thing has yet to be done. Other themes such as the Black man hustling (working multiple jobs) to make ends meet and take care of his girlfriend and baby boy, kids playing in the streets getting wet by the fire hydrants on the hottest day of the summer, and Black men sitting on the corner just talking and "cracking" jokes (usually about one another) all resonate with the African American community.

The height of the film, when Radio Raheem is killed in an altercation with police officers over a slice of pizza and disrespect from the White owners of the pizza shop, is similar to May 25, 2020, when George Floyd was murdered by Minneapolis police officer Derek Chauvin. In the film, the officer applied a chokehold with a baton. In Floyd's case, Chauvin used his knee on the back of Floyd's neck to squeeze the life out of him. Typically, scenes in films remind us of what may have happened in real life. That was Lee's intent as he based Raheem's character off Michael Stewart, a graffiti artist in New York who was killed in a similar fashion as Eric Garner was in 2014. Floyd's murder, although it reminds many of what has happened to African American men and women in recent years, also reminds us of Radio Raheem and Garner. Instead of a baton, it was a knee on his neck. It seems in this case, it was life imitating art. Viewers of both were traumatized, outraged, and grieved by these images of anti-Black violence.

While *Do the Right Thing* was remembering and recalling events that preceded it, it turned out to be a prophetic warning of things to come if the nation did not heed the titular imperative. The video of George Floyd's murder forces us to remember not just Radio Raheem but also the Trayvon Martins, Eric Garners, Tamir Rices, Philando Castiles, Sandra Blands, Amadou Diallos, and countless others. The question is, after continuing to view videos of the same anti-Black (and anti-Brown) violence since Floyd's and Arbery's videos and Breonna Taylor's unseen killing took place, for how long and to what extent will Floyd's video be a warning? The prophetic use of filmmaking necessarily demands both of society. It demands that we remember and be warned of a repeat of these results because of continued behavior until society no longer accepts the behavior. The power in Lee's filmmaking is that he literally brings the audience uncomfortably close enough to the reality to ink the image in their consciousness so that the collective soul of the nation yearns for new/different/alternative.

In Lee's directorial style, his characters often look directly into the camera, with tight shots capturing the intensity and range of emotions the characters embody. They speak directly to the camera as if to invite the audience to sit and have a conversation with them in that neighborhood in Brooklyn. Consider the proximity in which Lee brings the audience to the characters and the scene; he immerses or "baptizes" them in "the real"—the living, breathing, day-to-day reality (of the Black experience).[24] He is both missional and prophetic in his art. He confronts and criticizes the injustice and brings it to the audience, inviting them to "gaze" or contemplate "the real," and he energizes a countercommunity in the process. In his own words, he says, "I told everyone, we want people to be sweatin'."[25]

Viewing *Do the Right Thing* through a theological lens, Lee does not answer any ultimate questions; instead, he inspires more and leaves the audience to wrestle in lament and hope. "The real" of the crucifixion of Jesus included tragedy, injustice, and power dynamics followed by the beauty of the resurrection, which involved ultimate justice and the ultimate power of God on display. Lee confronts his viewers with the African American version of "the real." Lee does not, however, provide a "resurrection" scene. He seems to leave that to the audience to decide. The film's ending suggests an ongoing gaze. It implies that the narrative does not end; there is more to the story. This is also the essence of the gospel. It is an ongoing narrative that requires contemplation and that inspires activism as *Do the Right Thing* attempted to do.

The power of Lee's filmmaking in *Do the Right Thing* juxtaposed with the tragedy of the racial reality in America is that if the film debuted in 2020, aside from obvious evidence of the era it was shot in—the clothes, music, and urban vernacular of the day—it eerily and accurately speaks to the current social crisis. This film is not a statement of the event of "the real" upon which the audience and society at large must take a long, loving look, but it is a statement about the longevity and enduring breathing power of "the real" that must demand a reoriented "gaze."

What does a reoriented "gaze" mean? For the "gaze" upon Black bodies, it means a look of empathy rather than judgment or condemnation. It is a look that is capable of seeing oneself in that black skin rather than a look of othering. It is a look of appreciating and honoring its beauty rather than fetishizing it. Lastly, it is a look of indignation and lament at the violence that Black bodies have been (and still are) susceptible to rather than a look of indifference. Lee brings the audience to "choice points" throughout the film where they have to decide whether they will turn away from the blatant and subtle violence or be witnesses to it, sharing in the suffering. Will they turn their eyes away when there are no African American pictures on the wall in the pizza shop that is unquestionably supported by African Americans in the neighborhood who patronize it daily? Will they turn their eyes away from Radio Raheem's eyes while he's being choked to death, his body with no life left in it? Will they continue their gaze upon the Black experience just as the narrative around the Black experience continues after the film ends?

Many critics of the film were too concerned about potential riots that the film may have influenced to pause, consider, and value a newly oriented gaze. The fear that has long been projected onto African Americans extended to the art created by African Americans. Many people feared the film. They feared what the film could potentially energize the African American community to do. Fear of riots and violence was a projection. Historically, when a "controversial" film about race produced by African Americans was released and viewed, it was White people who responded with violence and riots targeting the African American community. The "riots and violence" narrative was the cover for fear of an energized and disruptive countercommunity. But violence would not be this film's legacy. Truth-telling would be its legacy. Truthfully telling the gamut of the Black experience—the beauty, humor, and tragedy—amid oppressive social conditions is its legacy.

Not everyone will appreciate this legacy though. Lee, in his conversation at TIFF in 2019, remembers reviewers lamenting the loss of Sal's Pizzeria in the film. He shares his disappointment in people putting more weight on the loss of

White-owned property than on Black lives. This should not have been a surprise, given the value placed on the status of White people over and above non-White people. Therefore, by extension, there is an expectation that their property is assigned the same value. Even within a drama around violence against Black bodies, many White people are unable or unwilling to see beyond the White social "screen" through which everything before their gaze is filtered. In addition, because of the supremacy placed on White bodies—and by extension, White property—in the dominant consciousness, the value of Black bodies is deemed, by default, secondary to the value of any entity with the qualifier *white* preceding it.

Lee reflects on his own work in *Do the Right Thing* and its relevance today, given the context of the rhetoric of the forty-fifth president of the United States, the rise in hate groups, and the perpetual disparities in justice and treatment of African Americans at the hands of law enforcement. He claims, "This film is relevant today. . . . It's not a history lesson or a relic, you can say it's ripped from the headlines."[26] Through the eyes of his camera lens, Lee reminded, warned, challenged, gave language to, and demanded of all, on behalf of the Black community, to hear us, see us, stand with and for us, and "do the right thing."

Ava DuVernay

Ava DuVernay, an African American woman with an ability to tell Black stories in such profound ways, is a torchbearer of beautiful cinematic prophetic brilliance. In a miniseries she directed, *When They See Us*, she reintroduces some and introduces others for the first time to the humanity of a Latino and four young African American teenagers (now men) who had their humanity stripped away when they were profiled, falsely accused, and imprisoned for the attempted rape of a White female jogger in Central Park in 1989. Thirty years later, as the miniseries about their lives and shared ordeal was about to be released, DuVernay tweeted, "Not thugs. Not wilding. Not criminals. Not even the Central Park Five. They are Korey, Antron, Raymond, Yusef, and Kevin. They are millions of young people of color who are blamed, judged, and accused on sight. May 31. A film in four parts about who they really are. WHEN THEY SEE US."[27] These five young men were neither seen nor heard. This was the failure that preceded the series of events that changed their lives and the lives of their families, friends, and communities. These young boys were never "seen" until it was time to find suspects. Even then, the extent of their visibility was limited through the white supremacist lens, unable to detect their humanity, just figures with the deficit of black and brown skin. They fit the White narrative of menacing boys who were suspects just for being Black and Brown and close enough to the crime scene that they were never a part of. They not only fit the narrative, but they also experienced its violence and trauma.

DuVernay's *When They See Us*, unlike Lee's *Do the Right Thing*, was not a fictional story but a narrative reenacting a true event. She confronts the real structural racism embedded in the United States that stole the freedom of five young, innocent Latino and African American teenagers. The five young men, formerly known as the "Central Park Five" (now the "Exonerated Five"), were falsely accused and imprisoned for a rape and assault of a White woman. There was no DNA evidence or fingerprints that could connect the young boys to the crime scene. The confessions were coerced, as the boys and some of the parents were manipulated into owning a crime they did not commit. They were not seen. Their humanity was hidden behind their skin. They were not heard. It was as if they were mimes without the white makeup. But the good news is they have names and voices. The tragedy of their wrongful incarceration did not annihilate their dreams and hopes. The film reenacts a resurrection story for Yusef Salaam, Korey Wise, Kevin Richardson, Antron McCray, and Raymond Santana. (Pause here. Honor them before reading on, and say their names out loud.)

DuVernay's film, while chronicling the tragic injustice that the young men experienced, communicated a "gospel" of its own. The later episodes of the film seem to go further than where Lee ends in *Do the Right Thing*. Much of the series focuses on the activism—legally and socially—that failed initially, then prevailed by the end. The good news or "gospel" here is the activism. It was a mission that confronted and exposed injustice, endured the counterresistance that sought to seal the young men's collective fate, and offered a counternarrative of truth, liberation, and power to the narrative that was campaigned for by institutions (e.g., media, law enforcement, justice system) and individuals (e.g., Donald Trump) of power. With reflection, in DuVernay's series, the young Black and Latino men's experience can be seen as analogous to that of the central gospel figure, Jesus. Jesus was unjustly accused, arrested, interrogated, imprisoned, and executed. Divine activism raised him from the guarded tomb intended to seal Jesus's fate and assure eternal death. The empty tomb is evidence of the counternarrative of truth, liberation, and power that prevailed over the royal narrative of injustice. Often filmmaking takes on the function of cultural critic. *When They See Us* is more than a critique of a racist justice system; it is prophetic confrontation. It is prophetic in its forthrightness and, for the reason mentioned above, is linked to divine superintendence and activity where justice ultimately prevails.

The film's titular message invokes the idea that through this medium, these young men—and more broadly, African American and Latino American men—have long been on a mission to affirm their humanity to White people. It begs the question, "Where should we place the inflection point in the title?" "When" suggests there *will* be a time, indeed *must* be a time when Black (and Brown) selfhood is fully acknowledged and respected. Who is "they" in the title referring to? White power structures? White-dominant law enforcement and justice systems? White people in general? "See" implies historically, and at present, Black and Brown people and their pain and suffering have been invisible. Invisibility has the tendency to justify indifference to racial injustice in the minds of many. Invisibility is exclusive to the ones made invisible by the dominant group and consciousness and insulating to the dominant group, generally shielded from racial oppression. "Us" may be the most threatening word in the title. It points directly to the radical other to whiteness. It makes no space for color blindness or the universality of human beings, sidestepping the particularity of racial experiences. It points to humanity in black and brown skin. Much like post-resurrection Jesus went unrecognized by the two people walking on the road to Emmaus (Luke 24:13–35) and was not believed to be resurrected by Thomas until he saw Jesus's scars, so it is with white supremacy to blackness. The mission, the conversion, the "good news" narrative is incomplete without seeing "us" and feeling the textures of our scars.

What DuVernay does, just as Lee did, in the miniseries is bring their lives beyond the event that they were accused of to the forefront. Dramatizing blackness is more than just telling the story of Black struggle at home, at work, or in society. It is showing the natural conflict of fighting to be seen, understood, and treated as human. It is the struggle for Black and Brown humanity first, then for liberation and justice in a White-dominant land. It is the struggle to counter the systematic stripping away of Black and Brown identity, worth, beauty, and potential. Essentially, it is filling in the blank spaces left behind by the erasure of blackness. In telling this story, she reclaims their humanity and the richness of their blackness and brownness rather than just telling a story of what happened to these five Black and Brown boys-turned-men.

As writer, director, and creative executive producer, DuVernay gave the young men their voices and names back. The original working title was *Central Park Five*, but DuVernay insisted on changing the name. She explains to Oprah Winfrey that "Central Park Five" was something that was imposed upon them by "the press, prosecutors, and police . . . it took away their faces, it took away their families, it took away their pulses and their beating hearts . . . it dehumanized them."[28] Not only did the film title change; they no longer had to carry the burden of the dehumanizing label "Central Park Five," as it was erased to make space for the more appropriate "Exonerated Five." What this film accomplished under DuVernay's direction was restoration. It restored the names, dignity, and humanity of these five young men, but it did the same for every young Black and Brown man, indeed every Black and Brown person.

The dramatization of blackness challenges White people to make the choice to fight for their own humanity.[29]

They must fight for their humanity being snuffed away by the idolatry of whiteness and the ideology of white supremacy. The dramatization of blackness is disorienting for many White people because true humanity, even their own, is unfamiliar to them, since it has been historically distorted by whiteness. As disorienting as it may be, it is in the dramatization of blackness that "White" people can regain their humanity. It is when the drama of blackness penetrates the seemingly impenetrable wall of white supremacy that White people have a pathway to be disentangled from its satanic grips. In this sense, blackness is liberating for us all.

Conclusion

When Johnny Carson invited Harry Belafonte to host his show in his absence, Belafonte filled the show with African American activists and liberal politicians. It was noted that he lost the majority of his Southern audience.[30] Carson took a risk in welcoming Belafonte on his show as a guest host. He likely knew what the optics created by the picture of a successful, beloved African American actor in a position of prominence and authority in front of the camera lens would mean for White people and African Americans. He invited Belafonte to trespass many White Southerners' living rooms. I use *trespass* here because he was not invited by them. This would be a watershed moment in media. Carson knew it. Belafonte knew it. Belafonte did not need to use words to speak a new narrative to the nation about African American equality and excellence. His presence communicated as much.

The growing presence of African Americans in front of and behind the camera dramatizing blackness through film and television is important to complete the Black and American stories. Lee and DuVernay are but two filmmakers in a lineage of African American filmmakers who have used the camera as a prophetic weapon against white supremacy. They chose to retell Black stories to remind viewers of the history of anti-Black racism in America and to cast a true vision, a more complete story for African Americans to see themselves more wholly represented. They also allow White Americans to see themselves more wholly, from angles and perspectives upon which they are not accustomed to reflecting. The dramatization of blackness is necessarily prophetic—speaking truth back to power, countering false narratives, inspiring activism—and is refreshingly liberating.

The lens in the hands of White filmmakers has historically simplified what it means to be Black. To be Black and acceptable has meant to portray certain African Americans as docile, subservient, and entertaining. To render blackness to these categories is to make blackness safe. These are "good" African Americans. To be Black and unacceptable, however, has meant to portray certain African Americans as threats because the lack of subservience equates to being a troublemaker, disruptor, or immoral. In this light, blackness is perceived as a threat to the well-being of White Americans and others. Hence the need for the white savior/hero.

Dramatizing blackness, as I am using it in this chapter, means to show the whole spectrum of what it means to be Black. It is to reveal the conflict that comes with fighting for Black humanity. It means to put in proper context our suffering and our joy. It means to show how we love and nurture one another. It means to capture the truth about the respective sources of our trauma and our resilience. African American filmmakers have vigilantly done this work of making the liminal, unseen existence of blackness visible for the world to gaze upon, be moved by, and be inspired by to align themselves with God's preeminent call for justice.

CHAPTER 9

Documenting the Image

The Power of the Visual

In 1993, just two days before Christmas, one of my best friends, Melvin Williams, was shot and killed in Charleston, South Carolina, just forty-five minutes away from our hometown of Georgetown. It was one of the most heartbreaking nights of my life. It was the first time most of our friends had a chance to meet up since graduating from high school eighteen months earlier. Everyone was excited to see one another as we prepared for a night of partying. The only one missing was "Mel," as we affectionately called him. We waited for him to arrive. Once he did, the entire "crew" would be together, and the night could officially begin. Soon, we got the news that Mel had been shot. Initially, I was not sure if he died or was in the hospital wounded. It quickly became clear that Mel was gone. The rest of the evening is a blur at this point. There was crying, anger, yelling, suggestions of going to Charleston to seek revenge, and every profanity-laced tirade imaginable. For me, though, there was still a sense of hope that maybe he was still alive, fighting for his life in the local hospital. I held onto hope until I saw the news with my friend's name displayed on the screen while the anchorwoman shared minimal details. I then knew with certainty that a "man," Melvin Williams, was murdered. Seeing his name on the news solidified the fact that he was dead. I had heard it and sensed it was true, but I still needed to see something definitive.

I did not attend the funeral, since it took place after I had returned to school in Greensboro, North Carolina, and it was not safe to travel back home because of dangerous, icy roads. I imagined those at the funeral experiencing an even deeper pain when they finally saw his body lying in the casket. There is something about seeing the visual of Mel's name on the news and his body lying in the casket that penetrated the soul in ways that a message from a friend could not achieve.

This is why Mamie Till's decision to have an open casket for her son Emmett Till's body to be seen by everyone was so profound and significant for catalyzing the Civil Rights Movement. To only *hear* about the disfiguration of his body and to have to imagine the extent of the brutality in which he was murdered provides a buffer of insulation from the reality of the tragedy. David Jackson stills the moment where Mamie Till is viewing her son's body. Almost unrecognizable because of the brutality of the murder, this image is important for the nation, according to Bryan Stevenson, because in it, "she is giving witness to victimization and violence."[1] As much as the nation needed to see Till's body, the fruit of White violence, they needed to see his mother's grief. Just as Till's body stirs outrage, his mother viewing her son's body should stir lament. The mother/son visual in the photo, both bearing the evidence of White violence—Emmett in his lifeless body, Mamie in her countenance—is an image that eliminated buffering and "made it impossible for White people to stay indifferent."[2]

When it comes to racial violence, especially anti-Black violence, any buffer allows one to rationalize, without the hard evidence of visual imagery, that the Black victim may have played a role in their own death. To only *hear* allows one to convince themselves of less gruesome imagery, avoiding the more discomforting and disorienting embodied response to this reality. The buffer justifies, for some, the response (rather, unresponsiveness) of apathy after an African American encounters violence of any kind. Insulation from the liminal, unseen reality of blackness is achieved and sustained by not having to *see*. A person can hear and still rationalize a completely different reality. To see, however, undermines those efforts.

Simone Biles is considered to be the greatest gymnast, man or woman, of all time. She is commonly referred to as "the GOAT"—"greatest of all time." In the 2021 Summer Olympic Games in Tokyo, she withdrew from competition in most of the events she was scheduled to compete in. She admitted that she had been experiencing the "twisties." The twisties are described as a gymnast losing their sense of space and dimension while in the air, causing them to lose control of their body.[3] She cited mental health as the larger reason behind her withdrawals. The "mental blocks" that come with twisties more than cause a gymnast to be "off" in their performances but can cause serious injury. While she received much support for her decision, she was also met with much backlash. Many people did not consider her mental health concerns equal to physical health concerns.

Had Simone Biles walked out with a bandage around her knee, ankle, or even around her head, people would have likely been more understanding. If she had visible scars and bruises, most would have rallied around her and praised her for her sacrifice to perform on behalf of the United States in the Olympics and for entertaining them throughout her career. They would have been able to *see* there was an injury that prevented her from performing. But because there is no way for them to quantify the extent to which her mental health may have been compromised, many found it hard to empathize with or have compassion for Biles. The power of the visual can potentially enable people to make more appropriate associations between theory and practice or event and consequences.

Since the Crimean War in 1853, cameras have been used to document war and conflicts. Its truth-telling capacity renders the camera invaluable in our ability to accurately account for major events that have culture-changing effects. The camera is the undeniable witness to modern history.[4] Images are compelling and evoke sentiments of compassion for those suffering as well as indignation for the injustices causing the suffering. But the images demand more than sentiment; they require fully embodied action by the collective viewers, whether on a local, national, or global level. Ellen Thornton captures the camera's powerful potential: "We cannot deny the visual evidence of the photographed event. The image says this human rights abuse happened and the photograph of it is now part of the history and memory of that time and place. When that documenting is supported by the appropriate social and political response, the power of the image to effect change can achieve a powerful currency."[5] The camera has done its part. The cameraman or camera woman has initiated the prophetic ministry. It is now up to citizens and those allies from within domains of power to participate conscientiously in prophetic movements.

Government propaganda attempts to sway public opinion to land support from the masses. Usually, the aggressor in the conflict seeks to hide the extent of suffering, especially of those who are collateral damage in the conflict (this is the Vladimir Putin playbook evidenced during his invasion of Ukraine in February 2022). When the prophetic voice is aroused, power structures construct counternarratives and tactics such as gaslighting—the psychological manipulation of a person or a group that causes them to question the legitimacy of their own thoughts, insights, or perspectives. The antidote to gaslighting from agents of power structures—clergy, politicians, pundits, or celebrities—is the visual imagery from the camera. Its testimony is true and beyond contest. Whether in the court of public opinion or the courts of the justice system, the camera's testimony must be taken seriously as the voice of the victimized.

This does not assure gaslighting and other forms of propaganda will cease. Just as the prophetic ministry is creative and improvisational, so are the strategies from the royal regime. The prophetic ministry is necessarily a network of operatives, institutions, and mediums. Collaborative efforts to maintain the production of truth from the margins must be persistent. Photos must continue to be taken. Videos must continue to be recorded. Content must continue to be published.

The Imagery on Trial

Every individual with access to the video of Floyd's murder has the choice and privilege to create or maintain a buffer by not watching the video, turning away from it if they see it on television, or scrolling past it on social media to avoid further trauma from the images. The disturbing, raw footage rubbed against old, hardened scars as well as fresh, raw wounds. Viewing the Derek Chauvin trial on television was also taxing enough for many US Americans, especially for most African Americans. Having to sit in the courtroom, however, and hear every testimony, view all the footage repeatedly, and parse every segment of it had to have taken a tremendous toll on the jurors selected to hear the evidence and make a unified decision of guilt or innocence. On October 28, 2021, several jurors were interviewed on television by CNN's Don Lemon. They shared honest thoughts, particularly about the impact of Darnella Frazier's video footage. Often through visceral reactions to remembering their time on the jury, they seemed to have sensed the trauma in their own bodies as they responded to Lemon's questions. Four of the jurors' responses speak to the potency of visual imagery:

> LISA CHRISTENSEN: Without Darnella Frazier's video, it would not have gotten to this level. Pictures are worth a thousand words.
> JODI DOUD: The video was the most compelling evidence in the trial.
> SHERRI BELTON HARDEMAN: Seeing the video and hearing George Floyd call out for his mom just broke my heart. It's something that haunts me.
> BRANDON MITCHELL: I wanted to close my eyes. I didn't want to watch it.[6]

The gaze of the camera lens as the key eyewitness in the Chauvin trial was clearly impactful for influencing the jury's verdict of guilty and, for some, establishing a degree of justice for Chauvin's senseless murder of George Floyd. The same impact of video images can be true working in favor of the person accused of killing another person in front of the camera's gaze. Kyle Rittenhouse, a then-seventeen-year-old

White teenager, decided to leave his home in Antioch, Illinois, to play the role of medic and police officer at the protests in downtown Kenosha, Wisconsin, following the shooting of Jacob Blake by White police officers.[7] He traveled across state lines in possession of an AR-15 semi-automatic assault weapon. The potential for violence was expectedly realistic considering the emotions and outrage among African Americans and non-Black allies angered by yet another unnecessary police shooting of an unarmed African American. The violence that millions of people will remember involved the seventeen-year-old Rittenhouse with his illegal military-style weapon when he killed two people and injured another who were pursuing him during the protests.

In his trial, Rittenhouse pleaded not guilty because he was acting in self-defense. The jury agreed with him. Rittenhouse's attorneys made their case for self-defense, but had it not been for the video that captured the whole incident between Rittenhouse and protesters, he may not have been so fortunate to have been found guilty. Shimon Prokupecz, a crime and justice correspondent for CNN, asserted, "Really, the video painted such a picture, such a chaos, such a scary scene in some ways for many of these jurors."[8] Like the effects Frazier's video had on the jurors in the Chauvin trial, so was the effect of the video caught on camera phones and drones on Rittenhouse's jury.

This imagery provided enough evidence to convince the jurors—not without twenty-five hours of deliberation—that Rittenhouse's actions were in defense of his life when he was being chased by protesters. The question that must be considered is, What if Rittenhouse were Black? If an African American girl, boy, woman, or man crossed state lines illegally carrying an AR-15 machine gun and went to a protest in another state to assume the role of "security" to keep the peace, what would the outcome be? If an African American, after shooting three people, approached law enforcement with that AR-15 across his or her body, even with hands raised, what would have likely been the outcome? Of course, these are hypothetical inquiries, but history narrates a story of white privilege versus the assumption of Black threat and guilt.

Just three months before the George Floyd murder and less than one month before Breonna Taylor was killed, in February 2020 in Brunswick, Georgia, Ahmaud Arbery, a twenty-five-year-old African American man while jogging, as was his normal activity, was confronted by a father and son who believed he was a thief guilty of a string of burglaries in their neighborhood. Travis McMichael and his father, Gregory McMichael, two White men, chased Arbery down in their truck. They attempted to stop him, claiming to make a citizen's arrest at gunpoint with no evidence to prove or even suspect he was the one committing the crimes. When Arbery tried to defend himself, he was shot and killed.

A third man, William "Roddie" Bryan, also White, who proved to be the key figure in this injustice (because he brought his phone to record), was a short distance away trailing in his car, filming the tragedy on his phone. Initially, he claimed he was trying to do the right thing by following the McMichaels and filming the pursuit of a criminal, but it turned out after further investigation by the Georgia Bureau of Investigations (GBI) that he was part of the plan to chase and apprehend Arbery based on assumptions. The investigation details that Bryan attempted to block Arbery as he jogged when they initially encountered him.[9] Ultimately, his recording provided the footage that angered millions across the nation and was the first of the three high-profile murders that year (along with those of Taylor and Floyd) that lead to the multiethnic coalition of Black Lives Matter protests.

Unfortunately, but not surprisingly, the Glynn County police chief, George Barnhill, dismissed the murder as not worth pursuing an arrest against the McMichaels and Bryan, even after viewing the video. In addition, Georgia district attorney Jacqueline Lee Johnson, who was later charged with violation of oath of a public officer and obstruction of a police officer, told two police officers not to arrest Travis McMichael.[10] It was not until the video was leaked to the public that justice began to take its course. Whatever their strategy was, it backfired on them and became the key evidence that led to the McMichaels's arrests (and subsequently, Bryan's arrest) about two and a half months later. Prior to the release of the video, the case was dormant. It was the publishing of the video recording that changed the course of events. Had there not been a video, these three men that killed Ahmaud Arbery would have further received the benefit of the doubt from the broader White community.

Bryan believed he was helping his friends and protecting his neighborhood from Ahmaud Arbery the criminal. He believed it was his duty to aid in the citizen arrest-turned-murder of this young African American man who they suspected violated White space and property. By documenting the encounter between Arbery and the McMichaels (and himself), Bryan assumed a position of righteousness inherent to white saviorism. Together, these men decided—whether consciously or unconsciously is irrelevant—it was better to sacrifice the one (Arbery) for the salvation of the many (their White neighborhood). This is a pattern in US American history that explains why James Cone demands that we see Jesus as Black. This is why he makes the analogy between the cross and the lynching tree, forcing us to juxtapose the two symbols, the two bodies, and the two experiences as a marginalized body amid a dominant group and consciousness.

Jesus was also the victim of a dominant group and consciousness that believed that his public crucifixion—documentation of the event—along with two known criminals was in the best interest of many. Caiaphas, the high priest that year, makes two statements before Jesus's crucifixion. He says in John 11:50 (ISV), "It is better for you to have one man die for the people than to have the whole nation destroyed." He reiterates this in John 18:14 (ISV): "It was better to have one man die for the people." Although this is not articulated verbally by any of the men as to this being their motivation, their actions caught on camera betray them. They were willing to go to the extent of killing this one man for the sake of "saving" the community. They proved they were willing to kill Arbery by the fact that they were armed and gave chase and by the tone and choice of words hurled at Arbery. Gregory McMichael yelled for Arbery to stop or he would "blow his fucking head off." Bryan, the McMichaels, and Caiaphas were willing to take the lives of innocent men, and they were willing to document it as well. They each understood the power of visual images to support their cases.

The Potency of the Visual Image

Visual images have the power to influence thought when used as pedagogical tools or as evidence to support testimony. In a sense, that is what Yahweh was doing with Pharaoh through the "signs" performed through Moses. This is what Nathan did to convict David and bring him to repentance. This is what Jesus's word-pictures of the parables were used for.

No person in human history has used visual imagery as effectively to change the course of history as God has. Scripture teaches that God is unseen. No one in history has ever "seen" the Creator (John 1:18, 5:37; 1 John 4:12). To do so would be to their demise (Judg 13:22). This is attributed to the holiness of God. The significance of God's holiness eludes human understanding. It is often taken for granted. Given the fact that no human being is holy enough to be granted the privilege of seeing such a god, no one has seen the invisible but living Creator. God maintained existence, in the Old Testament since the beginning of creation, in the invisibility and mystery of the Spirit. Yet God's presence was still heard, felt, and known by supernatural acts through humans, animals, or nature. God made Godself known through fire, wind, storm clouds, and even a donkey. These events would leave the people who encountered them awe-struck and more convinced of the reality of God. Although God continued to operate supernaturally through nature, that reality was modified in the person of Jesus.

"In the beginning was the Word, and the Word was *with* God, and the Word was God" (John 1:1) . . . "and the Word *became flesh* and dwelt among us" (John 1:14). It is in the becoming flesh that God unveiled Godself and gave human beings a visual image by which they could see, touch, and respond to God's presence. Jesus was "*the* image of the invisible God" (Col 1:15). Jesus said himself, "If you had known me, you would have known my Father also. From now on you do know him and have *seen* him" (John 14:7). Through the words, attitude, actions, character, and essence of who Jesus was and the acts Jesus performed, humanity could see, rather than just imagine, God. If the thought of God produced the fear (dread and reverence) of God, how much more potent is the visual of God to produce visceral responses in individuals and cultural change in humanity as a whole?

The second iteration of God using visual imagery to change the course of human history was through the very public suffering, crucifixion, and execution of Jesus. This event is not without its critique and debates about God's own ethics. We see the wrath of God (in response to sin) and the love of God (for humanity) intersect publicly at and in the physical body of Jesus. I would note that the choice of execution was human initiated, but in God's foreknowledge, God manipulated the event to serve divine purposes. What the Jewish leaders and Roman officials meant as punitive is understood to be grace in God's economy. What was meant to be a deterrent for future insurrectionists and criminals by those human leaders was co-opted by God to mean the satisfaction of all human sin and the corridor to reconciliation with God in that one suffering body. No doubt it would have been traumatizing for those who witnessed the gruesome execution. God, however, had the final say, in the form of the resurrection of Jesus's body just three days later, to signify the ultimate healing of humanity and all of creation in that same body.

Whether through the signs performed through Moses to initiate the Israelite exodus out of Egypt or the crucifixion of Jesus, God understands human limitations and the human tendency to respond to visual images. God becoming flesh and then crucifying that same flesh changed the course of human history and undermined human-constructed and human-managed power structures. To become like Christ, which is a commonly repeated Christian exhortation, is to become more human *and* more divine, as Jesus embodied that sacred intersection. Just as Jesus hung from the cross (a symbol) and became the sign, the visual image, so must humans—namely, Christ followers—become the sign, not to be worshipped, but to point to their Creator. While no human will ever be the "perfect" human, to be like Christ is to continue to mature into the human being God intended. For human beings to be more divine manifests in an ever-deepening intimacy with the spirit of God to bear the Spirit's fruit and to move more in sync with the Spirit's movement. Rather than the crucifixion intimidating a small group of Jesus followers, it ignited a religious (and, one could argue, a social) movement that continues to this day. A religious/social movement that, over the course of history since the first-century Christians, has continually emerged from the shadows of the margins to resist networks of power that form ethno- and socioeconomic dominant structures that have colonized and stripped nations and have oppressed entire people groups globally.

Visual images, like anything else, can be used for good or bad and can inspire moral or immoral behavior. In the same way that God recognized the human need to see in order to feel in their bodies and be convinced of something, humans recognize that instinct in themselves and act accordingly. One of the prohibitions among many in the whole of God's law for Israel is to not "turn to idols or make for yourselves any gods of cast metal" (Lev 19:4). Idolatry—elevating the creature to the status of God, is more than just the worship of idols made of materials like stone, metal, or wood.[11] It can be expanded to any created thing—animals, artwork, people, ideology, and symbols from the human imagination. Each of these categories have proven, over the course of history, to be the objects of cultlike allegiance, veneration, and source of security, provision, peace, or joy. In this way, these created or imagined things are given a deified status and have been used to sanction and justify immorality in order to preserve them or maintain allegiance to them.

Once this deified status is unchallenged and permanently assigned, consciously or unconsciously, to ideology and ideas like race or whiteness, all that's required are signs or symbols as images toward which the individual or group may orient their allegiance and their lives. These symbols, even in the form of persons or "kinds of persons" (e.g., White, male, wealthy, etc.), become the reference point to which one postures themselves to embody and express such allegiance. Media, literature, art, and other mechanisms that present White people in particular, and whiteness in general, as superior and sovereign have effectively and powerfully sustained this idol for hundreds of years. This physical, emotional, and intellectual posturing before the god of whiteness gave birth to a movement that many have been willing to die to preserve.

January 6, 2021, is an example of this degree of loyalty to the ideology of whiteness under the guise of patriotism. The nation watched in real time as thousands protested outside of the Capitol while hundreds illegally entered the building to try to stop the certification of the 2020 presidential election. There was no shame in the intruders' public criminal activity. After peace was restored hours later, the investigation began to get the identities of those who entered the building. In many cases, their own video footage provided the evidence of their involvement. In other cases, people actually spoke into cameras boasting of their mission in response to the former president Trump. The video images of police officers being assaulted, the anger that permeated the mob, and the sheer violence that intoxicated Trump's loyalists were on display. He is their messiah, their (false) prophet.

The revelation from the true prophet's mouth is intended to not only expose idolatry but puncture it and disable its practice in the community of God's people. The revelation from the camera's eye functions in a similar prophetic fashion. The camera disorients peoples' allegiances. In this case, whiteness (its purity, holiness, superiority in morals and civility, even its beauty) is now challenged by the video capturing whiteness in its element and essence. What is featured in its footage is not compatible with the idolatrous view of whiteness and its goodness that has enjoyed multi-generational transmission.

The power of visual imagery is its capacity to disorient. By *disorient*, I mean "to confuse by removing or obscuring something that has guided a person, group, or culture, as [in] moral standards."[12] What is disorienting about the visual images of the camera documenting anti-Black violence is that the ideas of intrinsic White goodness, benevolence, and moral superiority are obscured. While this can be traumatizing, it is potentially liberating. It can be liberating for those with idolatrous bondage to whiteness and enlightening to those who are oblivious to the unseen violence of the Black experience. Yet it is simultaneously affirming to African Americans who have cried out from the depths of their collective being about the impact whiteness, embedded in culture and institutions, has meant for their lives.

Visual images have been used for transmitting information and influencing thoughts from the time children are born. This is not lost on leaders of social movements like

Martin Luther King Jr. and this generation's leaders of Black Lives Matter and others. They each understand the potency of visual imagery. The appropriation of visual images to cause cultural shifts is not new. A form of visual imagery was even critical in the abolition of the slave trade in Britain.

There were individuals such as William Wilberforce—a British politician and abolitionist—and Thomas Clarkson who were unashamedly vocal about their antislavery stances. Clarkson succeeded in his cause to end the slave trade by interviewing sailors on the slave ships and gathering evidence to refute merchants, plantation owners, and government officials, those with vested interests in the slave trade. But it was his "diagram of the slave ship *Brooks*, which showed 482 'tight-packed' slaves distributed around the decks of the vessel, [that] eventually helped the movement abolish the slave trade."[13]

Like the British after seeing the diagram of the true conditions of the slave ship, after recent videos of anti-Black, state-sanctioned violence and the Capitol insurrection were released, White Americans were forced to reconcile what they understood about whiteness. They could reflect on what they were viewing on camera or choose to believe in an alternate reality that creatively denies what has been revealed, even to their own peril. They needed to discover the words for the persistent violence they were now witnessing that African Americans had encountered for centuries. But this was a foreign language to many of them.

Subversive Language

Language is foundational to all social realities and institutions. John Searle claims that "all of institutional reality [or societies] is created by linguistic representation."[14] While words are not essential to express language, symbols do serve as linguistic representation. Visual imagery is a type of language on its own. Language is necessary when someone or some group needs to point to something beyond themselves. Visual imagery is more than the image itself but also points to a larger narrative, pattern, or reality that necessitates communication. Beyond language expressed in words and sentences, visual imagery encapsulates meaning, narratives, values, and even morality, to name a few. So much of what we understand about antiquity can be gleaned from cave paintings, archeological findings, and art. They sent messages to the future through stories told through images.

If language, verbal or nonverbal, is essential to the creation and the progress of social realities and institutions, then can new languages, modes of language, or even interpretative linguistic methods play critical roles in disrupting oppressive institutions and creating alternative social realities? I believe these published images that reveal the oft-hidden anti-Black violence committed by White people have a linguistic function. The images can either be the signs and symbols or they can spawn them. This is because, as Willie Jennings asserts, "images create and carry so much power. For us, image and word, body and text, are inseparable, merging together, mutually constituting."[15] George Floyd, without forfeiting his humanity, lives on as a symbol. The image of his face in artwork or forms of media point to more than the event surrounding his murder. It communicates the reality of a culture of anti-Black policing, anti-Black violence, and anti-Black belonging in a society that claims "liberty and justice for all."

The image of his body beneath the body of Chauvin reminds viewers of a history and warns of a regressing future unless there is an alternative consciousness. The interaction of Floyd's Black body and Chauvin's White body on camera captures the historically normalized and accepted view of the Black/White relationship by adherents of white supremacy. Today, however, it is understood as abnormal. It forces White people who have been insulated from having to think about this interaction to have to grapple with this disorienting language. Prior to this and other videos, the cries and testimonies of African Americans had landed on deaf ears and sounded like an indiscernible language to the minds and, more importantly, souls of White people. Bryan Stevenson is correct when he says, "Imagery and photography are important tools. Without the [language of] imagery there would be no one who's prepared to believe some of the violence that we've witnessed."[16]

Language, as a requisite for creating and re-creating social reality, is not lost on God. It is through language that the spirit of God would manifest in a supernatural fashion at Pentecost. As a mechanism for divine power, language is used to signify or evidence the presence of the Spirit.[17] God immersed the community of disciples in the Spirit and gave them languages of the Jewish "others" around them who were present "from every nation under heaven" (Acts 2:5). This would be the witness of power Jesus alerted them to just a chapter earlier, before his ascension. Language, once a barrier, had been co-opted by God and used as a point of connection, orienting all who are present heavenward. It was hearing and seeing the event as an image that marked Jews who were from other lands. It is true that "to speak a language is to speak a people," but before language unites, it must disrupt.[18] It must disrupt that which divides and leads astray—narratives, ideologies, structures, and systems that are antifamilial and excommunicative.

The language of the Spirit is prophetic utterance (verbal) and prophetic embodiment (nonverbal). It is the prophetic ministry that disrupts existing hierarchical social structures. To share a common language is to be in community, one that thrives on interdependence. Language is characteristically familial.[19] The idea of family (beyond blood relatives) is antithetical to existing hierarchies of the first-century church and US society today; therefore, language, compatible with God's appropriation of it, is antithetical to hierarchy. The language of hierarchy is one of dominance, control, oppression, manipulation, and labeling. The language of family is liberation, solidarity, truthfulness, gentleness, and affirmation. The language of hierarchy as espoused by power, royal regime, or the dominant consciousness is one that is adversarial. The language of family, an alternative consciousness, is one of hospitality.

I analogize the visual baptism of the Floyd and Arbery murders to the spiritual baptism at Pentecost. When the Spirit fell at Pentecost upon the disciples, they experienced individual and collective baptism of the Spirit. They were immersed in the Spirit, and it gave them a new language and a new collective consciousness. It is then that Jesus says they would have the power (ability) to be witnesses (Acts 1:8). The videos of Floyd and Arbery "baptized" the nation, even the international community, in such a way that many began to speak the language of urgency, solidarity, allyship, and systemic racism that they had once dismissed. Many began to see differently after reemerging from the waters of hidden violence drenched in the reality that none had clean hands. New language, new consciousness, and new eyes imply that a new prophetic witness was required of all so that, as Jennings claims, "image emerges here fully encased in witness" and not in empty speech alone.[20] This new witness, however, inspired a new song from the shared lament while still desperately clinging to hope!

The language of prophetic ministry is inextricably tied to doxology.[21] Following the prophetic acts of God to liberate the Israelites from Egypt, Moses and the people sang a song of praise to Yahweh. Embedded in the glossolalia witnessed at Pentecost was praise to God. Each of these transformative events in the life of God's people involved the language of song. This is true in the African American community as well. The pain, suffering, and cries of the people become both the inspiration and melody for songs of hope.

"Amazing Grace" was written by poet, clergyman, and slave-trader-turned-abolitionist John Newton. While he is credited with penning the lyrics to the hymn, its melody was inspired by the Spirit-infused groans of the enslaved Africans from the belly of the ship. Negro spirituals narrating the experience of the enslaved contained coded subversive messaging (especially along the Underground Railroad route to freedom in the North) and helped sustain a sense of hope despite the despair in their existential reality. Christa K. Dixon encapsulates the significance and vitality of the spirituals:

> An explanation of even a few of the spiritual texts open up new and unexpected dimensions of understanding about how God's Word can become incarnate, take on flesh, in human—and inhuman—situations, even today. We begin to see that the spirituals are as faith-engendering and life-affirming for us in our time as

they were for the community of believers that originally created, shaped, and preserved them. Old songs can be sung with new meaning, and new songs can be created so that the burdens which weigh us down can be made lighter—as bearable as those of the slaves who actually experienced freedom from their chains while singing praise to him who has "the whole world in his hands."[22]

During the Civil Rights Movement, African American voices were heard singing "We Shall Overcome" while marching through Southern streets enduring White mob violence. They conveyed the lingering reality of oppression but also what it looks like to cling to hope for change. Even after George Floyd's video surfaced, there were several songs written by African American artists that spoke truthfully about his murder and directly to the royal regime of whiteness. Certainly, many African Americans in the Black church, as is our custom, after grieving the Floyd video, sang hymns of praise to God and hope in Jesus to "make it make sense."

So what does language really have to do with visual imagery? First, language is not just oratorical, but it is often embodied. Whether verbal or nonverbal, language is performed. It involves posture, countenance, energy, and interaction between performer and audience. It elicits a response. Second, visual imagery is language. It does the same, if not more so, as the spoken language. Doxology, tethered to prophetic ministry, is a language that is necessarily performed. It is born out of the belly of pain and suffering and matures in hopefulness to praise. Praise conceived by this language may sound like songs of joy or cries of lament.

The argument can be made that Floyd's refrain calling out to his mother is reminiscent of prophetic doxology. This underscores Brueggemann's claim that "doxology is the last full act of human freedom and justice."[23] The last full act that Floyd could perform before taking his last breath was to cry and groan for his mother who had already passed away. It was the injustice of the moment that evoked those cries. He was crying out for God by crying out for his mother, who represented the unconditional love of God for him. As a minister himself, he knew this Jesus who suffered for him and who, too, turned to his mother while on the cross. This image of Floyd's chorus of cries for his mother, the language of doxology, is what gutted many who otherwise kept their eyes and ears closed to Black suffering. The visual and the cries/song/language of his suffering cannot be divorced.

The language embedded in Frazier's video footage is the language of the suffering of Christ who died an unjust death. It is the language of hospitality that invites us to see Black suffering within White power structures. It is the language that invites us to then turn heavenward with an alternative consciousness and speak the alternative language of family by challenging us to see ourselves, all humans, in Floyd. It also invites those who see themselves in Chauvin, postured with knees on another human's neck until his life expired, to repentance. Only then can we all speak the universal and solidaric language of liberation.

Conclusion

There was a profoundly impactful scene in the movie *A Time to Kill*, which starred Matthew McConaughey, Sandra Bullock, and the incomparable Samuel L. Jackson, along with a star-studded cast. The story line follows that a ten-year-old

African American girl was kidnapped, beaten, raped, and hanged by two White men in a small town in Mississippi. The hanging attempt failed, and they left her by a river to die. The men were arrested, and while entering the courthouse for arraignment of the charges, Samuel Jackson's character, Carl Lee, afraid they might get away with the crime, avenges his daughter's rape and attempted murder by killing the two rapists. While on trial, with the death penalty over his head, Carl Lee hires a White lawyer—Jake Brigance, played by Matthew McConaughey. The trial ensues with an all-White jury. In his closing argument, Brigance asks the jurors to close their eyes while he walks them through the crime of the men who raped Carl Lee's daughter. He goes into detail, painting a vivid image, recreating the event for them. The camera pans the jury box, and visceral reactions are seen on the jurors' faces and in their bodies. At the end of the monologue, Brigance catches them and everyone in the courtroom (and I suspect the audience watching the film) by surprise when he says, "And imagine she's White."

The visual of seeing a little White girl being beaten, raped, and left for dead was jarring for the all-White jury. He forced them to have to see the humanity of the African American girl just as they would if she were White. The countenance of the jurors spoke volumes. Brigance had won them over. What looked like a sure guilty verdict was surprisingly a not guilty one. According to the jurors' collective body language and friendly interaction with the prosecutor during the movie trial scenes, the evidence against Carl Lee made it appear to be an open-and-shut case. The imagery presented to the jurors, however, spoken in a language they would likely have to respond to, was more potent than the case against Carl Lee. Lee admittedly hired Brigance because he was White. Even the visual of a White man standing before them, rather than an African American man or woman, would have potentially been disarming and would have given Lee a chance at a not guilty outcome. Brigance was hired because he could speak the language of the White jurors in appearance (nonverbal), tone, and words (verbal).

The power of the visual image on human thought and behavior is immeasurable. Humans are visual creatures. To see something is to be present with it. There is an intimacy that visual imagery provides that audio or secondhand information cannot, or they do so with limitations. Luke 11:34 claims, "Your eye is the lamp of your body. When your eye is healthy, your whole body is full of light, but when it is bad, your body is full of darkness."[24] The eye is the gateway for cravings, desires, and repulsions. The relationship between the eyes and the body's systems—nervous, muscular, neurological, vascular, and so on—is not to be taken for granted. The body senses and responds, through these systems, what the eyes consume. Each visual image has its own fingerprint, leaving a mark on the being, the soul of a person. They will either pursue or retreat. They will either remember or suppress the memory to forget the image. The body knows the potency of visual imagery.

Saul (before his name changed to Paul) saw and felt the presence of Jesus on the road to Damascus. His peers traveling with him merely heard a voice. This is an appropriate analogy to what is happening in this age. There are those who are insulated and oblivious, by choice or circumstance, and do not hear, see, or feel what is happening in the hidden, in-between experience of blackness. There are some who hear but do not see or feel. Finally, there are those who hear, see, and feel. Where people land among these categories depends on their individual or collective proximity to the actual event(s) or the violence depicted in the visual imagery supplied by the camera.

Certainly, for most in the African American community, and hopefully for the broader US American society, videos of unarmed African Americans leave an indelible mark on the collective conscience of the nation. This was King's intent and Frazier's instinct. They both, with prophetic efficacy, invited all to witness the drama of anti-Black violence and confronted the royal regime of whiteness / white supremacy / white sovereignty. The drama, though, continues in the individual and collective responses to the video images. The drama of royal consciousness and the alternative consciousness, oppression versus liberation, ensues.

Conclusion

T he body politic of the United States has been sick. Its illness has been self-inflicted, suffering from the "chronic inflammation" of whiteness. Whiteness has been the disease that has crippled the nation's ability to live up to its ideals of liberty and justice for all since its inception when these ideals were established. Inflammation in the human body is the appropriate analogy for whiteness as inflammation in the social body for several reasons. Inflammation is unseen until it manifests in pain, rashes on the skin, fatigue, fever, premature aging, or even depression. Its roots are unseen to the naked eye at the cellular level, and it plays a role in the development and progression of disease. One way of identifying inflammation in the body at the "root" level is through magnetic resonance imaging (MRI) or ultrasound. The images can detect early signs of inflammation that can eventually prevent individuals from experiencing the joy and fullness of life without the ever-presence of pain. Unfortunately, many people simply learn to live with the effects of chronic inflammation in their bodies, or they continue to participate in the habits that exacerbate it.

The chronic inflammation of whiteness shares similar traits. It is difficult for some to observe until it manifests in violence, bigotry, discriminatory attitudes and actions, and social structures. These symptoms are compounded with the pain they cause, the fatigue they induce, and the despair in which they suffocate groups of people. Like the MRIs and ultrasounds used to detect the signs of inflammation in the human body, the camera—used for still shots and video images—identifies and exposes whiteness-in-action within the social body. For African Americans, identifying the cause of the disease (whiteness) so that there is a proper diagnosis (white supremacy, anti-Black racism) and follow-up treatment (activism) is crucial to their survival and flourishing.

The irony of the Civil Rights Movement was that it needed the violence of whiteness to show itself for the Movement to be effective. If white supremacy operated in stealth, it would have been difficult to capture the violence that African Americans in the South were experiencing. It would have been challenging for the nation to gaze at "the real" of blackness and at the inflammation of whiteness. That which traumatized the community is the very practice that proved to be what led to the cultural transformation. Cultural change, however, was only achievable because of the creativity, resiliency, and discipline of a King-led revolution that co-opted the cameras that were present to photograph and/or record on video the terror of White violence.

What made the Civil Rights Movement so effective? Was it the charisma of Martin Luther King Jr.'s rhetoric? Was it the unwavering resilience of African Americans demonstrating in nonviolent fashion? Perhaps it was both and other factors not mentioned here. But without the national exposure provided by the news networks' cameras present to document and publish the injustice audaciously executed by White Southerners, most Americans would have still been left in the dark and ignorant of the reality for African

Americans in the South. I believe it was the violence of whiteness that contributed to the effectiveness of the Movement. Without Southern Whites doing their part and performing for the camera, there would have been nothing to capture. The camera was crucial in documenting whiteness on display. Without it, where would the Movement be?

The humanity of a nonviolent Black community standing courageously before the inhumanity of whiteness and its hatred and violence was a startling but inspiring image that captured the heart of the nation, and indeed the world. The camera in this context was an indispensable and prophetic weapon for Black moral agency. Martin Luther King Jr. served as not only lead rhetorician but creative producer and director of the drama that unfolded then, and he continues to remind the nation of our wounds and power as Black people. He gave the template. Technology only needed to catch up with him and democratize the camera so that any of us can be the initiators of creative tension that targets the collective conscience of the nation for social change.

The nation, specifically White people, needed to see the unseen and untold reality of the Black experience. James Baldwin warns us why this is imperative. He says, "People who shut their eyes to reality simply invite their own destruction, and anyone who insists on remaining in a state of innocence long after that innocence is dead turns himself into a monster."[1] The land of the free cannot be truly free until all are. White America, too, is in bondage to the idolatry of a dehumanizing worldview of whiteness and the ideology of white supremacy. If Baldwin is correct, whiteness is self-destructive for its White adherents—those practicing explicit racism *and* those in silent indifference. White Americans who are well-meaning and are potential allies must be relocated, brought closer to the social underbelly of racial history and present anti-Black violence. The camera functions to provide that invitation.

What will non-Black Americans do with the invitation? Will people of Color reflect on what the African American experience can reveal about their own experiences? What coalition will be formed and sustained from this reflection? Will White Americans sit in the discomfort long enough for an alternative consciousness to be formed in them? Or will they fall in line with the American ethos of "moving on" and "selective amnesia" once the emotional dust settles?

It is not necessary to continue to watch the traumatizing videos and pictures of anti-Black violence. What is necessary, however, is that all would reflect on (and not reject) what those images are revealing. Just like the Israelites rejected the prophets in the Old Testament who published a hard word from Yahweh, White Americans have too often rejected the prophetic ministry today. King was rejected until he was assassinated. His speeches are cherry-picked today to tell a different narrative than the one he told. The cries of African Americans were rejected as baseless complaints until the series of videos, culminating with George Floyd's murder, surfaced. It cannot continue to require the death of Black people for White Americans to become anti–white supremacists and participate in the prophetic ministry that confronts the royal regime.

After George Floyd's murder, amid the thousands of people worldwide protesting injustice, there was also a memorial in his name at the location where it all happened. While many came to protest injustice, what cannot get lost is the fact that they were also gathering to remember him and honor his life. It was a space for lament. It was a space to affirm the value of his life. Photographer Uzoma Obasi captured the essence of that space when he said, "I was there [at protests after Floyd's murder] for the family documenting the humanity of George."[2] The camera, in his hands, had healing purposes. But only for those who dared to gaze at the images he captured. The gaze will allow time for deep reflection to honor the life, but to enlist one's life for the cause of justice.

Where would we be without the camera? The images of Emmett Till taken by David Jackson both traumatized and energized the African American community, beginning with Rosa Parks. The violent drama of water hoses and batons meeting black skin as seen through the lens of the camera was proof that what Black folks were saying all along was the truth. Rodney King tormented by police officers, Ahmaud Arbery murdered while jogging, and George Floyd murdered with a White man's (police officer's) knee on his neck all serve as testimonies in a lineage of violence at the hands of White people. Their testimonies deserve a greater verdict than those deliberated upon and handed down to the individuals responsible. They demand more than a decision of guilt. The camera's testimonies cannot bring back those who have lost their lives, nor can they reverse what has already occurred. They demand compensatory and restorative verdicts of repentance, anti–white supremacy commitment, and a transformed culture of equality and equity. They demand change at the root level of society, within the institutions but also in the collective hearts of the group least involved in change—White Americans.

The challenge for all is to locate where the dramatization of blackness and its liberative possibilities begin. The challenge I have offered to White Christians is to heed the counsel of James Cone and begin at the cross and see the drama of Jesus's suffering as the drama of Black suffering. They must be willing to see Jesus as "Black." To reimagine Jesus as Black is to abandon the European Jesus who was invented to anchor white supremacy. If Jesus is "Black," then God is no longer White. This is the alternative paradigm, language, and ultimately consciousness that can liberate all, including White people, from the chokehold of whiteness. Jesus came into this world poor and humble, suffered unjustly, and was wrongfully executed. His life in thirty-three years is analogous to that of the Black experience in the United States for four hundred years. Cone boldly claims, "Until we can see the cross and the lynching tree together, until we can identify Christ with a 'recrucified' black body hanging from a lynching tree, there can be no genuine understanding of Christian identity in America, and no deliverance from the brutal legacy of slavery and white supremacy."[3]

So far, I have written about blackness as an experience shaped by the dominance of whiteness. Cone claims that this experience of blackness is an "ontological symbol and a visible reality which best describes what oppression means in America."[4] "Blackness" is not a framing of suffering exclusive to the African American experience (though this is its focus in this book), but "it stands for all victims of oppression" at the hands of whiteness.[5] Dwight Radcliff says the Black experience with racism, because of the history and degree of racial violence African Americans have been subjected to, *is the barometer* by which all other racial groups' experiences with racism are measured.[6]

Liberation from whiteness is tethered to an understanding and vision of this Jesus with this narrative. An alternative vision of God has the capacity to offer an alternative racial imagination that can transform society. Through the lens of the camera, can Jesus be seen as George Floyd with a Roman soldier's knee (Chauvin's) on his neck? Through the camera's lens, can Jesus be seen running toward or away from a gun pointed at him before bullets pierce his body like the nails that were hammered through his hands and feet? What prophetic truths can be revealed through the lens of the camera in the hands of African American "withstanders," activists, and filmmakers that can liberate the United States and move us toward a more just society?

Notes

Introduction

1 Marvin Gaye, "Can I Get a Witness," Lyrics.com, accessed February 8, 2022, https://www.lyrics.com/lyric/8150424.

2 Shelly Rambo, *Spirit and Trauma: A Theology of Remaining* (Louisville, KY: Westminster John Knox, 2010), 3, 7. Rambo describes trauma as an "event [or events] that exceeds categories of [human] comprehension; the human capacity to take in and process the external world. . . . Trauma is an open wound" (7). I will draw from this definition as my foundational understanding of trauma when I use this term throughout this book.

3 Nancy Dillon, "White Neighbors 'Upset' No Charges Filed for Fatal Shooting of Breonna Taylor: Lawyer," New York Daily News, September 24, 2020, https://www.nydailynews.com/news/national/ny-white-neighbors-upset-no-charges-filed-for-breonna-taylor-death-20200924-u2ei6use7jgvdpwtzmwqefvcre-story.html.

4 Dylan Lovan, "Q&A: What Were the Results of Breonna Taylor Investigation?," ABC News, September 24, 2020, https://abcnews.go.com/US/wireStory/qa-results-breonna-taylor-investigation-73215505.

5 Dillon, "White Neighbors."

6 Will Smith made the comments on the *Late Show with Stephen Colbert* in 2016. "Will Smith: 'Racism Is Not Getting Worse, It's

Getting Filmed,'" Yahoo, August 3, 2016, https://www.yahoo
.com/entertainment/smith-racism-not-getting-worse-getting
-filmed-151248092.html.

7 Michel Foucault, *Power/Knowledge: Selected Interviews and
Other Writings*, ed. Colin Gordon, trans. Colin Gordon, Leo
Marshall, John Mepham, and Kate Soper (New York: Vintage,
1977), 82.

8 Paul Tillich, *Theology of Culture*, ed. Robert C. Kimball (New
York: Oxford University Press, 1959), loc. 514 of 2094, Kindle.

Chapter 1

1 In this book, I use *Black* interchangeably with *African American*.
In the same ways and for the same reasons I would capitalize
African American, I capitalize the word *Black* when used in
those contexts. I capitalize the term *Black* (and *White*) when
using it in the same way I would use *Asian*, *Latino/a*, or *Jew*.
There are times when I do not capitalize the terms when *black* or
white are used more descriptively, like in *blackness* or *black skin*,
for example, or when it is a term that stands on its own, such
as *white supremacy*.

2 Lexico, s.v. "violent (*adj.*)," accessed February 9, 2022, https://
www.lexico.com/definition/violent.

3 Online Etymology Dictionary, s.v. "violation (*n.*)," accessed
February 9, 2022, https://www.etymonline.com/word/violation.

4 Peter Paris, *The Social Teachings of the Black Church* (Philadel-
phia: Fortress, 1985), 1–20.

5 "Emmett Till's Accuser Admits She Lied," Equal Justice Initiative, January 31, 2017, https://eji.org/news/emmett-till-accuser
-admits-she-lied/.

6 "The 1619 Project," *New York Times Magazine*, accessed February 9, 2022, https://www.nytimes.com/interactive/2019/08/
14/magazine/1619-america-slavery.html.

7 Marcus Rediker, *The Slave Ship: A Human History* (New York: Viking Penguin, 2007), loc. 141 of 8906, Kindle.

8 Rediker, loc. 338 of 8906.

9 Rediker, loc. 787 of 8906.

10 Rediker, loc. 1140 of 8906.

11 Rediker, loc. 141 of 8906.

12 Rediker, loc. 814 of 8906.

13 Rediker, loc. 787 of 8906.

14 Robin Blackburn, *Making of New World Slavery: From the Baroque to the Modern, 1492–1800* (London: Verso, 2010), 350.

15 Frederick Douglass, *The Narrative of the Life of Frederick Douglass* (Boston: Anti-slavery Office, 1845), loc. 247 of 1568, Kindle.

16 Victoria Adams, interviewed by Everett R. Pierce in Work Projects Administration, "Victoria Adams," in *Dem Days Was Hell: Recorded Testimonies of Former Slaves from 17 U.S. States* (Prague: e-artnow, 2017), loc. 5718 of 8012, Kindle.

17 Equal Justice Initiative, "Documenting Reconstruction Violence: Known and Unknown Horrors," in *Reconstruction in America: Racial Violence after the Civil War, 1865–1876*, accessed February 9, 2022, https://eji.org/report/reconstruction-in-america/documenting-reconstruction-violence/.

18 Leah Douglass, "African Americans Have Lost Untold Acres of Land over the Last Century," *Nation*, June 26, 2017, https://www.thenation.com/article/archive/african-americans-have-lost-acres/. See also Abril Castro and Caius C. Willingham, "Progressive Governance Can Turn the Tide for Black Farmers," Center for American Progress, April 3, 2019, https://americanprogress.org/article/progressive-governance-can-turn-tide-black-farmers/.

19 C. Vann Woodward, *The Strange Career of Jim Crow: A Commemorative Edition* (New York: Oxford University Press, 2002), 17, Kindle.

20 Woodward, 70.

21 *Merriam-Webster*, s.v. "ghetto (*n.*)," accessed December 21, 2021, https://www.merriam-webster.com/dictionary/ghetto.

22 *Merriam-Webster*, s.v. "ghetto (*n.*)." The etymology of the word *ghetto* was formerly the subject of much speculation, but today there is little doubt that the word comes from the Italian dialect form *ghèto*, meaning "foundry." A foundry for cannons was once located on an island that forms part of Venice, where in 1516 the Venetians restricted Jewish residence. The word *ghèto* became the name for the area and was borrowed into standard Italian as *ghetto*, with the meaning of "section of a city where Jews are forced to live." From there, it passed into most other European languages. Since the late nineteenth century, the meaning of *ghetto* has been extended to crowded urban districts where other ethnic or racial groups have been confined by poverty or prejudice.

23 Richard Rothstein, *The Color of Law: A Forgotten History of How Our Government Segregated America* (New York: Liveright, 2017), 59, Kindle.

24 Michelle Alexander, *The New Jim Crow: Mass Incarceration in the Age of Colorblindness* (New York: New Press, 2012), 6, Kindle.

25 Samuel R. Gross, ed., *Race and Wrongful Convictions in the United States*, National Registry of Exonerations (Irvine, CA: Newkirk Center for Science and Society, 2017), 6, http://www.law.umich.edu/special/exoneration/Documents/Race_and_Wrongful_Convictions.pdf.

26 Alexander, *New Jim Crow*, 1.

27 For example, when formerly enslaved Africans were no longer confined to the plantations of the slave system, "Black Codes" were created to further perpetuate social control over Black bodies for the benefit and dominance of White Americans, particularly in the South. Those "Black Codes" gave White authorities license to arrest African Americans for just about whatever reason they could think of to not only restrict their freedom but take it away completely. They were designed to "legally" continue the enslavement of African Americans. See Alexander, 28, 36.

Chapter 2

1 Matt 7:15.

2 Love Sechrest, Johnny Ramírez-Johnson, and Amos Yong, eds., introduction to *Can "White" People Be Saved? Triangulating Race, Theology, and Mission* (Downers Grove, IL: IVP Academic, 2018), 12.

3 Sechrest, Ramírez-Johnson, and Yong, 13.

4 Charles Mills, *The Racial Contract* (Ithaca, NY: Cornell University Press, 1997), loc. 101 of 2530, Kindle.

5 Joe R. Feagin, *Systemic Racism: A Theory of Oppression* (New York: Routledge, 2006), 237.

6 Willie James Jennings, "Can White People Be Saved? Reflections on the Relationship of Missions and Whiteness," in Sechrest, Ramírez-Johnson, and Yong, *Can "White" People Be Saved?*, 27.

7 Sechrest, Ramírez-Johnson, and Yong, *Can "White" People Be Saved?*, 8.

8 Nell Irvin Painter, *The History of White People* (New York: W. W. Norton, 2010), 30, Kindle.

9 Painter, 33.

10 Painter, 47.

11 Painter, 45.

12 Painter, 56–59.

13 Antonio Damasio, *The Strange Order of Things: Life, Feeling, and the Making of Culture* (New York: Pantheon, 2018), 24.

14 Holly Yan, Devon M. Sayers, and Steve Almasy, "Virginia Governor on White Nationalists: They Should Leave America," CNN, August 14, 2017, https://www.cnn.com/2017/08/13/us/charlottesville-white-nationalist-rally-car-crash/index.html.

15 See footage of Fox News commentator Laura Ingraham's comments in response to LeBron James and Kevin Durant's statements about former president Donald Trump. Martenzie Johnson, "What Laura Ingraham's Attacks on LeBron

James Really Means," Undefeated, February 16, 2018, https://
theundefeated.com/features/what-laura-ingrahams-attack-of
-lebron-james-really-means/.

16 Jeannine Fletcher Hill, *The Sin of White Supremacy: Christianity, Racism, and Religious Diversity in America* (Maryknoll, NY: Orbis, 2017), 12, Kindle.

17 Hill, 14.

18 Ian Haney López, *White by Law: The Legal Construction of Race* (New York: New York University Press, 2006), 79, Kindle.

19 Finis Jennings Dake, *Dake's Annotated Reference Bible* (Lawrenceville, GA: Dake Bible Sales, 1981), 8, 9, 36, 40, cited in Cain Hope Felder, *Race, Racism, and the Biblical Narratives* (Minneapolis, MN: Fortress, 2002), loc. 86 of 330, Kindle (emphasis mine).

20 Peter Randolph, "Plantation Churches: Visible and Invisible," in *African American Religious History: A Documentary Witness*, 2nd ed., ed. Milton C. Sernett (Durham, NC: Duke University Press, 1999), 63, Kindle.

21 Hill, *Sin of White Supremacy*, 12.

22 Gloria J. Browne-Marshall, *Race, Law, and American Society: 1607–Present*, 2nd ed. (New York: Routledge, 2013), loc. 1109, Kindle.

23 W. E. B. Du Bois, "The Freedman's Bureau," *Atlantic Monthly* 87 (1901): 354–65, cited in Browne-Marshall, *Race, Law, and American Society*, loc. 1125.

24 Andrew Greif, "Doc Rivers: 'It's Amazing We Keep Loving This Country, and This Country Does Not Love Us Back,'" *LA Times*, August 25, 2020, https://www.latimes.com/sports/clippers/story/2020-08-25/doc-rivers-loving-this-country-and-does-not-love-us-back.

25 Resmaa Menakem, *My Grandmother's Hands: Racialized Trauma and the Pathway to Mending Our Hearts and Bodies* (Las Vegas, NV: Central Recovery, 2017), 60, Kindle.

26 Menakem, 71.

27 Anthony P. Carnevale and Jeff Strohl, *Separate and Unequal: How Higher Education Reinforces the Intergenerational Reproduction of White Racial Privilege* (Washington, DC: Georgetown University Public Policy Institute, 2013), 23, http://cew.georgetown.edu/wp-content/uploads/SeparateUnequal.FR_.pdf.

28 National Center for Education Statistics, "Race/Ethnicity of College Faculty," accessed February 11, 2022, https://nces.ed.gov/fastfacts/display.asp?id=61.

Chapter 3

1 Matthew W. Hughey and Emma González-Lesser, introduction to *Racialized Media: The Design, Delivery, and Decoding of Race and Identity* (New York: New York University Press, 2020), 7.

2 Hughey and González-Lesser, 7. Hughey and González-Lesser make this observation from analyzing sociologist Stuart Hall's encoding/decoding model of communication.

3 Roslyn Satchel, *What Movies Teach about Race: Exceptionalism, Erasure, and Entitlement* (New York: Lexington, 2017), 31, Kindle.

4 Ralph Basui Watkins, "A Brief Introduction to the History of Civil Rights Photography and Select Photographers" (lecture, Rochester Institute of Technology, Rochester, NY, February 17, 2021), https://www.youtube.com/watch?v=YQ-2Hs_VkEI.

5 Satchel, *What Movies Teach*, 55.

6 Angela Y. Davis, *Women, Race, and Class* (New York: Random House, 1981), 6.

7 Mark E. Benbow, "Birth of a Quotation: Woodrow Wilson and 'Like Writing History with Lightning,'" in "Native Americans and Indian Policy in the Progressive Era," special issue, *Journal of the Gilded Age and Progressive Era* 9, no. 4 (October 2010): 510.

8 Benbow, 510.

9 Benbow, 511.

10 Benbow, 512.

11 Ralph Basui Watkins, "Introduction to Black Theology" (lecture, Fuller Theological Seminary, Pasadena, CA, July 2016).

12 Felder, *Biblical Narratives*, loc. 78 of 330.

13 Felder, loc. 80 of 330.

14 Willie James Jennings, *The Christian Imagination: Theology and the Origins of Race* (New Haven, CT: Yale University Press, 2010), 58.

15 Jennings, 58.

16 Felder, *Biblical Narratives*, loc. 87 of 330.

17 Roger Ebert, "Mandingo," RogerEbert.com, July 25, 1975, https://www.rogerebert.com/reviews/mandingo-1975.

18 Ibram X. Kendi, "The 15 Most Racist Oscar Films of All Time: Here's Why #OscarsSoWhite Is Not a Surprise," Salon, February 24, 2016, https://www.salon.com/2016/02/24/the_15_most _racist_oscar_films_of_all_time_heres_why_oscarssowhite_is _not_a_surprise/.

19 Kendi (emphasis mine).

20 Quote by Woodrow Wilson in D. W. Griffith's *The Birth of a Nation*; Khalbrae, "The Birth of a Nation—Full Movie (1915) HD—the Masterpiece of Racist Cinema," YouTube, 3:13:17, August 1, 2015, https://www.youtube.com/watch?v= ebtiJH3EOHo (emphasis mine).

21 Darnell Hunt and Ana-Christina Rámon, "Hollywood Diversity Report 2020: Part 1: Film," UCLA College Social Sciences, 2020, accessed February 21, 2022, https://irle.ucla.edu/ wp-content/uploads/2020/02/UCLA-Hollywood-Diversity -Report-2020-Film-2-6-2020.pdf.

22 Jonathan Dunn et al., "Black Representation in Film and TV: The Challenges and Impact of Increasing Diversity," McKinsey & Company, March 11, 2021, https://www.mckinsey .com/Featured-Insights/Diversity-and-Inclusion/Black

-representation-in-film-and-TV-The-challenges-and-impact
-of-increasing-diversity.

23 *Kryptonite* is a fictional word of the Superman series meaning
"something that renders a person or thing helpless"; "presents
a particular threat to one that is otherwise powerful"; and can
seriously weaken or harm a person or thing. *The Free Dictionary*,
s.v. "kryptonite (*n.*)," accessed February 15, 2022, https://www
.thefreedictionary.com/kryptonite.

24 Andrew T. Draper, "The End of 'Mission': Christian Witness
and the Decentering of White Identity," in Sechrest, Ramírez-
Johnson, and Yong, *Can "White" People Be Saved?*, 177.

25 Gen 1:26, 28.

26 Khalbrae, "Birth of a Nation."

27 Satchel, *What Movies Teach*, 56.

28 Claude Steele and Joshua Aronson, "Stereotype Threat and the
Intellectual Test Performance of African Americans," *Journal
of Personality and Social Psychology* 69, no. 5 (1995): 797.

29 Satchel, *What Movies Teach*, 48. Satchel offers context for
how "binary opposition" is used in media: "To represent
racial difference, media stereotyping utilizes a splitting
strategy—binary oppositions—that depicts what is acceptable and what is unacceptable. In excluding anything that the
majority considers unacceptable, media content also symbol-
ically annihilates certain groups in popular culture" (48).

30 Adrian Bardon, "Corona Responses Highlight How Humans
Are Hardwired to Dismiss Facts That Don't Fit Their Worldview," Conversation, June 25, 2020, https://theconversation
.com/humans-are-hardwired-to-dismiss-facts-that-dont-fit
-their-worldview-127168.

31 Bardon.

Chapter 4

1 Foucault, *Power/Knowledge*, 93.
2 This chapter draws upon an article I published in the journal *Mission Studies*: Phillip Allen, "The Prophetic Lens: A Missiological Function of Film for Black Social Movement from Martin Luther King, Jr. to the Camera Phone," *Mission Studies* 38 (2021): 350–71.
3 L. Michael Lee, phone interview with author, October 29, 2021. Director L. Michael Lee says the cinematographer "ensures that the shots planned during pre-production are being done correctly so that the story is being told properly (visually speaking)." Frazier, by her location and proximity to Chauvin while he was on Floyd's neck, assures that the clearest shot of the murder was captured on her phone. This would prove to be crucial given the initial statement (story) by the Minneapolis Police Department that contradicts what she recorded.
4 Tim Darnell, "Read What Minneapolis Police Originally Said about George Floyd's Death," *Atlanta Journal-Constitution*, April 21, 2021, https://www.ajc.com/news/nation-world/read -what-minneapolis-police-originally-said-about-george-floyds -death/6U46PPB6RFBZNFEKTYBHDXO2KY/. Original statement posted by Jake Tapper, news anchor at CNN. Jake Tapper (@jaketapper), "Seriously, read it again knowing what we know," photo, Twitter, April 20, 2021, https://twitter.com/ jaketapper/status/1384622849562873856.
5 F. D. Bluford Library, "The A&T Four: February 1st, 1960," accessed February 15, 2022, http://www.library.ncat.edu/ resources/archives/four.html#:~:text=The%20A%26T%20Four %3A%20February%201st%2C%201960.%20On%20February ,in%E2%80%9D%20at%20the%20whites%E2%80%93only %20lunch%20counter%20at%20Woolworth%E2%80%99s.
6 Walter Brueggemann, *Prophetic Imagination* (Minneapolis, MN: Fortress, 2001), 3.
7 Brueggemann, 21.

8 To keep the language compatible in this chapter with the language that Brueggemann uses, when I use the term *empire*, I am referring to the dominant group with the most access to power—White power structures, agents of white supremacy, or the White community as a collective. This does not mean *every* White individual is complicit with empire, but the White collective is the focus here. White people as a group either benefit from, perpetuate, or have familial links to the architects and perpetrators of the various degrees of violence from these power structures.

9 Brueggemann, *Prophetic Imagination*, 21.

10 Brueggemann, 3.

11 Brueggemann, 32.

12 Brueggemann, 4.

13 Brueggemann, 3.

14 Martin Luther King Jr., "Letter from Birmingham City Jail," in *A Testament of Hope: Essential Writings and Speeches of Martin Luther King, Jr.*, ed. James M. Washington (New York: Harper One, 1986), 292.

15 Brueggemann, *Prophetic Imagination*, 3.

16 Brueggemann, 4.

17 Richard Delgado and Jean Stefancic, "Norms and Narratives: Can Judges Avoid Serious Moral Error?," *Texas Law Review* 69 (1991): 1929.

18 Avery F. Gordon, "Some Thoughts on Haunting and Futurity," *Borderlands* 10, no. 2 (2011): 2, cited in Sadhana Bery's chapter "Making Whiteness in Reenactments of Slavery," in *The Construction of Whiteness: An Interdisciplinary Analysis of Race Formation and the Meaning of a White Identity*, ed. Stephen Middleton, David R. Roediger, and Donald M. Shaffer (Jackson: University Press of Mississippi, 2016), 140, Kindle.

19 Bery, "Making Whiteness," 140.

20 Brueggemann, *Prophetic Imagination*, 100.

21 Brueggemann, 3 (emphasis mine).

22 Nolan D. McCaskill, "'A Seismic Quake': Floyd Killing Transforms Views on Race," *Politico*, June 10, 2020, https://www.politico.com/news/2020/06/10/george-floyds-death-transforms-views-on-race-307575.

23 Janie Haseman et al., "Tracking Protests across the US in the Wake of George Floyd's Death," *USA Today*, June 18, 2020, https://www.usatoday.com/in-depth/graphics/2020/06/03/map-protests-wake-george-floyds-death/5310149002/.

24 McCaskill, "Seismic Quake."

25 McCaskill.

26 Dana Brownlee, "Do White People Have the Stamina for Racial Justice? This White Guy Thinks So," *Forbes*, November 15, 2021, https://www.forbes.com/sites/danabrownlee/2021/11/15/do-white-people-have-the-stamina-for-racial-justice-this-white-guy-thinks-so/?sh=3a9d12da1c0a. Brownlee quotes Jared Karol from his book *A White Guy Confronting Racism: An Invitation to Reflect and Act* (self-pub., 2021). According to a USA Today / Ipsos poll conducted in June 2020 on CNN.com, weeks after Floyd's murder, 60 percent of respondents described Floyd's death as murder. Less than a year later (March 2021), only 36 percent described it as such. Nicole Chavez, "White and Black Americans Are Divided over George Floyd's Death and Whether Race Relations Have Improved, Poll Finds," CNN, March 8, 2021, https://www.cnn.com/2021/03/08/us/race-relations-george-floyd-poll/index.html.

27 Brueggemann, *Prophetic Imagination*, 1.

28 Robert O'Harrow Jr., Andrew Ba Tran, and Derek Hawkins, "The Rise of Domestic Extremism in America," *Washington Post*, April 12, 2021, https://www.washingtonpost.com/investigations/interactive/2021/domestic-terrorism-data/.

29 O'Harrow, Tran, and Hawkins.

30 Zachary Evans, "FBI Director Warns of Metastasizing Domestic Terrorism," Yahoo News, March 3, 2021, https://news.yahoo

.com/fbi-director-warns-metastasizing-domestic-141142633
.html?fr=yhssrp_catchall.

31 Brueggemann, *Prophetic Imagination*, 32, 35.

32 Brueggemann, 36.

33 Brueggemann, 29.

34 Brueggemann, 4.

35 Watkins, "Brief Introduction."

36 Online Etymology Dictionary, s.v. "nurture (*v.*)," accessed February 15, 2022, https://www.etymonline.com/search?q=nurture&ref=searchbar_searchhint.

37 Online Etymology Dictionary, s.v. "nourish (*v.*)," accessed February 15, 2022, https://www.etymonline.com/search?q=nourish&ref=searchbar_searchhint.

38 Brueggemann, *Prophetic Imagination*, 1.

39 Black bodies are a prophetic disruption to whiteness because whiteness must acknowledge truths that contrast or contradict its declared narrative. It must consider what it means to be fully human and not measured against whiteness. Its comfort is interrupted because it must now share space with the unfamiliarity of a radical other. It must grapple with the untenable stance of a worldview that places greater value on White bodies, thought, beauty, and so on over Black bodies. It must also rethink its theology with Eurocentric roots and its entanglement with white supremacy that has shaped a narrative about who God is and what God cares about; a God of evangelism must also be a God of justice and equity for the least of these. Black bodies in White spaces evoke reflections on these truths.

40 Rothstein, *Color of Law*, 56.

Chapter 5

1 This chapter draws upon an article I published in the journal *Mission Studies*: Allen, "Prophetic Lens," 350–71.

2 Alexis C. Madrigal, "When the Revolution Was Televised," *Atlantic*, April 1, 2018, https://www.theatlantic.com/technology/archive/2018/04/televisions-civilrights-revolution/554639/.

3 National Park Service, "Bloody Sunday," last updated August 9, 2018, https://www.nps.gov/semo/learn/historyculture/bloody-sunday.htm.

4 King, "The Case against 'Tokenism,'" in Washington, *Testament of Hope*, 109.

5 King, "Letter from Birmingham City Jail," 295 (emphasis mine).

6 Madrigal, "Revolution Was Televised."

7 Robin DiAngelo, *White Fragility: Why It's So Hard for White People to Talk about Racism* (Boston: Beacon, 2018), 40, Kindle.

8 King, "Letter from Birmingham City Jail," 291.

9 King, 291.

10 King, 295.

11 King, 296.

12 King, "Showdown for Nonviolence," in Washington, *Testament of Hope*, 68.

13 Maurice Berger, "Malcolm X as Visual Strategist," *New York Times*, September 19, 2012, https://lens.blogs.nytimes.com/2012/09/19/malcolm-x-as-visual-strategist/.

14 Berger.

15 James H. Cone, *Martin and Malcolm and American: A Dream or a Nightmare* (Maryknoll, NY: Orbis, 1992), loc. 124, Kindle.

16 Cone, loc. 48.

17 "Covering the South: A National Symposium on the Media and the Civil Rights Movement" (conference, University of Mississippi, Oxford, MS, April 3–5, 1987), comments by Robert Schakne, panel 1, pp. 34, 35 (hereafter, "Symposium"), cited in

Robert J. Donavan and Ray Scherer, *Unsilent Revolution: Television News and American Public Life* (Cambridge: Cambridge University Press, 1992), 5.

18 Peter J. Boyer, *Who Killed CBS?* (New York: Random House, 1988), 229.

19 Donavan and Scherer, *Unsilent Revolution*, 5.

20 "Symposium," panel 1, p. 34, in Donavan and Scherer, *Unsilent Revolution*, 5.

21 Donavan and Scherer, 6.

22 Donavan and Scherer, 7.

23 Donavan and Scherer, 9.

24 Donavan and Scherer, 10.

25 Joy DeGruy, *Post-traumatic Slave Syndrome: America's Legacy of Enduring Injury and Healing* (Stone Mountain, GA: Joy DeGruy, 2017), 38–39.

26 King, "The Power of Nonviolence," in Washington, *Testament of Hope*, 12.

27 King, 13.

28 Watkins, "Brief Introduction."

29 King, "Power of Nonviolence," 13–14.

30 Donavan and Scherer, *Unsilent Revolution*, 14.

Chapter 6

1 Frederick Douglass, "West India Emancipation," in *Frederick Douglass: The Most Complete Collection of His Written Works and Speeches* (n.p.: Northpointe Classics, 2011), loc. 21613 of 23534, Kindle (emphasis mine).

2 *Merriam-Webster*, s.v. "democracy (*n.*)," accessed February 11, 2022, https://www.merriam-webster.com/dictionary/democracy.

3 Alexis de Tocqueville, *Democracy in America*, trans. Henry Reeves (Champaign, IL: Project Gutenberg, 1999), 9 (emphasis mine).

4 Foucault, *Power/Knowledge*, 93.

5 Foucault, 102.

6 J. K. Smith, *Desiring the Kingdom (Cultural Liturgies): Worship, Worldview, and Cultural Formation* (Grand Rapids, MI: Baker Academics, 2009), 40, Kindle.

7 Jer 26:4–6.

8 Jer 26:8.

9 Jer 26:9, 11.

10 Jer 7:5–7.

11 Jer 28:9.

12 "Printing Press," History.com, last updated October 10, 2019, https://www.history.com/.amp/topics/inventions/printing -press.

13 "Printing Press."

14 Exod 19:21–25.

15 Exod 20:18–19.

16 Jer 31:33.

17 Col 1:15.

18 Phil Allen Jr., "Power-Full Black Bodily Resistance: Reimagining Kaepernick's Protest through King's Nonviolent Direct Action," *Journal of Religious Leadership* 19, no. 2 (Autumn 2019): 39.

19 Elisha Fieldstadt, "Black Ohio Police Officer Whose White Chief Put KKK Note on His Coat Breaks His Silence," NBC News, November 11, 2021, https://www.nbcnews.com/news/ us-news/black-ohio-police-officer-whose-white-chief-put-kkk -note-coat-breaks-s-rcna5253.

20 Deborah Ramirez, Jack McDevitt, and Amy Farrell, *A Resource Guide on Racial Profiling Data Collection Systems: Promising Practices and Lessons Learned* (Boston: Northeastern University, 2000), 10.

21 Roxane Gay, "Justine Sacco's Aftermath: The Cost of Twitter Out- rage," Salon, December 23, 2013, https://www.salon.com/2013/12/ 23/justine_saccos_aftermath_the_cost_of_twitter_outrage/.

Chapter 7

1 Associated Press, "Judge Upholds Ex-Cop's 20 Year Sentence for Killing Black Man," HuffPost, April 20, 2021, https://www.huffpost.com/entry/michael-slager-loses-sentence-appeal-in-walter-scott-shooting_n_607ec6f3e4b0df3610c065b3.

2 Eliott C. McLaughlin, "Like the George Floyd Witnesses, He Saw Police Kill a Man. Now He's a Part of the System Demanding Change," CNN, April 11, 2021, https://www.cnn.com/2021/04/11/us/walter-scott-shooting-witness-feidin-santana/index.html.

3 Phil Allen Jr., *Open Wounds: A Story of Racial Tragedy, Trauma, and Redemption* (Minneapolis, MN: Fortress, 2021), 87, Kindle.

4 1 Sam 13:14; Acts 13:22.

5 2 Sam 11:15.

6 2 Sam 12:1–4.

7 Judith Herman, *Trauma and Recovery: The Aftermath of Violence—from Domestic Abuse to Political Terror* (New York: Basic Books, 1997), 7.

8 *Merriam-Webster*, s.v. "bystander (*n.*)," accessed February 11, 2020, https://www.merriam-webster.com/dictionary/bystander.

9 Browne-Marshall, *Race, Law, and American Society*, loc. 2180, Kindle.

10 Browne-Marshall, loc. 2180.

11 Browne-Marshall, loc. 2180.

12 Kyle McGovern, "Deryl Dedmon Pleads Guilty in Mississippi Hate Crime Hit-and-Run of James Craig Anderson," HuffPost, March 22, 2012, https://www.huffpost.com/entry/deryl-dedmon_n_1372184.

13 McGovern.

14 David Close, "This Is the Noose That Was Found in Bubba Wallace's Garage Stall at the Talladega Speedway," CNN, June 26, 2020, https://www.cnn.com/2020/06/25/us/nascar-noose

-investigation-complete-trnd/index.html. Also in *E:60* documentary, "Fistful of Steel: The Rise of Bubba Wallace," interview with Ryan McGee, aired December 14, 2021, on ESPN.

15 Close, "Noose."

16 James H. Cone, *The Cross and the Lynching Tree* (Maryknoll, NY: Orbis, 2011).

Chapter 8

1 Kristal Brent Zook, *I See Black People: The Rise and Fall of African American-Owned Television and Radio* (New York: Nation, 2008).

2 John Landis, *The Eighties*, season 1, episode 1, "The Movies," aired July 8, 2019, on CNN.

3 Nadra Kareem Nittle, "How MTV Handled Accusations of Racism and Became More Inclusive," LiveAbout, January 14, 2020, https://www.liveabout.com/when-mtv-first-aired-black -videos-2834657.

4 *The Eighties*, season 1, episode 6, "Video Killed the Radio Star," aired May 19, 2016, on CNN.

5 Minjeong Kim and Rachelle J. Brunn-Bevel, "Political Economy and the Global-Local Nexus of Hollywood," in *Racialized Media: The Design, Delivery, and Decoding of Race and Ethnicity*, ed. Matthew W. Hughey and Emma González-Lesser (New York: New York Press, 2020), 34.

6 Earl James Young Jr., *The Life and Work of Oscar Micheaux: Pioneer Black Author and Filmmaker 1884–1951*, ed. Beverly J. Robinson (Sacramento, CA: KMT, 2003), loc. 241 of 3427, Kindle.

7 Young, loc. 167 of 3427.

8 Young, loc. 181 of 3427.

9 Young, loc. 167 of 3427.

10 "Oscar Micheaux," National Park Service, last updated May 17, 2021, https://www.nps.gov/people/oscar-micheaux.htm.

11 Young, *Oscar Micheaux*, loc. 567 of 3427.

12 Young, loc. 899 of 3427.

13 Sarah Whitten, "20 Black Filmmakers Who Have Changed Hollywood in the Last Century," CNBC, February 19, 2021, https://www.cnbc.com/2021/02/19/20-black-movie-directors-that-changed-hollywood-in-the-last-century.html.

14 Whitten.

15 Maurice Berger, "'Shaft?' We're Talking about Gordon Parks . . . and We Dig It," *New York Times*, May 24, 2019, https://www.nytimes.com/2019/05/24/lens/shaft-gordon-parks-photos.html.

16 Berger.

17 Berger.

18 Andy Grundberg, "Gordon Parks, a Master of the Camera, Dies at 93," *New York Times*, May 8, 2006, https://www.nytimes.com/2006/03/08/arts/design/gordon-parks-a-master-of-the-camera-dies-at-93.html.

19 Priscilla Frank, "The Importance of Photography in the Fight for Civil Rights," HuffPost, February 16, 2016, https://www.huffpost.com/entry/gordon-parks-civil-rights-photography_n_56c222c9e4b0b40245c7681a.

20 Kathleen Collins, "Extended Biography," accessed February 12, 2022, http://kathleencollins.org/about.

21 Collins.

22 Collins.

23 TIFF Talks, "Spike Lee on Do the Right Thing | TIFF 2019," YouTube, 46:39, July 22, 2019, https://www.youtube.com/watch?v=vL6xOlIaB-E.

24 Walter Burghardt, "Contemplation: A Long Loving Look at the Real," in *An Ignatian Spirituality Reader*, ed. George W. Traub (Chicago: Loyola Press, 2008), 92, cited in James Lorenz, "The Cinema Gaze as 'A Long Loving Look at the Real': Andrei Tarkovsky and Walter Burghardt's Theology of Contemplation," *Heythrop Journal*, May 19, 2020, https://onlinelibrary.wiley.com/doi/full/10.1111/heyj.13576#heyj13576-sec-0001-title.

25 TIFF Talks, "Spike Lee."

26 TIFF Talks.

27 Ava DuVernay (@ava), "Not thugs. Not wilding. Not criminals. Not even the Central Park Five. They are Korey, Antron, Raymond, Yusef, and Kevin," Twitter, March 1, 2019, https:// twitter.com/ava/status/1101499104834707456. Also found on http://www.avaduvernay.com/when-they-see-us/.

28 Ava DuVernay, *Oprah Winfrey Presents: When They See Us*, interview, directed by Mark Ritchie, 2019, Netflix.

29 George Yancy, *Backlash: What Happens When We Talk Honestly about Racism in America* (New York: Rowman & Littlefield, 2018), 21.

30 *The Story of Late Night*, season 1, episode 2, "Carson: King of Late Night," directed by John Ealer, aired May 9, 2021, on CNN.

Chapter 9

1 Bryan Stevenson, "The Body of Emmett Till | 100 Photos | Time," YouTube, 8:17, November 17, 2016, https://www .youtube.com/watch?v=4V6ffUUEvaM.

2 Stevenson.

3 Ashitha Nagesh, "Simone Biles: What Are the Twisties in Gymnastics?," BBC News, July 28, 2021, https://www.bbc.com/ news/world-us-canada-57986166.

4 Ellen Thornton, "The Art of Documenting War and Conflict," RTE, November 28, 2019, https://www.rte.ie/brainstorm/2019/ 0129/1026165-the-art-of-documenting-war-and-conflict/.

5 Thornton.

6 The interview with jurors from the Derek Chauvin trial was a CNN special with news anchor Don Lemon on October 28, 2021. These statements are direct quotes from the interview.

7 Julie Bosman and Daniel E. Slotnik, "Kyle Rittenhouse, Who Styled Himself a Medic, Said He Is Now Studying Nursing,"

New York Times, November 10, 2021, https://www.nytimes
.com/2021/11/10/us/kyle-rittenhouse-who-is.html.

8 Shimon Prokupecz, "Jury Finds Kyle Rittenhouse Not Guilty,"
CNN Newsroom, aired November 19, 2021, on CNN, https://
transcripts.cnn.com/show/cnr/date/2021-11-19/segment/07.

9 Victoria Albert, "Man Who Recorded Ahmaud Arbery Shooting Charged with Felony Murder," CBS News, May 22, 2020,
https://www.cbsnews.com/news/william-bryan-charged-felony
-murder-ahmaud-arbery-shooting-video/.

10 Doha Madani, "Former DA Indicted after Allegedly 'Showing
Favor' to Men Accused of Killing Ahmaud Arbery," NBC
News, September 2, 2021, https://www.nbcnews.com/news/
nbcblk/former-da-indicted-allegedly-showing-favor-men
-accused-killing-ahmaud-n1278416.

11 Richard J. Plantinga, Thomas R. Thompson, and Matthew D.
Lundberg, *An Introduction to Christian Theology* (Cambridge:
Cambridge University Press, 2010), 168.

12 Dictionary.com, s.v. "disorient (*v.*)," accessed on February 12,
2022, https://www.dictionary.com/browse/disorient.

13 Rediker, *Slave Ship*, loc. 193–206 of 8906, Kindle.

14 John Searle, *Making the Social World: The Structure of Human
Civilization* (Oxford: Oxford University Press, 2010), 17.

15 Willie James Jennings, *Acts: A Theological Commentary on the
Bible* (Louisville, KY: Westminster John Knox, 2017), 33.

16 Stevenson, "Body of Emmett Till."

17 Jennings, *Acts*, 28.

18 Jennings, 28.

19 Jennings, 28.

20 Jennings, 34.

21 Brueggemann, *Prophetic Imagination*, 16.

22 Christa K. Dixon, *Negro Spirituals: Bible to Folksongs* (Phila-
delphia: Fortress, 1976), x.

23 Brueggemann, *Prophetic Imagination*, 16.

24 I am using this verse as biblical precedence highlighting the
relationship between the eyes, what they see (or witness), and

their relationship with the rest of the body's systems that are triggered by those images.

Conclusion

1 James Baldwin, *Notes of a Native Son* (New York: Bantam, 1964).

2 Uzoma Obasi, "A Photographer Followed George Floyd's Family after His Death: This Is What He Saw," LX, December 9, 2021, https://www.lx.com/social-justice/a-photographer -followed-george-floyds-family-after-his-death-this-is-what-he -saw/46137/.

3 James H. Cone, *A Black Theology of Liberation*, 40th anniv. ed. (Maryknoll, NY: Orbis, 2010), 14.

4 Cone, 23.

5 Cone, 23.

6 Dwight Radcliff, "Tupac, Biggie, and Jesus," February 8, 2021, in *Intersections with Phil Allen Jr.*, produced by Phil Allen Jr., podcast interview, MP3 audio, 1:09:00.